INTRODUCING
MENTORING

A Guide for
Mentors and Organisers of Mentoring Schemes

GORDON HOLDING

BALBOA
PRESS
A DIVISION OF HAY HOUSE

Balboa Press books may be ordered through booksellers or by contacting:

Balboa Press
A Division of Hay House
1663 Liberty Drive
Bloomington, IN 47403
www.balboapress.com.au
1-(877) 407-4847

ISBN: 978-1-4525-0355-4 (sc)
ISBN: 978-1-4525-0356-1 (e)

Printed in the United States of America

Balboa Press rev. date: 04/10/2012

To my wife Christine,

for her advice,

support, and

patience.

Acknowledgements

I would like to thank Edward and Marjorie Burton for their careful proof reading of the text and Nicole and Mark Giandomenico for collaborating with me in the training of mentors and for sharing some of their experiences as mentoring scheme coordinators.

Mark Green of NSW Rugby kindly allowed me to use a photograph of him, mentoring my son Matthew, on the front cover.

Contents

Introduction

Dear mentor, prospective mentor, or mentoring organiser, this publication is designed to:

- help prospective mentors to understand the mentoring relationship and to consider whether they have the attributes needed to mentor successfully,
- introduce the basic principles and techniques of mentoring and to present some examples of mentoring in action,
- be a resource for existing mentors who wish to reflect upon and review their own mentoring experiences as they strive to become more effective,
- provide a framework for use by trainers of mentors and coordinators of mentoring schemes.

The term mentoring comes from Greek mythology where Mentor was trusted to oversee the development of Odysseus's son. It is a potentially powerful technique which is being used successfully across the world in very diverse settings.

It can be highly cost effective because it is often undertaken by unpaid volunteers or existing staff who mentor as a temporary addition to their usual work responsibilities. Since it draws upon the mentor's existing social skills and life experiences it only needs some modest initial training. However, to be successful, mentoring does require that people come to it with positive attitudes and a good understanding of its purposes and what it can and cannot achieve.

It is important to stress that mentoring is by no means always or automatically successful. Indeed it can do harm rather than good if its basic principles and techniques are ignored. In the chapters that follow you will be introduced to these principles and techniques.

The main text provides an explanation of the nature and scope of mentoring. It includes guidance on how to mentor and how to set up and operate a mentoring scheme. It is supplemented, in text boxes, by:

- examples and case studies,
- activities which can be used by trainers,
- materials which can be used whilst mentoring,
- examples of documents used in the organisation of mentoring schemes.

Please note that in the text either 'he' or 'she' is used to reflect the fact that mentors and mentees can be of either gender. Use of one or the other does not imply that one gender is more suited than the other to be a mentor or mentee.

This publication is designed as a general guide for practitioners. It is not a piece of academic research. Therefore it is not full of academic references but a general reading list is included at the end for readers who wish to investigate further. It is based upon the author's experience as a mentor, mentor trainer, and organiser of mentoring schemes in both England and Australia. It also draws on research from other countries, notably the USA.

The first five chapters introduce you to the basics of being a mentor. Chapters six to ten look at mentoring in different contexts. Chapter 10 looks at how we might support mentees with relationship problems and Chapter 11 is designed to assist with the setting up of a mentoring scheme.

Whilst each chapter has a particular focus, each one also contains material of general applicability. The chapter on careers for example includes material on identifying individual circumstances, needs and wants, decision making and action planning. It is worth looking at all the chapters even the ones outside your main area of interest.

As you read, you might start to think that much of the advice given is obvious or merely common sense. If it does strike you as common sense, that could be a good sign. Unfortunately, sometimes common sense leads us to sharply contrasting solutions, some of which may work whilst others could be disastrous. No doubt, you will be able to think of plenty of examples where 'obviously sensible' approaches have been ignored even by professional communicators such as doctors, managers, youth workers, teachers and government officials. Therefore it is worth taking time to reflect on what strategies work best when we try to support others. Hopefully the suggestions made here, being based on research and experience, will be helpful.

You may find the same themes repeated in different chapters as some basic techniques and principles are explored in different contexts. This is designed to reinforce learning not to irritate the reader.

Why become a mentor?

Mentoring in some form is as old as human history. For tens of thousands of years we lived in small bands and communities where support for individuals in need was provided by family, friends and neighbours. Contemporary life in western societies is more affluent and physically less demanding for most of us. However, it brings with it a series of psychological and social challenges. Social isolation is far more pronounced. We are reaching the stage, in some areas of cities in Europe and North America, where most households are single person. We can find ourselves confronted by large impersonal organisations, as both employees and consumers. Moreover, people are changing their jobs more frequently. Technological change has become more rapid. All this is accompanied by an individually competitive education and training system that can make great demands upon us and shape our life chances.

In response to these challenges professions have arisen to support individuals and families: medicine, teaching, social work, career counselling, clinical psychology and so on. Of course professionals are expensive to train and employ. Hence their services have to be rationed according to need and, in some countries, ability to pay. Consequently there is a great social need to fill the gap that exists between the informal help of family, friends and colleagues on the one hand and professional support systems on the other.

We all benefit from the support of others from time to time. This support may assist us to tackle practical tasks or to deal with emotionally distressing relationships. If our problem is not severe enough to need professional help and our network of family and friends cannot give us the kind of support that we need, a mentor may be the way forward.

Becoming a mentor is a generous gesture of support for others but it also has beneficial spinoffs for mentors themselves. Feedback from mentors suggests that being a mentor:

- gives us new insight into ourselves,
- increases our understanding of and tolerance towards others, particularly if they come from a different background and culture,
- challenges myths about other groups in society,
- improves social and communication skills,
- improves problem solving skills,
- widens knowledge of local community and community services,
- creates new networks of friends among fellow mentors and support agencies,
- increases self confidence and willingness to take responsibility,
- helps managers to become more effective leaders.

In summary mentoring can aid the personal growth of both mentees and mentors.

The following examples illustrate the potential value of mentoring. They are drawn from actual situations with some details and names changed.

Jas

Jas is twenty eight and has been with the firm for five years. At first it had not been easy. A rather shy person, he had found it hard to adapt and fit in. The prospect of coming to work each day had induced a sick, sinking feeling in his stomach. Yet the need for cash at home and the lack of any alternatives had fused with a persistence acquired at a tough inner city school, to see him through. Now things were much easier. Jas felt on top of the job, was accepted as one of the team and was even asked for advice by supposedly more experienced colleagues when technical problems developed. However, that feeling of inferiority persisted and was reinforced when a younger graduate recruit was fast tracked into management.

Wayne surveyed the paperwork piled precariously in his in-tray. The promised paperless office just seemed to generate more crap. He had had enough of policies and initiatives from that new woman at Human Resources—what was her name? Jemma double barrelled something— here only a few months and trying to change everything.

At least he had got the go ahead to appoint an additional supervisor in next year's budget. Should he look outside or promote one of his team? Jas seemed to be highly competent and got on well with all the guys without being too familiar. Perhaps Jas could do the job but was there enough drive and ambition there? Maybe they should try the new mentoring scheme that Jemma 'what not' was banging on about.

A few days later Wayne called Jas in and made the offer of a mentor from another department to help him look at options. Jas was a bit mystified. What was behind this? Better give it a go—a refusal would look bad.

Jas's mentor turned out to be Marco, an assistant manager who had been promoted about twelve months ago. After an initial chat Marco soon picked up on two key points. Jas was very capable, was on top of the job and had lots of potential but lacked self confidence and self belief. Jas would probably make a great supervisor but might not even bother to apply for a promotion if it came up. When the prospect of promotion emerged in discussion he was ambivalent. If he got the job—what would it mean?

Jas smiled at the thought of how proud mum would be. After all mum worked long, tough, hours as a cleaner and had brought up the kids on her own after dad died. It would mean more money to take home and a chance to put some of his ideas into practice at work. His former supervisor, Alf, disliked change and had refused to contemplate the suggestions that Jas and others had put forward at team meetings.

Wayne, as departmental manager, had some great qualities but giving his staff praise was not one of them. If you messed up you got a bollocking and then it was forgotten but when you did well it was just taken for granted. Jas did not realise how much Wayne relied on him to get difficult jobs right. Marco was able to get Jas talking and reviewing his time with the firm and identifying his positive qualities. He passed on to Jas the praise that Wayne had expressed when he briefed Marco as the mentoring was being set up.

Chatting on practically equal terms to a member of management began to subtly change Jas's feelings. This could be all right. They seem to have confidence in me. Perhaps I could do this. After seeing each other fairly regularly for three months, Marco was convinced that Jas could make a real success of the supervisor's role and Jas's fears had been much allayed. He decided to have a go when the new financial year brought an invitation to apply for that promotion.

Sandy

Sandy is fifteen and has been invited to apply to take part in a scheme at school which uses retired volunteers, from the local community, as mentors. Since it means missing a lesson on Thursday mornings she decided to give it a go. The school sent a letter home to get parental permission.

When Sandy's dad read the letter he rang the school to speak to the teacher coordinating the scheme. It appears that he is worried about Sandy's progress and hopes that a mentor can turn her round. She is uninterested in school work, insists on wearing make-up and a school dress that, in dad's view, is too short. Dad is unhappy with her friends who are mainly older than her, smoke and go to the pub. Sandy and her dad recently had a row that disintegrated into a screaming match because she wants to leave school at the first opportunity and get a job like her mates. Her aim is to earn money to get her own car and flat. Her dad reckoned that she did well at school up to year 8 and had hoped that she would be the first in the family to go to university. Now he feels he has lost all influence with her.

Jan has recently retired after 20 years working in local government. Having had three children of her own, including two daughters, she hopes she will have sufficient experience to be able to communicate with young people. She has agreed to spend an hour with Sandy each week for up to twelve weeks.

They start by getting to know one another, sharing stories and chatting about, boys, fashion, local shopping, TV soaps, boring lessons and overprotective dads who don't understand how daughters think. When Jan felt that that Sandy had developed some trust and liking for her, she gently turned the discussion towards Sandy's hopes and expectations for the future. They got the local paper, looked up the cost of renting flats and did a rough budget together. It soon became clear that a car and flat were out of the question on the income that she could realistically earn.

After spending a couple of meetings looking at other job options, Sandy felt that she would really like to work with children or with animals. Jan managed to fix up some work experience for Sandy at a day nursery managed by a friend. It was a revelation to Sandy who loved it and really felt grown up when she was treated as an adult by the other staff and the parents who called to collect their children.

At their next meeting Sandy soon came to the question "How soon can I leave school and get a job like that?" Jan had discussed this with her friend and was able patiently to explain that Sandy would need to do well at school and then win a place at the local college to get a child care qualification. Even when she got a job the pay would not be great so she would have to live at home for some time yet. Sandy went away to think about it.

At their next meeting Sandy was still keen on the child care option and quite liked the idea of going to college. "Being a college student would be cool. Have you seen some of the guys up there"? Her worry was her dad, who really wanted her to stay at school and go for university. Jan suggested that Sandy ring the college and make an appointment to see one of the child care teachers. Jan went with her. The teacher explained that the qualifications were at different levels and after getting an initial qualification, she could move onto higher levels of study if she wished, once she was working. If she got up to Diploma level that could even get her into university, some years down the track. "I am not sure that I will ever want that but it might help Dad to go along with it, if uni is a possibility". Jan and Sandy rehearsed the discussion that she was going to have with her parents when she broke the news to them.

The following week Sandy's Dad rang Jan. "I don't know what you did but whatever it was, we are very grateful. Sandy has found something sensible to aim at, at last. She actually went to school with a smile on her face this morning".

Sami

Sami was 68 years of age, living alone, and not in good health. She had been diagnosed with an aggressive form of cancer a few weeks earlier. In discussion with her specialist and with Kate, the hospital social worker, Sami was very reluctant to have the suggested treatment. The specialist proposed radiation treatment followed by chemotherapy. Sami had heard about the nasty side effects from these treatments: hair loss, nausea, extreme tiredness, pain. On top of all this she had a fear of hospitals and hated needles. Anyway, it didn't always work did it and what state would it leave her in? Life would never be the same again.

After several sleepless nights and days of worry she decided not to have the treatment and let the cancer take its course. Despite reassurance from Kate that side effects were much less severe these days, Sami was still very anxious and had deep misgivings. Kate decided to put Sami in touch with the local cancer support group. Chris, a member of the support group, was recovering well from the same type of cancer that was afflicting Sami and had gone through the same treatment pattern that was being proposed.

They met for coffee and gradually struck up a good understanding. Chris did not dive in with a detailed account of her own experiences. Instead she listened carefully to the fears that Sami expressed and answered her questions. Sami began to be reassured, as much by Chris's obvious jest for life and cheerfulness as her reassurance about the treatment. They shared a few jokes about Chris shocking her friends at work when she turned up in a wig and then whipped it off to show her shaven head. Somehow things didn't seem so bad if you could laugh about them.

Chris reassured Sami that she would keep in touch and visit her through the months of treatment and recovery. Sami decided to go ahead, have the radiation, the chemo. and "fight this damn thing".

In 2010 the President of the USA, Barack Obama, formally proclaimed January to be *National Mentoring Month*, focusing particularly on young people. The President in his proclamation declared:

"Many of us are fortunate to recall a role model from our own adolescent years who pushed us to succeed or pulled us back from making a poor decision. We carry their wisdom with us throughout our lives, knowing the unique and timeless gift of mentorship".

CHAPTER ONE

What is Mentoring?

A mentor is someone who offers personal support to others. If we are in need of support, a mentor is someone whose experiences we can draw upon and someone we can look up to as a role model. Our mentor will generously give of his or her time and will care enough to listen and offer a helping hand. Whilst there are numerous definitions of mentoring, in this publication it is seen as:

a relationship in which a more experienced person supports a less experienced one through a challenge, transition or difficulty.

We will call the former 'the mentor' and the latter 'the mentee'.

How is mentoring distinctive?

Whatever background we come from or lifestyle we lead, we can all experience new situations which leave us feeling vulnerable. We can all find ourselves facing challenges that we find hard to cope with. In these circumstances it is often the support of other people that sees us through. In difficult times we might be supported by a partner, family member, neighbour, colleague or a personal friend. We might also seek help from a counsellor, doctor, social worker, or psychologist. Are these people mentors? If not how is mentoring different?

Mentors often occupy the space between a professional tutor, counsellor, medical practitioner or advice worker on the one hand and a personal friend or relative on the other. Almost anyone can become a mentor provided that they come to it with the right attitudes and are able to build good relationships with other people.

The mentor/mentee relationship will be for a particular purpose and for an agreed period of time. Therefore, unlike a family member or friend, the mentor will not usually have had a long term close relationship with the mentee.

Many of us go through phases in our lives where the support of family and friends is not available or is not appropriate. Alternatively, the issue may be one where our friends and family feel that they lack any relevant experience or are not in a position to support us e.g. at work or in education. At the same time the situation may not be one where we feel the need to seek formal professional help.

Even when we do get professional help, some additional support from a non professional can be of great benefit to us. In these circumstances turning to a mentor for a while may be an answer.

The term mentor can be used very widely to refer to anyone whom we look up to and who provides us with guidance and support. Whilst much of what we cover in this publication will be of general interest, we will focus mainly on mentors who are supporting other people within an organised mentoring scheme. Such mentors will be expected to follow the scheme's guidelines and code of conduct. The mentor within a formal mentoring scheme has a role which is distinctive. It will have boundaries which distinguish it from the other relationships mentioned above.

We trust that mentors will be warm and friendly towards their mentees and that together they will develop a trusting and rewarding relationship.

However, experience suggests that they would be wise to keep their private lives separate from their mentoring role. Moreover, it is not always a good idea for a close family member, friend or neighbour to become the formal mentor. Why not?

- They may be too emotionally involved to see all sides of a question and may be inclined to push the mentee to make particular choices.
- The mentee may need the perspective of someone outside the situation.
- The mentee may not wish friends or members of the family to know about the private matters to be discussed with the mentor.
- They may have a personal interest in the mentee making certain decisions.
- It may raise the emotional temperature at home and make it difficult for the mentee to relax with family or with friends.
- It may be difficult for family and friends to maintain confidentiality.
- Family members may have some power or authority over the mentee.
- The mentor needs some protection from excessive demands by the mentee and vice versa.

Of course, once the agreed period of mentoring is over, a mentor and mentee may find that they enjoy each other's company and they may become personal friends (if the mentee is a child or young person, the scheme rules may impose restrictions on such friendships).

If you become a mentor, you and your mentee are strongly advised to identify a purpose for your meetings together and to agree a time limit. In a formal scheme the purpose may be set by the scheme that you are part of. Here are some examples of schemes to illustrate the range of settings in which mentoring can take place and aims which can be pursued.

- Mentoring a new employee to assist that person to adjust to their new work role. The pair agree to meet for half an hour each work day morning for the first week followed by a meeting once each week for a further four weeks. The employer sets up the arrangement after consultation.
- Mentoring of an employee seeking promotion by an experienced head of another department within the organisation.
- Mentoring of an unemployed man, by an unpaid volunteer, within a scheme run by a local community centre. The pair agree to meet twice weekly for up to two months to help the mentee find suitable work.
- Mentoring of a 17 year old high school student, fortnightly for three months, by a community volunteer whilst she explores possible career paths.
- Mentoring of a small group of adult students returning to a technical college course after being away from study for many years. This is built into the college timetable and takes place weekly during term time for the whole duration of the one year course. The mentee may be a member of the college staff from another department or a student from a year ahead. The emphasis here is not upon teaching a subject but upon helping students to plan their study and to give emotional support to encourage students to persist with their studies.
- Mentoring by volunteers from a local church of a group of refugees who can only speak the language of their home country. This starts intensively for a month and continues fortnightly for up to 12 months. The purpose is to assist the refugees to adjust to a new culture, to assist with their language learning and to plug them into support networks including government agencies.
- Mentoring of retired socially isolated men, by mentors from an older men's group, to introduce them to new people and to a range of groups and activities operating in their area— such as the Men's Shed (see later for more detail).

- Mentoring of women struggling to cope with breast cancer by mentors from a support group who have gone through the same course of treatment themselves.
- Mentoring of individuals struggling with an emotional disorder by volunteer mentors working with the local mental health service.
- Mentoring of juvenile offenders by mentors recruited by a juvenile justice service.
- Mentoring of ex offenders recently released from prison who are struggling to cope 'on the outside'.
- Mentoring of young Aboriginal men from single parent families, by Aboriginal Elders.
- Mentors from a local environmental awareness group who support people wishing to make their homes more energy efficient.
- Peer mentoring in a High school where older students support new students making the transition from primary school. This helps the newcomers to settle in and reduces bullying.
- Mentoring of school students by mentors employed full time to work in schools. The mentors give emotional support and encouragement to students whose attendance is poor, do little homework and are underachieving.
- Mentoring of a salesperson colleague, based in another region of the country, using email and a planned weekly video conferencing session.
- Mentoring of the owner of a new small business by an experienced and successful local business owner as part of a government funded enterprise scheme.
- Mentoring by university staff of new students from underprivileged backgrounds who have no family history of undergraduate study (evidence from the UK suggests that students from such backgrounds are more likely to drop out of university before completing their degrees).
- Mentoring of twelve and thirteen year old boys who have been identified by the police as users of soft drugs. The

mentors are older men who, after special training, have agreed to mentor the boys for a period of 12 months to assist them to stay away from drugs.

- Sponsorship of senior executives in a company by Board members as a part of a succession planning programme which will see the mentees replace the board members as they reach retirement.
- Senior players in a professional sports club mentoring younger players. This is separate from coaching and includes support to cope with the emotional and social challenges of being in the public eye.

The above examples are very diverse but they all have a clear purpose and take place inside an organised scheme. Underlying all of them are the personal circumstances and the emotional needs of the mentees. Emotional support, confidence building and raising self esteem are crucial features of the relationship which we will explore in detail later. However, here it is important to remember that mentors are not trained counsellors, social workers or psychotherapists. If we try to take on these roles we may do more harm than good. By all means, as a mentor, give emotional support in pursuit of your shared purpose but if you suspect that your mentee has a serious emotional disorder or is suffering from a severe trauma, refer your mentee on for professional help (unless of course you are a specially trained mentor who is working with a mentee referred to you by mental health workers).

The above examples also point to the importance of some modest initial training. Mentors usually derive great benefit from such a course before starting to mentor. The length and intensity of the training needed will depend upon the backgrounds of the mentors and the aims of the particular scheme they are entering. The first example above might only require a day of training for experienced employees. The sixth example would demand much more. For volunteer mentors in a school situation a two day training programme might well be sufficient to start off. This could be followed by some later, one off sessions, as they gain more experience.

The absence of guidance and training in some mentoring schemes is a matter for concern. This book should help scheme organisers to prepare a worthwhile training programme. In some countries formal courses and qualifications (or units of qualifications) have been developed as we shall see in chapter 11.

Where schemes support people struggling with significant emotional problems mentoring relationships can become very intense and stressful. Moreover, the commitment might be relatively open ended. We need to tread very cautiously here and understand the limitations of our role.

Rather than attempting to act as a counsellor in these circumstances, mentors should liaise with mental health professionals and try not to usurp their roles. Mentors can work with the caring professions to offer additional support but must not undermine them.

You may have also noted that example five above refers to a small group rather than an individual. Usually mentoring occurs one to one to give some privacy in case the mentee wishes to share confidential feelings, experiences or information. However, sometimes mentoring a small group of people, together, can be beneficial because they may share the same concerns and can support each other. There is a danger here. A strong or opinionated group member may lead others in a direction that, had they thought about the issue more carefully, they would not want to go. A choice of school subjects or even of a career would be examples. The group mentor must always be alert to this danger and be willing to see the mentees individually if necessary.

Most people can become successful mentors but some individuals have such poor social skills or ingrained prejudices that they need to be steered away from the role. Others may have such strong convictions about correct and incorrect actions that they would find it difficult to step back and allow their mentees make their own decisions. Such people would not find it easy to follow the approach to mentoring which is explained here.

If we formalise mentoring doesn't it become teaching, coaching or counselling?

Mentoring can overlap these other roles but it is distinctive from them.

Counsellors, teachers and many coaches usually have a lengthy period of very demanding training leading to a professional qualification. By contrast some mentors may only have a relatively short period of training, an initial briefing or short notes of guidance to explain the mechanics of the scheme.

Counsellors typically work with people who are experiencing very distressing emotional problems. As mentioned above, mentors may help to support people in these circumstances but should also encourage their mentees to seek the assistance of qualified counsellors when professional help is needed (see chapters nine and ten). However, mentors are often to be found helping people to tackle practical issues, such as engaging with new responsibilities at work. There may be powerful emotions involved here too but they are not necessarily causing the level of severe emotional distress which would require professional help. An overlap with counselling is perhaps most noticeable in some of the attitudes which we should display, such as being non directive, which will be explored in subsequent chapters.

Successful mentoring is a learning experience for both parties.

Learning is central to mentoring but ideally it is collaborative, side by side learning, in which the mentor has more experience than the mentee. The mentor can offer information, suggestions, advice and experience but the mentee is free to accept or reject any of these. Learning by the mentee often involves learning how to learn, learning to manage emotions and relationships, and learning rational decision making skills.

It differs from the role of a qualified school or college teacher, workplace instructor or coach. These latter roles involve an element of direction and of assessment of the work of the student, trainee or athlete. To some degree the professional trainer or teacher has a curriculum which must be followed and exercises some formal authority. The mentor on the other hand cannot give instructions to the mentee, dictate the agenda, set assignments or formally assess the mentee's performance. However, there is a degree of overlap since many of the skills involved in teaching and coaching are also valuable in mentoring. Indeed it could be argued that mentoring is an egalitarian and informal form of teaching that does not necessarily require professional qualifications; although it can benefit from them.

Megginson et al make a useful distinction between two models of mentoring. One is sponsorship mentoring which usually takes place inside organisations. Here mentors are senior to mentees and assist their career development by sponsoring them and passing on their knowledge and experience.

The other model is called developmental mentoring where the emphasis is much more upon a relationship of equals, one of whom has rather more experience in a certain area but perhaps not in others. It is a side by side relationship not a power relationship. It encourages personal growth and tries to develop the independence of the mentee.

Sponsorship mentoring can be a valuable tool within an organisation but It is the developmental model of mentoring that is the main focus of this book.

The diagram which follows shows some of the dimensions of mentoring. In one dimension it can have a predominantly practical aim such as choosing a career path. At the other extreme it could be about emotional support. The other dimension contrasts mentoring within an organisation such as a workplace or school with 'community mentoring'. In the former case the mentoring may be part of that organisation's policy to support its staff or its students. In the latter, the focus is on the mentees' private concerns. Of course these are not mutually exclusive. During mentoring both emotional and practical issues may be discussed as might working life and private life. However, the main focus will differ from scheme to scheme and from individual to individual.

The duration of a mentoring relationship can vary greatly from a few weeks to several years. Where it is in the bottom left hand side of the diagram, mentoring may need frequent and regular contact over a lengthy period of time—perhaps weekly or fortnightly for many months or even a year or more. To the right hand side of the diagram where specifically practical issues are tackled a much shorter period might suffice.

Two Dimensions of Mentoring

Work	
e.g. Coping with exam stress	e.g. Gaining promotion at work
Emotional	**Practical**
e.g. Relationship breakup	e.g. Managing money
Personal/Private	

Mentoring Cultures

Each scheme will have its own distinctive approach and way of operating. Lets us look at two extreme possibilities.

In a traditional hierarchical commercial company, there might be a very detailed and comprehensive policy framework producing a highly structured mentoring operation with strict budget and time constraints, supervised by a senior manager. It might take place in an office environment during working hours. Mentoring plans might be required from each mentor together with regular written progress reports. The whole thing would be expected to be brisk, business like and to produce measurable outcomes showing clear benefits to the organisation.

In contrast, a local mentoring scheme run by a group of retired friends to help refugee families to settle into their area, might have a very different culture of relaxed informality at the local church hall. The mentees might bring their children with them. Time might not be a serious constraint and lots of tea and cakes might be consumed. Coordination might be shared by a couple of friends and formal paperwork be kept to the minimum. In practice the skills, experience and network of local contacts enjoyed by the mentors might produce a highly effective scheme.

One mentoring culture is not superior to the other. They simply reflect different aims, settings and styles of operation. However, underlying all effective schemes are some common principles and techniques which we shall explore in subsequent chapters

Can Mentoring Be Compulsory?

Since it should not be a relationship where one person has power over another or can direct another against their will, mentoring should always be voluntary on both sides. No one should be forced into a mentoring scheme. However, we know that in practice this rule is not always followed. Students in schools and colleges can be timetabled as mentees. An employee could be allocated a mentor whom she distrusts but she accepts the situation because she feels that her manager would look unfavourably on her if she refused.

Usually, mentoring will fail if the mentee does not really wish to participate and therefore enters it with a negative attitude. This may be related to the choice of mentor. In an organisation where the mentee already knows the available mentors, it is helpful to give the mentee a choice of mentor. Usually this will greatly increase the chances of trust and rapport developing between them. On the other hand the coordinator of the scheme should avoid placing a couple of mates together who will simply use their meetings as a social occasion rather than as a serious attempt to tackle an issue.

Is the Mentor an Employee or Volunteer?

Mentoring is an element of many employees' responsibilities. For a few it is central to their role. In England for example full time mentors are employed in some schools where levels of achievement are well below national norms, in attempt to boost pupil attendance and motivation. In industry and the public service in general, mentoring of colleagues often takes place but it is usually only a small element of the work load.

It is perhaps in unpaid community work where volunteer mentoring is particularly prominent.

But what would I actually do as a Mentor?

In essence, mentoring is a one to one conversation. Through this conversation mutual trust and rapport is developed which enables mentor and mentee to share experiences and explore an issue together. They reflect together on the issue and by doing so gain a greater understanding of it. Ideally mentees (and often mentors) will also gain greater insight into themselves and their situation. The conversation should lead to the development of personal goals and a strategy for achieving them. This sometimes leads to follow up action by the mentor on behalf of the mentee. At its best, it leads to personal growth and development.

As in all conversations mentoring involves listening, speaking, questioning and answering, exchanging experiences, information and opinion. Sometimes the mentor will challenge the mentee to look at the situation from another angle. It can also include periods of silent reflection. The skills involved will be discussed in chapter two.

Initially mentor and mentee must get to know each other and establish a positive atmosphere of mutual respect and trust. Hopefully, they will develop mutual empathy. This may take some time and should not be rushed.

A frequent error made by inexperienced mentors is to attempt to resolve the mentees issues at first meeting by coming up with, what seems to the mentor, a sensible way forward. However, what the mentee often needs at this stage is the time and space to talk things through with a sympathetic listener. The mentor (as listener) should ensure that the mentee thoroughly reviews the situation and identifies the alternative courses of action and their likely consequences before rushing to decisions.

The most important activity occurs when the mentee talks and the mentor listens.

Where the mentee is struggling to make a decision or to find a solution to a problem, it is not the task of the mentor to come up with 'the answer'. Rather, the mentor should be supporting the mentee to make his/her own decisions. In developmental mentoring these may well be different from those preferred by the mentor. However, the mentor has a crucial role in trying to ensure that the mentee does not simply decide on the first course of action that comes to mind. Remember that our decisions can lead to unintended consequences for others, which an outsider such as a mentor might be able to alert us to.

As mentors, our role is to ensure that any decisions made by the mentee have been thought through thoroughly and that all the various options have been identified and considered. Explaining to a mentor and responding to questions from a mentor forces the mentee to clarify the issues and the alternatives in order to put them into words.

Once decisions have been made the mentee may need some support carrying them through. Our task here is to empower the mentee. As far as possible we help them to develop the skills they need to implement their decisions themselves. Although from time to time we might need to act as their advocate or to use our networks of contacts to bring in additional support.

The key elements of a mentor's role

These will be explored in more detail as you work through this book.

As a mentor I will:

- be a trustworthy supporter for someone for a limited period of time, within a mentoring scheme,
- be a role model, showing positive attitudes to my mentee and to the future,
- listen sympathetically to my mentee and encourage her or him to talk by sharing stories and asking questions,

- encourage my mentee to set some personal goals and gain a sense of direction in his or her life,
- research and explore alternatives with my mentee and help her or him to evaluate them,
- try to make sure that any choices made are genuinely the mentee's own,
- help my mentee to develop good personal organisation at work, in study and in private life,
- help my mentee to think through personal issues and anxieties,
- support my mentee to gain a sense of self worth,
- maintain my values but not be judgmental of my mentee,
- give advice when needed but not dictate,
- challenge my mentee to see other points of view,
- assist my mentee to improve his or her communication skills by practicing them together,
- use other mentors and my outside contacts to help my mentee obtain information, assistance and opportunities,
- if necessary, help my mentee to speak up for herself or himself although on occasion I may need to act as an advocate for my mentee,
- maintain confidentiality except where I have a legal or moral responsibility to pass information on to a designated person (see code of conduct in chapter 3),
- give my mentee the experience of having a successful relationship,
- abide by the rules and code of conduct of the scheme,
- liaise with the person coordinating the scheme and seek their guidance if I have any difficulties.

If you are wondering whether you could become a mentor, ask yourself "Could I make a reasonable attempt to do the things asked for on the above list?" If you think that you could, give it a go.

Do Mentoring Programmes Work?

Numerous studies around the world have identified a range of benefits from mentoring. They have also pointed to the ineffectiveness of poorly run schemes.

The world's largest mentoring programme is thought to be the 'Big Brother Big Sister' programme originating in the USA which claims to help over 280,000 children, between the ages of five and seventeen around the world, through professionally supported one-to-one relationships. This programme started in 1904 and now has affiliates in thirteen countries. It is worth looking at the website: www.bbbsi.org. A number of positive evaluations of this programme have been published. One example is *Making a Difference: An Impact Study of Big Brothers Big Sisters* which was published in 1995. It concluded that among mentored young people in the study:

46% were less likely to begin using illegal drugs, 27% were less likely to begin using alcohol, 52% were less likely to skip school, 37% were less likely to skip a class, 1/3 were less likely to hit someone. Generally mentees were more confident of their performance in schoolwork and were getting along better with their families.

In the UK learning mentoring played a big part in the Government's 'Excellence in Cities' programme which aimed to improve educational performance in disadvantaged neighbourhoods. After feedback suggested that it was one of the most effective strategies for raising school performance, the learning mentoring programme was expanded with over 3,500 mentors appointed to secondary and primary schools.

A word of caution is needed here. Mentoring schemes are not automatically successful. The author is aware of schemes that have been miserable failures. If they are to be effective they must be properly and efficiently managed. Mentors should be carefully selected and trained to exclude unsuitable individuals. Background checks are essential for those working with children to prevent exploitation and abuse. Moreover the mentors will need ongoing support from coordinators. If they feel unsupported or the scheme is inefficiently run, volunteer mentors will simply pull out and workplace mentors will just go through the motions.

Getting There—an illustration of key principles

Mentoring is like an experienced traveler, Andrew (the mentor), supporting Tania (the mentee) who is planning her first trip abroad. Andrew can provide information, offer advice and give warnings. They can look at alternatives together and discuss the various advantages and disadvantages of each destination but it is Tania who makes the final decision. Together they can research alternative routes and forms of transport, where Andrew can offer advice. Yet it is Tania who makes the final selections.

Andrew may withdraw at this point or he may accompany Tania on the early stages of her journey but it is Tania who reaches the destination.

When Tania is planning future journeys she may not need Andrew because she has gained self confidence, learned how to plan and how to make rational decisions that meet her personal needs.

Andrew also will have learned from the research that they have done together and both may have enhanced their relationship skills.

Chapter Two

Process, Skills and Attitudes

The word 'Process' is used here to indicate that the mentoring relationship develops over time. It differs from an ongoing friendship because it has a specific goal that is chosen and tackled. It has a finishing point in mind.

The Stages of Mentoring

Although each mentoring relationship is unique there is a characteristic set of stages that mentoring relationships tend to go through. Writers on mentoring differ about the number of stages in the process and they can overlap but they are generally along the following lines.

1. Preparing before the first meeting, liaising with the scheme coordinator, getting some basic information about your mentee, considering possible times/places to meet, deciding what boundaries to set and which ground rules to propose, deciding what issues to raise in discussion.
2. Agreeing, at the first meeting: the arrangements, some ground rules and how you will use your time together (sometimes called a mentoring plan).

3. Getting to know each other and creating mutual trust and empathy.
4. Understanding the issues faced by your mentee and discussing any personal matters which your mentee wishes to raise.
5. Researching and exploring together, identifying alternative goals and actions for your mentee to consider and thinking through the likely consequences.
6. Supporting your mentee to make decisions, set goals, and create a personal action plan.
7. Supporting your mentee to carry out the plan and actions decided upon.
8. Closing the mentoring relationship.

In reality the process is not as neat and tidy as this list indicates. Stages will overlap. In Stage 3 for example you may spend time just getting to know one another but this may deepen as you progress through all the subsequent stages. The mentee may have a change of mind leading to backtracking. New issues may also arise during the process and you may need to digress in order to address them.

We will explore these in subsequent chapters. However it is worth noting at this point that aiming to produce a personal action plan together, to guide the mentee through his or her next steps, is often a good idea. This plan is likely to extend beyond the life of the mentoring relationship. Indeed, in some cases producing a plan may be the reason for the relationship. Depending upon the type of mentoring scheme, the plan may be quite formal (e.g. in a workplace or college), or relatively informal. It could be set out on paper or just agreed in discussion. A format for a formal plan is set out below. A completed version of this plan is shown in chapter seven.

ACTIVITY: Create a plan to tackle one of your goals

My Action Plan			
Name .... Date			
My Goal for .... Year's Time			
Steps towards my Goal	Action to be taken and sources of information/help that I will need	Time Scale	Done

Time and Place

The following fictional example illustrates the importance of identifying an appropriate time and place for mentoring.

Annette

Annette is employed in the office of a large and very busy commercial company called Newbright Industries. She works in an open plan office with about 20 other staff. A new colleague, George, has just started in the same office. Following company policy Grace, the departmental manager, asks Annette to be George's mentor for the next few weeks to help him settle in.

Since it is now 10.00 a.m. on a Monday morning everyone in the office is working flat out. Phones are ringing, people are continually coming in and out and an impromptu meeting is being held at one side of the room to discuss a problem that has arisen in one of the branches over the weekend.

Annette welcomes George with a friendly smile and handshake and they grab a quick coffee before sitting down for a chat. Annette sits behind her large desk with her computer running and a pile of paperwork perched precariously in a tray next to it. She invites George to take a seat opposite her on the other side of her desk and explains "You will get used to all the action in here. It seems like chaos at times but it gives me a real buzz. I love the fast pace and challenge of the job". She asks George about where he has worked before but as he starts to answer, her phone rings. After a rapid fire conversation she turns again to George. "Now where were we?" As George gets into his explanation he sees Annette's attention wandering to her computer. Clearly an email message is causing her some amusement. "Sorry' she says, "Carry on. I am used to doing two things at once. We women have to do this all the time".

Annette asks George if there is anything in particular that he wishes to know. Although he has been through an induction with Grace the previous week he still has a mental list of things he would like to discuss and starts to work his way through them. After a few minutes a colleague, Tim, comes over to Annette and asks for an update on a new project that Annette is responsible for. Annette apologises to George "Sorry but it really important that I get Tim up to date on this. He has a meeting with the Boss in half an hour where this will be discussed. You don't mind do you. Look I am here most of the time, if there is anything you need just sing out, OK?"

Over the next couple of weeks George manages to catch Annette from time to time with a particular query which she does her best to answer between meetings, phone calls etc. However, George feels rather lost and isolated in the organisation. He fears making a major blunder and his self confidence has taken a knock. He is not sure that he will be able to cope. He sees that Annette goes off for lunch with a group of friends most days and is reluctant to intrude. She seems so confident and in control that he does not want to appear stupid by expressing his feelings, particularly in an open office environment where other people might hear.

From Annette's point of view she has been friendly to George and is always ready to answer any questions that he has got when she has a spare minute. So when asked by Grace, she replies that is not aware of George having any significant problems. She is confident that she is a good mentor a good role model. She sees herself as welcoming and friendly. She feels that she has positive attitudes and shows commitment, efficiency, hard work and good team working skills.

In the author's experience, scenarios like this one are not uncommon. Organisations may allocate the task of mentoring to staff that have not been trained and have not fully appreciated its importance and potential value. Lets us see what Annette could have done.

Annette is employed in the office of a large and very busy commercial company called Newbright Industries. She works in an open plan office with about 20 other staff. A new colleague, George, has just started in the same office. Following company policy Grace, the departmental manager, asks Annette to be George's mentor for the next few weeks to help him settle in.

Since it is now 10.00 a.m. on a Monday morning everyone in the office is working flat out. Phones are ringing, people are continually coming in and out and an impromptu meeting is being held at one side of the room to discuss a problem that has arisen in one of the branches over the weekend.

Annette welcomes George with a friendly smile and handshake and they grab a quick coffee. Annette finds a quiet area of an unoccupied room where they can talk undisturbed for a few minutes. She makes sure that they sit in similar chairs at right angles to each other with no desk in between. Annette has remembered from her training that this is an indication to George of openness, informality, and equality. Moreover she gives George her full attention.

Annette explains that Monday morning is not the best time for an extended discussion and suggests that although she will answer any urgent questions, it might be best to wait until the end of the day when they can spend an hour together and talk in more depth.

She suggests that they meet for an hour or so each Friday afternoon over the next few weeks where they can talk without interruption but that if any issues arise in the mean time not to hesitate to approach her.

She says "I am here to help, so if you come across any issues that you are unsure how to tackle, seek me out and we will look at them together. It took me a few weeks to find my feet when I first came. No doubt it will be the same for you. I had a mentor who helped me settle in and I will be glad to do the same for you if I can. ".

George feels reassured that he has a potential ally in the organisation. He is happy that he will be able to raise any worries in a confidential conversation where his mentor will give him her full attention.

You must be able to give your full attention to your mentee, for an agreed period of time, if you are to establish empathy and trust. To do this you will need to find a place free from distractions where you are unlikely to be interrupted. Remember that your mentee may wish to discuss personal feelings and concerns. So you will need a space where your private conversation cannot be overheard. Yet there are dangers here.

The mentee can misconstrue a meeting in a private room with a closed door where you are going out of your way to be friendly. The mentee may fear too much intimacy, particularly of a sexual nature. In rare cases the mentee can become infatuated with the mentor and imagine a sexual element to the relationship. If rejected they could make accusations of impropriety by the mentor. This is a particular concern if you are mentoring young people. To avoid any problems of this kind you should consider mentoring in a place where you can be seen by others but where your conversation cannot be overheard. For example if you are mentoring in a private office, it would be a good idea to leave the door open. Alternatively a corner of a staff common room could be used and your colleagues informed that you will be having a private mentoring meeting for forty five minutes and should only be disturbed in an emergency. Once this becomes part of the organisation's culture, most of your colleagues will understand and give you the time and space that you need.

As a mentor, planning and diarying your meetings should give you the time that you need and may avoid your mentee frequently interrupting you with non urgent matters.

Your proximity to each other and use of furniture can send unconscious messages about the relationship. If you sit behind a desk on a higher, more comfortable chair, you are asserting your superiority and importance. Whereas sitting without a barrier between you in similar chairs implies a relationship of equality. It is best to avoid sitting directly opposite one another since this can convey challenge and confrontation. However sitting close and side by side can feel uncomfortable because it seems too intimate. Ideally, position your chairs at right angles to each other just outside touching distance.

Essential Skills and Attitudes

During the mentoring process we are using the skills and attitudes that we have developed in our everyday lives to build relationships, to gain the trust of others and to communicate effectively with them. It is likely that people who have volunteered or been selected to be mentors, already have well developed skills of this kind. Yet their skills may be intuitive rather than being deliberately directed to achieve consciously thought out objectives. They may not be aware of the skills and attitudes that they project and use each day.

It is worth specifying these skills and attitudes and taking time to reflect upon them to help to refine them and avoid some of the pitfalls that could make us less effective. This might also help to identify areas where our mentees could be more effective in their own relationships.

- Establishing Trust, Empathy and Rapport

The mentor should aim to put the mentee at ease and to give the mentee some confidence that the relationship will be friendly, collaborative and non-threatening. This will provide a basis for the gradual build up of trust and empathy. Empathy is the ability to imagine oneself in the other person's position, seeing things from their point of view and being able to feel something of what they feel.

Rapport develops from empathy. It is the feeling of 'being on the same wavelength', of communicating really well and understanding and sharing the same thoughts and feelings. It is often based on shared values and a similar outlook on life. Hence rapport may not be fully achieved in all mentoring relationships but mutual trust and a degree of empathy should be present if the mentoring relationship is to succeed. How can we work towards these goals?

To do so we must choose a suitable time and place, create the right physical environment and we must communicate friendliness, interest and trustworthiness through our appearance, non verbal communication and use of language. Once we get started our most important skill will be to show our concern for our mentee by the way in which we listen, the responses we make and the questions we ask.

- Patience

A person who is impatient, very task focused and anxious for quick results could soon become frustrated as a mentor. It is a collaborative, negotiated process where there may be changes of mind and false starts which some mentors will find frustrating. It is important to recognise before you start that extended discussion will be central to the process. Some mentee's will approach issues in an unsystematic and indecisive manner and may take some time to find a way forward. Part of the role of mentor is to help the mentee to explore alternatives and to think things through with greater clarity and this demands patience.

- Know Your Limitations

It is tempting as a mentor to think that you know more than you do and to be flattered by your mentee turning to you for an opinion. Don't pretend to have knowledge that you don't have and don't feel you have to come up with an answer. If you feel that your knowledge may be outdated admit this and look up the latest information for next time. Remember that you are not there as a teacher or supervisor. One of the best things that you can do is to find things out together, perhaps by an internet search or by consulting a colleague.

If your mentee comes to you with a personal issue where you feel out of your depth and unable to help don't be afraid to admit this. Perhaps the coordinator can find an alternative mentor or you can refer your mentee on to a qualified counsellor.

- Non Verbal Communication (NVC) and Paralanguage

When we meet someone for the first time we must sum them up instantly to be able to react to them. As they approach us are they a threat? If they smile do you smile back or avoid them. Are they senior to you? Are they a client? Are they a homicidal manic? Do they need your help? We could respond in many different ways but we must respond almost instantaneously. We can't afford to spend five minutes thinking about it. On what basis do we select our response? What information do we use?

The experts claim that most of the data that we instantly take in about others is non verbal. The meanings of the words that others say are a relatively small influence on us. What matters most is what we see and what we smell, together with the tone of voice and any accent that they use. Regardless of the words that they say, if a person gives off body odour, has grubby torn clothes and a loud aggressive tone of voice, we will probably see them as a potential threat. We will treat them with caution. Obviously this is an extreme example. In practice our perceptions of others are very subtle and often unconscious. We just get positive, negative or perhaps indifferent feelings about others. We act on these feelings instantly without time for thought. Of course they can change as we get to know the person. Yet if we start by feeling negative this will show in our response and may trigger a cycle of mistrust and dislike between us which takes some time to overcome.

It follows that we should make a conscious effort to present ourselves in a friendly and positive light and should try to avoid making premature judgements about our mentee based on first intuitive impressions.

In mentoring schemes which focus on helping people with a personal issue of some sort, we often find that the problem comes down to, one or more difficult relationships. For example a mentee might have difficulty finding work because he or she makes a poor personal impression at interview. Much of this may result from personal appearance or from displaying a body language which gives off very negative impressions.

If we can gain the trust of our mentee we may be able to do some practice interviews and encourage a more positive approach. What can make the difference? Let us look at a fictional example.

Tom

Tom is 17 and having left school is struggling to find work. He is invited to join a scheme which uses community volunteers as mentors. Jean has volunteered to be a mentor. She works in a credit union branch and her manager has agreed to give her an extended lunchbreak on Wednesdays to enable her to mentor. The credit union society sees this as part of its presence in the local community and a way of fostering a good image for the organisation.

Tom turns up for mentoring in a red football shirt, denim shorts and old scuffed sandals. His hair is untidy. Tom does not make eye contact and slumps into a chair with his arms tightly folded across his chest and his legs crossed so that his body is turned away from Jean.

Jean attempts to be friendly and get a conversation going. Gradually Tom starts to relax as he realises that Jean is genuinely interested in him and wants to get to know him. As they gradually become more comfortable in each other's company Jean realises that Tom is rather shy and has very low self esteem. After months of trying to find work unsuccessfully he has become depressed and morose. He seems very distrustful of others. Jean can't inquire too deeply into his background and circumstances to discover the reasons for this but she realises that he will have to change his approach if he is to find work. Jean's dilemma is that if she immediately tries to instruct him in how to behave towards a potential employer he may well become resentful and withdraw.

Over the next few meetings Jean and Tom gradually build up a mutual respect and Tom opens up more about his home and school experiences. Jean gradually gets a good impression of the kind of lifestyle that Tom feels would suit him. She turns the conversation towards jobs and they decide to explore some websites together. Tom has good IT skills and so Jean encourages him to take the lead. Having found a couple of suitable vacancies Jean works with Tom to update his C.V. (resume) and complete application forms.

The following week Tom announces that he has got an interview. Jean sees her opportunity and suggests that they do a practice interview together the following day. She now feels able to raise the issue of what Tom wears and suggests that he comes to the practice in a clean ironed shirt with a collar, tailored trousers, and with polished shoes. Wanting to please his new friend Jean, Tom obliges.

Jean is able to show Tom how to approach his employer by offering to shake hands, making eye contact and waiting to be invited to sit down. She shows by example an upright, relaxed and alert body posture.

They practice answering typical interview questions and select some questions for Tom to ask, to demonstrate his interest. Tom has not magically been transformed into a different person but if he can remember a few basic tips he will make a much better impression and will be able to approach the interview showing much more confidence, with a real hope of being successful.

Jean is careful to point out that he might not get the job but if he makes a good impression this will stand him in good stead if further vacancies arise with that employer. She also reminds him to take a comb.

The key features of non verbal communication include:

- *Appearance and Dress.*

Clearly this will vary according to the situation. For example, when mentoring an unemployed young person at a youth centre, a mentor may decide to dress very casually (in contrast to mentoring a colleague at work). However, if a mentor comes straight from work to a mentoring session, work clothes may be a positive since they remind the mentee that the mentor is voluntarily giving up time for them. The key is to put yourself in the other person's position and think in advance of the kind of impression which will give the mentee confidence in you. Turning up grubby and scruffy is not a good idea. Some older mentors, including teachers, make the mistake of thinking that if they dress (and talk) like teenagers, young people will accept them more easily. This can often rebound as the youngster quickly spots insincerity. It is not just the clothes that you wear which communicate your personality. Hairstyle, glasses, make up, beard, possessions, home, car, all reflect your values and personality and help others to make judgements about you.

All this should not inhibit mentors too much. Expressing personality through clothes, appearance and possessions shows a unique distinctive individual that others can relate to. There is no need to be dull as long as you avoid appearing threatening or untrustworthy.

- *Body Posture. and Proxemics*

How you stand and how you sit, unconsciously reflect your attitude to the person that you are with. Getting the right posture and setting helps to build trust.

As mentors we are trying to show interest in the other person, respect for them, and equality in the relationship. We also wish to be friendly, open, relaxed and to put them at their ease. We want to avoid any suggestion of dominance, submissiveness, disinterest, deception, rejection, or stress. Ideally, what posture do we adopt?

As suggested earlier it is a good idea to sit in similar comfortable chairs at right angles to each other, at about arms length away. Turn your hips towards the other person. Find a comfortable relaxed position but sit upright to show that you are taking this seriously and it is important to you. Avoid crossing your arms and try not to fidget too much.

Proxemics is about how physically close you get to others and what physical contact takes place. It varies by culture, your status, and the circumstances. Each culture has its own proxemic norms (taken for granted, unwritten rules). Of course these are largely unconscious until they are infringed because we grow up with them and take them for granted i.e. they are 'normal' in that society. In some societies, or sub cultures within societies, it is normal for friends to stand or sit very close to one another, frequently touching arms or backs in animated conversation. In other sub-cultures personal space is sacrosanct and touching is frowned upon.

When mentoring, it is safest to avoid touching except for a handshake (some cultures may even avoid this). This is particularly important when mentoring young people and people of the opposite sex. However, when someone is seriously upset, perhaps after receiving some bad news, a squeeze of the hand by a female mentor to a teenage girl or a touch on the arm of an older man by a male mentor, could be valuable gestures of concern.

Mirroring is a technique that mentors can use. This builds on the insight that individuals in a conversation often copy each other's posture. This is almost like a dance that they unconsciously perform. If you observe people talking you will often see this happening. One person leans forward so the other copies her. One crosses their legs then the other follows. If, for example, you find that your mentee has a tense protective posture where he is leaning away from you and crossing his arms, copy this posture. Then after a few minutes adopt a more open and relaxed posture with your hands in your lap. Often your mentee will automatically copy you and will feel more relaxed as this more relaxed posture is adopted. Give it a try.

- *Facial Expressions and Eye Contact*

Facial expressions such as smiles and frowns enable us to show emotions. It is amazing how tiny movements to our facial muscles, leading to small subtle changes in facial expression, can convey very different messages. Joy and horror with open mouth and staring eyes can be very similar and yet most of us easily pick out the difference. An expression of intense concentration can look similar to annoyance but to most of us, most of the time, the distinction is clear. Slightly raised eyebrows can show surprise or curiosity depending on the shape of the mouth. It seems that most facial expressions are universal across all humans and mean the same thing in contrasting cultures.

Much of the time we unconsciously show our expressions and hence reveal our moods and inner feelings to others. Of course, some of us have much more expressive faces than others. No doubt we all learn to hide our deeper feelings as a means of self protection. Some people go much further. They are talented actors and are very skilled at hiding their real feelings by giving 'false' impressions. In effect they manipulate other people's emotions to make them behave in a particular way. Have you had the experience of approaching a salesman who appears extremely open, friendly and interested in you? Yet once the sale is made the charm switches off us and is directed to the next prospective customer. Touching your face can send unintended messages. A hand over the mouth or rubbing the nose is thought to show lying or dishonesty.

What is the relevance of all this to mentoring? Is it legitimate for us as mentors to deliberately alter our body language to hide our true feelings, in order to manipulate the feelings of our mentees? We all have a right to keep our emotions private which may involve making a conscious effort not to show certain feelings. Your mentee may tell you about something which they have done or experienced which shocks you profoundly. Their behaviour may go against some of your deepest convictions. Yet if you show emotions of shock or rejection you may quickly lose their trust and they will clam up. This relates to the principle of being non-judgmental which will be discussed in the next chapter.

The experts in this field always stress the importance of eye contact but it is important to recognise that, unlike our basic facial expressions, this does vary between cultures. Generally in western society we make eye contact when we meet and begin conversations. It is easy to get the wrong impression here. Eye contact does not mean continuously staring into the other person's eyes (except perhaps for infatuated lovers). Indeed if someone does that to you it can be very disconcerting. Instead we make eye contact from time to time in conversation to check the understanding of the other person and to exchange the conversation; to indicate that you have finished speaking and invite the other person to speak. We do this unconsciously but it makes for a smooth interaction. Failure to make eye contact can be subconsciously interpreted as rejection, disinterest or that the person has something to hide.

In some cultures the rules are different. For example when the author first taught a class including Aboriginal girls, they refused to make eye contact and turned away when approached. Usually a teacher uses feedback from eye contact to check that students are listening and showing interest in the topic. The feedback from the body language of your students immediately tells you how well the class is going. So, if some students won't make eye contact, you immediately and intuitively feel that something is going awry. In the case of the Aboriginal girls, a colleague was able to explain that in the culture of that particular group, eye contact between young unmarried females and older men was frowned upon. The same applies in some Middle-Eastern societies. Similarly a handshake between older men, is not a part of some Aboriginal cultures. Hence if you offer your hand it might be briefly touched at best.

If you are supporting a mentee from a culture where eye contact and handshaking is not normal practice you will need to discuss this together. If you were mentoring someone who is seeking a job or promotion at work, you might want to offer to practice handshaking and eye contact with them, particularly if they are preparing for an interview.

When you meet your mentee for the first time you may be a little cautious. If this leads you to avoid eye contact and you fail to give a warm smile, your mentee may feel that you wish to keep the relationship more formal and distant. Whereas if you can give a firm handshake, smile warmly and make eye contact, you are immediately sending a message of openness and friendliness. You may be exaggerating your real, more ambivalent feelings, but you are doing so for a positive reason rather than to mislead.

Remember that the Intended message is not always the one received.

- *Gestures and Paralanguage*

Gestures can be used as substitutes for words. A single gesture may communicate more meaning than several carefully chosen sentences. They can also be used to emphasize a point and to show your feelings. Hence they can liven up a rather dull speech or wake up a languid audience after a good lunch. In mentoring conversations they are particularly useful as a way of giving feedback when your mentee is talking. A gesture with the hand or a nod of the head can confirm that you are listening and have understood. They can show sympathy or disagreement.

Paralanguage can fulfill a similar function. This refers to sounds (other than spoken words) which convey a message, including murmurs, sighs, laughter, tears, throat clearing, and sniffing. Murmuring 'ah ah' and nodding the head can be used to encourage the mentee to continue talking. The danger here is that unconscious throat clearing or sniffing can give the impression of impatience or disagreement.

The speed of speech also affects meaning as does an emphasis on particular words. A soft tone can show sympathy and is non-threatening whereas loud and rapid speech can be interpreted as an attempt to assert dominance. Obviously accents can indicate ethnicity, class or regional origin and trigger prejudice and stereotyping; if we are not alert to the danger of making unfair assumptions.

Sometimes within a mentoring conversation the mentee can benefit from taking a little time for silent reflection. Silence also communicates a message. It can be companionable when accompanied by the right body language. Mentors often feel uncomfortable if there is a pause in the conversation and try to fill it. However if the mentor just sits in silence for a minute or two the mentee will often pick up the conversation.

The purpose of raising these issues is to encourage mentors to become more self aware. However, this can go too far.

We don't want to suppress individual personality, make lively people dull or force quieter, more thoughtful, people to try to be louder. In fact it can be useful to have a team of mentors with contrasting personalities which can be matched with the needs of mentees.

It would of course be very false and artificial if you were constantly checking your body language. Yet, at key points in a relationship it is useful to be aware of the impression that you could be giving and consciously make some adjustments to build trust and confidence.

- Listening and Questioning

The ability to put a person at their ease and to listen supportively to them is the most important quality that a mentor can possess.

If a person is struggling to cope with a distressing situation, explaining their worries and feelings to someone else is the best way to make sense of them and to start to deal with them. The process of explaining to a mentor will force the mentee to put confused thoughts, feelings and anxieties into words. To do so necessitates some degree of rational thought. At first the explanation may come out in a jumble; although the mentee will usually be aware of this and will try again to produce a more coherent account.

Carefully phrased questions from the mentor, when the mentee pauses, can help the mentee clarify his or her thoughts.

The mentor can also feedback a summary of what has been said to check understanding and this will often provoke a further refinement from the mentee. Gradually the mentee will be able to produce a more coherent account of his/her emotions and concerns. This is often followed by the mentee's explanation of how the situation arose. In other words by explaining something to someone else we can get it clearer in our own minds and perhaps get it into perspective. It is important to realise that this can take time and the mentee may want to return to the issue in successive mentoring sessions.

We saw in the last chapter that often an issue will involve a relationship that has gone wrong. To make sense of this the mentee may need to begin to see things from the other person's point of view—to develop some empathy for them.

Here the mentor can often help by asking questions such as

"Why do you think George got so upset when you . . . ."
"How do you think your mother will be feeling now?"

Empathy is not only a quality that a mentor needs. Often the mentee also needs it in order to mend a damaged relationship. By your listening and questioning you can help your mentee develop it. You are mentoring by example and acting as a role model.

'Active listening' is a useful phrase to describe the skills of listening effectively to a mentee or indeed to anyone.

In your daily life you may find that some people listen to you very passively. They may sit there quietly whilst you talk but they give you no indication of whether they are interested in what you are saying or what they think about it. Other listeners are selective. They make assumptions in advance about what you are going to say. Consequently they don't give you their full open minded attention. Instead they pick on only those points that you make which fit their preconceptions and only respond to those. These selective listeners will often interrupt you before you have given a full account (does this remind you of TV interviewers?).

Attentive listeners avoid the pitfalls of the passive and selective listener. They concentrate on what you are saying, give you to time to explain, and ask questions to clarify anything that is unclear. They use non verbal communication to show interest and concern for you. Active listeners will also pick up on their mentee's emotional state (e.g. of sadness or delight) and reflect that back by showing similar feelings themselves. This sharing of feelings will promote empathy and strengthen the relationship. However one more element needs to be added to attentive listening to make it active listening. This element involves being receptive to hidden messages.

When mentoring you will occasionally have a mentee who is rather cautious about fully revealing the problems and emotions that he/she is struggling with. These feelings may involve things that they are ashamed of, or incidents that are highly confidential. Alternatively, they may fear becoming very emotional and losing self control. Yet they may also want to share their worries and let out the stress that has built up inside them. In these circumstances the mentee may want tentatively to test you out by hinting at the existence of the problem and by dropping little asides into the conversation or using such phrases as "of course that wouldn't interest you", "that's all in the past, I am over it now" or "she doesn't like me anymore but I don't care". When someone says they are "over it" or that "they don't care", it often indicates that they are still very hurt and they are (perhaps only semi consciously) inviting you to follow this up and ask them about it. The *active listener* will pick up on these hidden messages and give the mentee an opportunity to explore them further.

It is important not to take this search for hidden messages to extremes. There may be no hidden messages or your mentee may genuinely not want to discuss these private matters. Do not press the issue. You mentee has a right to keep secret anything that he or she wishes to. You have no right to probe their private lives and feelings. Give people the opportunity to talk about sensitive issues if they wish to but don't try to force them to.

Have you noticed that some people can ask questions subtly to get a response without causing irritation whilst others seem to be nosey and intrusive? Some questioning seems to open up the conversation whilst others seem to be more like an interrogation.

We can use questions to:

- obtain information

"What did they give you to do on your work experience placement"?

- clarify any ambiguity in what your mentee has just said,

"How do you feel about your ex girlfriend now"?

- give feedback to show understanding

"I am really impressed that you have not given up on this. How have you managed to keep such a positive attitude"?

- help the mentee to think about things in a new light

"How would your life be different if you . . . ."?

- see things from another person's point of view

"If you were Allen, how you feel if one of your mates said that to you"?

- express your concern about your mentee

"I am worried that you have not thought this through. If you go ahead, how will you cope with a big cut in your income?"

The main types of question

Closed questions are ones asking for a simple yes/know or very brief answer. Sometimes you need to ask closed questions to get a clear answer such as:

'Do you have a part-time job?"

However, where you have a mentee who is shy or lacking in confidence other closed questions such as "Do you like school?" can simply produce a series of one word answers rather than a conversation. This soon becomes very hard work and leaves you feeling that you are making little progress in breaking down barriers between you.

Open questions that require fuller answers are much better:

"You said that you don't like school much. Could you explain why you feel this way?"

Scaling questions can be useful to clarify the strength of a mentee's feelings:

"On a scale of 1 to 10 how important to you is getting a promotion; if 1 is totally unimportant and 10 is extremely important"?

Alternate questions give the mentee a choice of answer. They can be useful as a way of helping the mentee to be clear about the options, when she or he is vacillating between alternatives. However, there is a danger that other possibilities might be excluded from consideration or that your mentee is being pushed to make a decision before they are ready to do so.

"Would you prefer to go to college to study horticulture full-time or would you prefer to study part-time and try to get a part time job?"

Hypothetical questions can be very useful to test out a mentee's reaction to a possible scenario.

"If your wife was willing to take you back, how would you feel?"

Rhetorical questions should usually be avoided since you are expressing an opinion and simply inviting your mentee to agree with you. They may do so to please you even if is not their true feelings.

"Wouldn't you agree that, looking back, being sent to a young offenders institution did you a lot of good, even though it was not a pleasant experience at the time?"

Testing questions are similar but do not imply an opinion by the mentor. They can be useful to clarify a mentee's views.

"I get the impression from what you have said that you felt really depressed throughout the Christmas period. Is that right?"

Probing questions should be treated with great caution since the mentee can feel that you are intruding into their private lives and may come to distrust your motives.

"How good was the sex last night?"

Third party questions appeal to the experiences of someone else. They can be useful but we should not assume that what suits one person will be right for another.

"Maria joined the University of the Third Age when she was left alone and it brought her a new set of friends. Wouldn't you like to try it?"

Direct Questions, which are closed ones, do need to be asked on occasion.

"You have said that you are feeling depressed. Does that extend to suicidal thoughts?"

Leading questions are those where the answer is implied in the question. See the box below.

Salesmen are particularly adept at using questioning to manipulate you into a direction that you might not otherwise want to go. As mentors we should <u>not</u> use this technique

Telephone salesman on a cold call:

Wouldn't it be nice to have a holiday break with your partner?

(answer: "I guess so")

A week away at the coast would be great wouldn't it?

(answer "I wouldn't mind that")

If you could get you a 50% price reduction at La Currunia boutique luxury resort would you see that as a good offer?

(answer "Of course")

Do you have any holiday leave due at work over the next six months?

(answer "I should have")

It would be a shame not to make full use of it wouldn't it?

(answer "I suppose so")

We are making this special promotional offer to selected couples and we have chosen you. No one in their right minds would pass up such an offer would they?

Could you please give me your card details for the deposit to secure the booking?

Here the questions are leading the potential customer to the required answer. Weak and vulnerable people can be led to make purchases that they did not intend to make. They are not genuine questions where the questioner really wants to know what the person thinks. As mentors it is important that we do not decide in advance what is best for our mentee and then ask leading questions to get them to agree.

Although mentors should avoid leading questions and rhetorical questions that push the mentee in a particular direction, the aims of some mentoring schemes can appear to be at odds with this principle. If the aim of a scheme was to encourage young people to continue in education or vocational training rather than dropping out as soon as the law allows, mentors might be tempted to denigrate the option of leaving to get an unskilled job or to live on state benefits. If we try to influence someone to stay on are we not infringing the principle of being non-directive? We will deal with this ethical dilemma in the next chapter.

ACTIVITY: Active listening and effective questioning check list

Practice these in your daily life to prepare for mentoring and reflect on how well you succeeded.

Show
- ✓ Interest in the mentee
- ✓ that you are following and understanding what mentee is saying
- ✓ concern for and empathy towards the mentee

Encourage
- ✓ mentee to express thoughts and feelings whilst respecting mentee's privacy
- ✓ mentee to think about the pro's and con's of alternative courses of action
- ✓ the growth of empathy by both the mentee and yourself

By
- ✓ removing distractions
- ✓ giving full attention
- ✓ non verbal signals
- ✓ paralanguage
- ✓ mirroring
- ✓ questioning to clarify meaning
- ✓ recapping the points made by mentee
- ✓ reflecting meanings and feelings back
- ✓ allowing pauses for silent reflection
- ✓ being alert for hidden messages
- ✓ questioning to encourage consideration of alternatives
- ✓ challenging sloppy thinking and negative attitudes
- ✓ questioning to encourage mentee to understand the feelings of others
- ✓ being slow to offer advice

Whilst Avoiding
- ✓ prejudging your mentee (stereotyping)
- ✓ dominating the conversation
- ✓ interrupting
- ✓ jumping to conclusions about what mentee will say
- ✓ finishing the mentees sentences for them
- ✓ topping (always having a better story to tell than the one the mentee has just recounted)
- ✓ making value judgements about mentee as a person (see chapter . . .)
- ✓ leading questions, probing questions, excessive use of closed questions
- ✓ directing the mentee towards opinions or choices favoured by the mentor.

- • Note Making

Mentors should be very careful about making notes while the mentee is talking. It can give entirely the wrong impression. The times to make notes are firstly, when mentor and mentee agree together that they need to jot down some information e.g. of available jobs when looking through an employer's website together. Secondly, to act as a reminder of some follow up action that they have agreed e.g. the mentor undertakes to find some information for the mentee to bring to their next session. No notes should be taken without first asking the mentee's agreement. All notes should be available for the mentee to see.

In some mentoring schemes Mentors write a brief written record after each meeting (see chapter 11. for further guidance).

- Advocacy

We have stressed the importance of supporting mentees to become more independent but there are occasions when a mentor might take a more interventionist approach. This could occur when a mentor is supporting an immature or emotionally vulnerable person who finds it hard to stand up for himself and be assertive with people in authority. Alternatively the mentee may have a disability or a chronic health problem which makes it difficult for her to present her own case. A mentee may try to be assertive but due to their low status in society or being from a minority group, those in authority are not listening or taking the issue seriously.

Mentors within properly organised mentoring schemes can often use the scheme coordinator or members of the management committee to advise on, or assist with, advocacy. These people may have greater 'clout' than the mentor acting alone because they have some standing in the local community or have the ear of key people such as local councillors or government officials. Here, we see the benefits of a scheme reaching out to stakeholders and having an effective network of community contacts.

For mentors there are several forms of advocacy.

- ❖ Talking directly to key decisions makers on behalf of a mentee to ensure that the mentee's case is heard and taken seriously.

- ❖ Recruiting influential people such as a local journalist or the local Member of Parliament to take up the mentee's case.
- ❖ Writing letters or emails on the mentee's behalf.
- ❖ Using the coordinator, management committee members, or fellow mentors to take up the mentees case.
- ❖ Accompanying the mentee to interviews with officials, Principals, lawyers, financial advisers, social workers, doctors etc.

It is important to point out that in most mentoring relationships, advocacy will not take place because a better alternative is to support mentees to present their own cases. In exceptional circumstances, after consultation with the scheme coordinator, a mentor may agree to advocate for someone who otherwise would not be able to get a fair hearing.

Communication Styles

To communicate successfully in mentoring is to create a relationship. As we have already seen it is not just about the obvious means of communication (writing, face to face speech, telephone, texting etc) or even the meanings of the words that we use. It is also powerfully influenced by a range of other factors including our appearance, smell, body language (including, eye contact, facial expressions, body posture and gestures) tone of voice, how we listen to others and the extent to which we question and interrupt. Even the possessions that we have on show, contribute to the messages that we send to others.

These messages are often unconsciously given and received but they produce an emotional reaction in others. As we meet them, we instantly trigger feelings in others and we have reactions to others which may be confirmed, refined or modified as we get to know each other better. This whole package of information that we give to others when we interact can be called a communication style.

Most of us have a range of communication styles that we vary as we move from situation to situation. For example we may use a different style at home with the family than in a work situation with an employer, different again when we are a customer at the local newsagent and yet another style when enjoying an evening out with friends.

We sometimes find that the person we are mentoring is not very aware of the impressions that they are communicating to others. One mentee may come across for example as rather aggressive, another may appear somewhat passive, yet another may give the impression of disinterest. Once trust has been gained we may be able to give our mentees some feedback on their communication styles and discuss ways in which they could present themselves in a more positive light. Obviously any feedback needs to be given to them with sensitivity and as positive suggestions for them to consider rather than as personal criticisms.

Whilst we all communicate with our own unique characteristics, there are some common patterns leading to a range of typical communication styles. Mentors can use this knowledge to reflect on how they communicate and how their mentees communicate.

By helping our mentees to become more self aware we may be able to support them to develop more effective relationships with other people. Let us look at some common styles.

- Aggressive

Aggressive people communicate angrily and try to dominate the conversation and can become bullies, often without realising it. Their NVC is hostile and threatening. When speaking they use emotionally charged language, blaming others, issuing orders and making unreasonable demands on others. They are quick to accuse and lack insight into their own behaviour. Obscenities may colour their language. The aggressive person will be insensitive to others and demand action regardless of the emotional or personal cost to others. They disrupt team working and produce fear and avoidance in others.

As mentors are we likely to be on the receiving end of aggression?

Mentees should be willing volunteers. If not the relationship is unlikely to work. Therefore it is very uncommon for aggression to be directed towards the mentor. However, if the mentee is feeling very upset and angry, perhaps feeling unjustly treated, anger can surface during mentoring meetings, usually directed at someone else. It is more common for the mentee to be concerned about aggression directed towards them. Hence they may want to discuss how they should respond. They may also be concerned that they have a short temper or can provoke aggression in others. Mentors can help by discussing the causes of aggression and by suggesting strategies to use with aggressive people or suggesting how to deal with our own aggressive feelings.

Aggressive communication usually results from frustration because the person concerned feels blocked in something that they are trying to achieve and can't overcome the obstacle. It could be that they are trying to communicate something very important and the other person seems to be rejecting the message; ignoring it or not responding to it. For example a customer is concerned that her order is not being given the priority that she thinks it deserves. She tries to explain this to the salesman but he keeps interrupting her with excuses. Her response is anger and aggression. She raises her voice and makes threats. The salesman responds with some ripe language and the conflict escalates.

Sometimes aggressive communication is seen in people who lack the skills to communicate effectively. They may struggle to explain themselves and their aggression results from the apparent inability of others to get the point that they are making.

Here, it is quite common for the aggressive person to continue to repeat the same statement over again more loudly and rapidly, perhaps with additional expletives added, rather than being able to explain more fully. The author has witnessed this in schools where irate parents arrive asserting that their child has been unfairly treated.

Shouting, for example:

"This school is absolute rubbish. The teachers here are a joke"

is hardly likely to get the parents a sympathetic hearing. A mentor to the young person concerned will have quite a challenge since the home may not provide a good role model of effective ways of relating to teachers.

When a person gets angry, physical changes are taking place in the brain and body which are immediately spotted by any other people present. If aggression is directed towards you, your brain and body automatically respond. If you lack personal insight and self control, you respond to aggression with aggression.

An aggressive, angry or a threatened person will have a faster heart beat and breathe more rapidly and shallowly, with blood being pumped to their muscles. This is clearly an automatic response to enable the person to fight or flee. The skin of the face and chest becomes red, eyes widen and the jaw tenses. The brain releases stimulants into the body, the voice becomes loud whilst thoughts and speech become rapid. Unfortunately rapidity of thought does not equal quality of thought. Judgement is impaired and risk taking behaviour can increase.

This is not the best state in which to show empathy, think clearly, solve problems, and have a sensible conversation. Active listening goes out of the window. We will look at some strategies for managing aggression in Chapter Ten.

- Passive

Passive communicators are often shy and lacking in self esteem and confidence. They are unwilling to challenge stronger personalities. They may fear conflict and hence be unwilling to stand up for themselves. Passive communicators may give little feedback when you talk to them. When a course of action is suggested to them they may outwardly agree even if they are not really convinced. Passive communicators can also take on the role of being helpless and appeal to others to complete tasks for them. A reluctance to take responsibility and to make decisions can be a real handicap in the workplace. It also can produce students who will not manage their own learning. Among the long term unemployed passive communicators can blame others for their situation and be unwilling to take effective action to change their circumstances.

Whilst aggressive people can become bullies, passive ones are vulnerable to being bullied. Passive communicators may agree to being mentored without having any real commitment to it. Hence they can be difficult to engage and get a response from. It may take some time before they trust a mentor and open up. Mentors can be extremely valuable to this group by helping to build their confidence and by showing them different ways to communicate which can be modelled in the mentoring meetings.

If we can support them to succeed in small steps, their attitudes can gradually change and their skills develop. In young people passivity may be a short term response to some of the changes brought on by adolescence. Mentors can support their mentees by showing them how to become more assertive and hence become more independent, making their own decisions and having the confidence to follow them through.

- Assertive

Assertive communicators will stand up for themselves and make their views clear. They will not allow themselves to be bullied into a course of action that they feel is wrong. Unlike aggressive people they strive to remain calm and do not attack others. They concentrate on describing their own feelings and on making constructive suggestions rather than attributing blame. Unlike passive communicators, assertive people often take the initiative. They have the self confidence to make proposals. However, they will do their best to see the other person's point of view and will actively solicit the opinions of others in order to try to accommodate them. Hence they will listen actively to others. Suggestions made by assertive communicators will seek to meet the needs and aspirations of others as well as their own.

By not attacking others and by listening to them actively, we reduce the likelihood of triggering an aggressive response. By making our own needs and wishes clear and by making constructive suggestions we show that we are no pushover. Of course this easy to write but can be difficult to do. We could be assertive in the words that we use but still give off aggressive messages in our non verbal communication and tone of voice.

It is much more difficult to avoid aggression or passivity if we are personally involved as a friend or relative than if we are a mentor. As mentors we are in a good position to help explain to our mentees about the dangers of aggressive or passive styles of communication and to offer them the opportunity to practice conversations where they try to become active listeners and are assertive communicators.

We can suggest to the potentially aggressive or passive communicators that they attempt this three step approach to convey an assertive message.

I feel   describe your emotional reaction to the situation, taking care not to attack others

I think   explain how you see the situation using facts to support your case

I suggest   make sensible proposals whilst taking other people into account

---

In this example of extracts from a conversation, Henry a seventeen year old is concerned about his parent's decision to move to another town. He feels that they did not take his views into account and that his schooling will be disrupted, damaging his prospects of getting a place at college.

Scenario one. Henry' s father announces one evening that he has been offered promotion at work but this means that the family must move to another town which is about a three hour journey away.

Henry "This is bullshit. You never think of me. All you care about is making more money. You can get stuffed. I am not bloody well moving. You can't make me".

Mother "Don't you talk to your father like that you ungrateful little prig. He works hard to bring money to this house and all he gets in return is abuse from you".

Father "This is great opportunity for me and your mother and I am not going to let you spoil it. We are going and you are coming with us and that is an end to it".

Henry "I am not a kid anymore—you can't tell me what to do. What about me and Amy (girlfriend)? You don't give a toss do you? You really piss me off".

Father "I don't know where we have gone wrong with you. If I had talked to my father like that I would have felt his belt on my backside. We have been too lenient by half with you. You will do as you are bloody well told".

Henry rushes out and slams the door behind him.

Scenario two

I feel Henry "Congratulations on getting promotion, Dad. You deserve it. But this is a bit of a shock to me. It is going to cause me big problems. I am really worried about my course and I don't want to leave my mates and Amy of course. I feel very churned up about where this leaves me".

Mother "I understand that this is not easy for you but your dad and I can't pass up this opportunity. Surely you can see that "?

<u>I think</u>

Henry "I can see that. Dad has got to go for it, obviously. Look, this is how I see it. I am half way through this course. If I switch to another school they might not use the same syllabuses and anyway they might cover the topics in a different order.

Also there is the course work which might be different. The other thing is that Amy and I have been seeing each other for three months and I really like her. I am not the greatest student in the world but over the last few months I have been getting my act together. If I move it might be hard to fit in. Is there any way we can get round this?"

<u>I suggest</u>

Henry "Would it be possible for me to stay here during term time? I could come over to see you sometimes at weekends and live with you during the holidays. It would only be for a year anyway because next year, if I do well, I will be going away to college.

Father "I suppose the Lawson's might put you up. They have plenty of space now that Gerry has left home. It's an option that we will need to think about."

Listening actively and communicating assertively can make a real difference to our relationships and will change how people see us and relate to us. They will view us in a more positive light and be more trusting of our judgement. Of course we can't expect to be a paragon of virtue in our private lives. We will get angry and get into arguments with those we share our lives with. But if we can learn the skills of active listening and assertive communication we will certainly be better mentors and be better able to assist our mentees to communicate more effectively.

So far we have considered three communication styles. A range of other typical styles have been identified, including:

- Collaborative

This person is a listener and peace maker who will offer help to others, responds sympathetically to the distress of others and is reluctant to criticise others. However, the collaborator may dislike conflict, suppress her or his own needs and shy away from controversy.

- Sociable

Every group need this kind of communicator. This person is warm, friendly and empathetic. He or she might also enjoy putting on social events. The sociable communicator can strengthen group bonds. However, beware of sociable gossip that denigrates colleagues.

- The Entertainer

An entertainer, comedian or practical joker can lighten a tense atmosphere and bring some fun to relationships. When taken too far, in a work place or classroom, the entertainer can be disruptive by using humour to avoid work or to avoid taking important issues seriously.

- Task Focused

Here setting targets, making plans and being competitive are common characteristics. However, this can lead to high levels of self imposed stress and can produce insensitivity to the needs of others.

- Passive/Aggressive

Finally, some individuals seem to combine aggression with passivity by quietly undermining others, spreading malicious gossip and being deliberately obstructive. They make the bullets and try to persuade others to fire them. The author has found that these people are particularly awkward to deal with because they are often full of resentment at what they see as unfair treatment by their colleagues or managers.

The above categorisation is an oversimplification but it can help us to be more self aware of the styles that we find ourselves using. It might also help us to think about the ways in which our mentee communicates. For some mentees, the communication style and non verbal communication that they have unconsciously developed over the years, may be at the heart of relationship problems.

Giving Advice and Information

There is a fine line between giving advice and persuading a mentee into a decision that is not his or her own. Remember, our role is to support mentees to make their own decisions. What would be right for us is not necessarily right for them. However, if we have relevant experience and knowledge we should of course, share it with our mentee. Advice based on this knowledge and experience is particularly useful when:

mentors issue warnings of potential pitfalls or the damaging consequences of proposed actions by the mentee—the mentor may be able to see problems looming which the mentor has not foreseen ("that could upset your colleagues in the marketing department"),

mentors advise on the most effective ways of implementing the decisions that the mentee has taken ("I suggest that you contact the hospital and ask to speak to a medical social worker about getting affordable accommodation whilst your daughter is being treated there").

Using Information Technology

Being confident with computers, using the internet, emailing and producing documents electronically are all useful mentoring skills. In some situations accessing IT may be required, such as supporting career development, but it is not essential that the mentor is the one with these skills. If you are a mentor lacking expertise or confidence in IT, do not despair. Your mentee may have the required skills. If not consult your coordinator or fellow mentors.

Being able to learn skills such as these from your mentee is a good way to build up a side by side relationship of trust and should help your mentee's self confidence.

If neither of you have this expertise you could try learning together to build your relationship. If you are in a formal mentoring scheme your coordinator will probably be able to arrange for someone with IT skills to assist you.

Additional Techniques

The techniques below will each be outlined in a particular chapter to illustrate its use in a context. They can, of course, be used in a range of other contexts and situations but to avoid excessive repetition they are only covered once in this publication.

- Analysis of mentees situation, skills and preferences (chapter seven—career).
- Action planning (chapter seven—career).
- Problem solving (chapter seven and chapter eight—workplace),
- Negotiating (chapter ten—relationship conflict),
- Dealing with aggressive behaviour (chapter ten).

You will find that they are actually 'skill sets' which incorporate the essential skills and attitudes that we have already outlined. Hence they draw upon active listening and questioning skills and are enhanced by an understanding of NVC and an assertive communication style. It will be seen that as we develop and learn, we acquire the ability to adapt our skills to suit the situation that we are in and the people we are communicating with.

A Checklist: Removing Communication Barriers to mentoring conversations (could be discussed with your mentees once you get to know them)

Be able to engage in friendly small talk about trivia. This reassures the other person that you are not weird or a threat to them. It can also fill awkward silences and confirms that you are a sociable person.

AVOID

- Using jargon or phrases that the other person does not understand.
- Mumbling.
- Sighing, yawning and looking bored.
- Jumping to conclusions and interrupting before the speaker has finished.
- Having physical barriers e.g. desks, shelves, or people in the way, sitting higher up or directly opposite a person.
- Having loud noise in the background.
- Looking away when you speak—no eye contact.
- Walking away as you speak.
- Having facial expressions that put people off e.g. smirking or frowning.
- Turning your body away from the speaker.
- Doing something else while they are speaking. For example, you may be answering the telephone, writing at a desk, sorting out shelves, or be looking at a computer screen. Don't look at your watch as if you have to be somewhere else.
- Allowing yourself to be interrupted by another person or by the telephone.
- Being sarcastic.
- Having an off putting appearance and poor personal hygiene.
- Not giving any feedback—the other person is not sure that you have understood.
- Appearing disorganised and giving this meeting a low priority e.g. arrived late without apology.

The First Mentoring Meeting

It is likely that you will both feel a little anxious before your first meeting. Your mentee may well feel cautious and nervous. When you meet you will want to confirm the main purpose of mentoring in your scheme and talk about the practical arrangements for your future meetings but you should also start to get to know one another. Remember not to rush this. Taking time to establish a good relationship, being able to joke and laugh together, will make it much easier to make progress when you start to tackle tough issues at your next meeting.

Sometimes the relationship gels very quickly and conversation takes off. For other pairs there may be a little initial awkwardness. One way of breaking this down is to use a short icebreaking activity. A useful one is set out in the Activity below. This is just a way of sharing some basic information about each other to find a point of connection that can stimulate a conversation. The main aim is to give you something to talk about but it also starts the process of finding out about each other. It is not designed to be an interrogation or formal interview. Therefore the mentor and mentee take turns to ask questions of each other. It must not be a one way process in which the mentor grills the mentee. Rather it is sharing knowledge about each other and beginning to gain trust.

You both have a right to privacy. As a mentor you have no right to know anything that your mentees do not want to tell you about themselves. The questions are very general to enable the mentee to avoid giving details that they may want to keep confidential. If the mentee appears reluctant to answer a question do not press them—move on to the next one. Do not probe into their private lives. When they trust you they will talk about their feelings and circumstances. You will find that some mentees are all too anxious to give you chapter and verse on all their family details and personal relationship problems without waiting to get to know you. Other will be cautious and reveal little at first until you have gained their trust whilst some will never let you into their private thoughts and feelings. This is ok! You have no right to know.

The mentee must be the judge of what to tell you. You will of course soon realise that you cannot be sure of the truth of what you are told. Where relationship conflicts are involved, always remember that you are only hearing one side of the story, so don't rush into judgment or condemnation.

Do NOT use this activity as an excuse for an ego trip or one upmanship. You do not want your mentee to feel that you are showing off your qualifications, lifestyle, or perfect family. Share information but be sensitive to your mentee and show restraint as necessary. Be willing to share but try to talk less than your mentee. Concentrate on *listening actively*.

The questions below could be printed out in advance for you both to look at, as a standard approach for everyone in the scheme. Alternatively you could just ask questions like these very informally and kick off by suggesting that you take turns to ask 'getting to know you' questions of each other.

ACTIVITY: Sharing Basic Information

Take it in turns to ask questions of each other. Adjust the questions to reflect the age group and what you know in advance of the circumstances of your mentee.

- Name (to get the spelling correct and discover any nicknames used)
- How easy was it for you to make our meeting today—is the day, time, place, convenient for you?
- How do you feel about having/being a mentor?
- What do you hope to get out of our meetings?
- How do you like living in this area? What do you like/dislike most about it?
- What family do you have?

- Does anyone else live at home with you?
- Do you have any pets?
- Are you working (studying, retired) at the moment? How are you finding it?
- What jobs have you had in the past?
- Where did you go to school/college? How did you find it?
- What are you favourite TV programmes (and/or films)
- What kind of music do you like?
- What is your favourite kind of food and drink?
- What was the best holiday that you have ever had?
- What is your favourite possession?
- Are there any sports or interests that you follow or take part in?
- Are you a member of any social or sports clubs?
- If you won the lottery how would you spend the money?
- If you could afford to live anywhere you wished, where would you choose?

You should talk together about mentoring and what it involves to check that you have an agreed understanding of it. Take the time to talk through any different perceptions. Ask your mentee what they expect from mentoring and outline your own expectations. This should help to lead you into a discussion about how you are going to work together including communication styles.

Make an initial assessment of your mentee's level of self esteem and self confidence. If it appears to be low, before your next meeting, think about what you can do to give support (chapter four should help).

Your first meeting should also include some discussion of ground rules. These should include how you will treat each other and the importance of listening to each other and showing mutual respect. You must explain the rules about confidentiality (see chapter three). Any required record keeping will also need to be considered.

ACTIVITY: Some Agreed Ground Rules

As a mentor preparing for your first mentoring meeting, identify the ground rules that you will propose to your mentee. These might include:

Identify the time, place, frequency and duration of each meeting. Agree that we will both commit to attend and be punctual. Agree to give notice to each other if circumstances beyond our control prevent us making an agreed meeting.

Agree how and in what circumstances we are going to communicate with each other between meetings (set boundaries and protect your private life).

Agree when our mentoring will terminate (e.g. at the end of March next year). You can always change this later by mutual agreement but it sets a boundary which can prove a useful target date to complete agreed actions.

Make a statement about confidentiality and mandatory reporting (you will need to read chapter three to do this).

State that we will both do any agreed preparation/action between meetings.

Treat each other with respect and consideration.

Listen to each other and do our best to understand each other's point of view.

Proceed by agreement—do not try to dictate or bully.

Seek to support the mentee to identify personal goals. We agree to develop together a plan to tackle them.

In the case of disagreements that we can't solve we agree to take the issue to the scheme manager/coordinator.

Make a record of our progress and give feed back to our scheme manager/coordinator.

Agree to cooperate with monitoring and evaluation.

NOTE: Once you have reached agreement on these rules you might wish to write them up as an agreement and both sign and date them. This will help to cover you in case of any disagreement later. This is particularly useful in a workplace and with young people.

A Mentoring Plan?

Also at your first meeting it is sensible to think about how you will use your future meetings. Sometimes the purpose of the mentoring is very clear and you can soon agree how you will spend your time together. This could be set out on paper as a simple mentoring plan. This motivates and gives you a sense of direction.

In some mentoring schemes there can be a requirement that a mentoring plan is submitted as a means of monitoring the progress of the relationship. Such plans have got to be open to amendment as the relationship develops. In other mentoring situations, particularly where the mentee is emotionally vulnerable, it may not be possible to create a mentoring plan until a later stage, if at all.

A Group Session

Another option is to have a group social event as the first meeting for a number of mentors and mentees, where key messages can be shared (such as the confidentiality rules) and where some fun, non-threatening, group activities can be used as icebreakers to kick things off. Don't forget the cakes! In this case most of the items on the checklist below could be postponed to the following session which would usually be one to one.

First Mentoring Meeting—Checklist

Some of these items will be explained in later chapters

- Prepare in advance—find out about your mentee, have written scheme aims and guidelines ready to share.
- Ensure uninterrupted time.
- Set up venue—room, chairs, refreshments, turn off mobile phone.
- Start to get to know one another—consider icebreaking activity.
- Explain aims of scheme—check mentee is OK with these and discuss personal aims.
- Discuss mentor and mentee roles and relationships.
- Tell mentor how to contact the coordinator if not happy.
- Explain confidentiality.
- Discuss how long the relationship will last.
- Agree methods of contacting each other.
- Agree how you are going to record your progress.
- Agree the remaining ground rules.
- Decide on time and place of future meetings.
- Decide what you are going to discuss at next meeting(s).
- Consider a mentoring plan.

Working With Your Mentee

We have identified stages of the mentoring process and have explored the skills and attitudes required. How we set personal goals and tackle them will depend very much on the characteristics of the mentee, the setting, and the transition or problem being addressed. The following chapters will focus on some of the more common settings and look in more detail at their characteristics, typical issues and how they can be tackled. Chapter six looks at ability and learning in education. Chapter seven on careers illustrates in detail how a mentoring relationship can move through stages. Problem solving is addressed in the workplace chapter (eight) and negotiation in chapter ten on personal relationships.

Closure

Sooner or later each mentoring relationship must be brought to an end. Managing that closure can be difficult if a genuine rapport has developed. How can we go about it? Effective closure should leave the mentee with a strategy to move forward. Sometimes the mentee's goal has been achieved and the closing session might look forward to new opportunities and challenges that, hopefully, the mentee is equipped to handle independently.

For others, mentoring will have helped the mentee to set personal goals and develop a plan but there may be still some way to go to complete it. The mentor may have supported the mentee to take the first steps but feels that the mentee can now move forward unaided. Remember that we aim to promote independence in the mentee not continuing dependence. There comes a point where our mentee needs to take flight.

If the recommendations made earlier are followed, a time frame was agreed at the first mentoring meeting. Hence both parties are expecting closure which should make it easier. If this was not agreed, closure can leave the mentee feeling hurt and rejected.

Closure ends the mentoring but it does not necessarily end the relationship between the people concerned. In a workplace they may continue to be colleagues. In other settings they may decide to continue as friends. Occasionally the mentee will move on to become a mentor and hence will join the network and meet their former mentor as a new colleague. Here the nature of the relationship will change but closure is less of a wrench. Some schemes have developed a policy setting out rules for continuing contact but it is difficult to see how these could be enforced.

The best way to close is to mark it with a review of the progress that you have made together followed by a celebration of your success. The review of progress involves looking back over the mentoring process and evaluating what has been learned, what has worked well and where improvements could have been made. In turn this should be fed back to the scheme coordinator. More information on the celebration, monitoring, evaluation and review is given in chapter eleven.

ACTIVITY: Have I Got What It Takes To Be A Mentor?

If you can honestly say yes to the following statements there is a good chance that you will find mentoring to be a rewarding and successful experience.

I feel that I could:	Yes,	Not yet
befriend another person for a limited period of time with an agreed objective		
show positive attitudes to my mentee's future		
listen sympathetically to my mentee and encourage her or him to talk by sharing stories, and asking questions		
share my experience and knowledge		
avoid stereotyping and support my mentee equally well regardless of social background, age, gender, ability, ethnicity and sexuality		
help my mentee to think through any personal issues and gain a sense of self worth		
encourage my mentee to set some personal goals and gain a sense of direction in his or her life		
use other mentors, and outside contacts to obtain information and opportunities to offer to my mentee		

ensure that choices made are genuinely the mentee's own		
explore alternative pathways with my mentee, helping him or her to evaluate the options		
as necessary, help my mentee to speak up for himself or herself and on occasion I could act as an advocate for my mentee		
maintain confidentiality*		
help prepare my mentee for the next steps in life		
give my mentee the experience of having a successful mature non-sexual relationship.		

*except for reportable information—see chapter three.

Mentoring Ethics

The term 'Ethics' refers to the code of behaviour of a particular occupation, organisation or group.

Ethics are derived from values and moral principles. They are the rules which tell us how we should apply our values and principles to the particular field in which we are working. Hence we have, for example, medical ethics which apply to doctors.

Most professions base their codes on these four basic principles:

- avoid doing harm to others,
- promote the wellbeing of others,
- treat others fairly and impartially,
- be trustworthy and loyal; keep any commitments that you make.

Since mentoring involves a personal relationship of mutual trust where mentees often reveal private information, it is important that mentors also follow a strict code of ethics. In practice a set of ethical rules is often called a 'Code of Conduct'. Such a code may also include some additional requirements, such as administrative procedures, that are not strictly about ethical standards.

Since our role as mentors is distinctive, we need our own distinctive ethical codes. The precise wording of such a code will vary somewhat from scheme to scheme but they will all address similar issues. In this chapter we will outline principles which you are likely to find in a mentoring code of conduct. If you are setting up a mentoring scheme these principles should help you to devise your own code. We will go on to look at some examples of the ethical dilemmas that mentors can face.

Firstly, it is important to recognise that we are not above the law. Any code of conduct must be compatible with the law and should assert our responsibility to keep within the law. This may seem obvious but it presents us with an ethical dilemma when we come to the principle of confidentiality, as we shall see later.

Our mentoring scheme may take place within a wider organization such as a college, commercial company, church, government agency or a charity. This organization will have its own rules which will usually be set out in one or more documents. As mentors, even if we are unpaid volunteers, we are also bound by these rules. Although it is conceivable that we could find a rule which clashes with our mentoring ethics, such an eventuality would be unusual. Reputable organisations will usually incorporate ethical principles into their rules.

We have a duty of care to our mentees. This involves being alert to any threats to their wellbeing and taking steps to avoid these threats. For example, we would not arrange to meet a female mentee, in the evening, at a location where she had to walk alone through an area of town known for the rowdy, drunken and aggressive behavior of local men. Generally we should assess the risks before suggesting any course of action to our mentee.

We should endeavor to be a good role model. Hence we should dress appropriately and take care with our personal hygiene. This may seem obvious but the author has experience of mentors turning up with obvious body odour and dressed in grubby clothes. However, work clothes such as overalls may be appropriate when mentoring in a workplace or where a mentor takes time out of work to visit a mentee (meeting in a training centre for example).

Turning up for appointments and time keeping are also obvious requirements of a role model. There will be occasions when we are unavoidably delayed but we should telephone ahead and apologize once it is clear that we are not going to make it on time.

Reference was made earlier to the twin objectives of promoting the independence of the mentee and ensuring that any decisions made are genuinely the mentees own. To make these possible we should abide by the principle of being non-directive. This principle recognises that if the mentee has not made his or her own decision and is not genuinely convinced that it is the best alternative, it is much less likely to be pursued successfully. Moreover it would contradict the fundamental right of individuals to exercise their free will within the law. This does not mean that we avoid making suggestions or offering alternatives. It does mean that we should not push a particular course of action if it is clear that the mentee is not comfortable with it. The exceptions to this rule would be where the mentee is clearly intending to commit a serious crime or is intending self harm or harm to others. Apart from such rare and exceptional situations we should be seeking to help the mentee to explore and evaluate alternatives. It is our job to help the mentee think about the possible consequences of proposed actions, both positive and negative. Questioning is often the best approach here.

"How would you feel if . . . ?" What if . . . . happened?" How would doing this affect your relationship with . . . . ?" "How would you pay for . . . . ?"

References to fairness and equity are found in many ethical codes. It is important to remember that these principles also apply to people that we are NOT mentoring. Where a mentee confides in us that he or she has been treated very badly by another person we should listen carefully and supportively to the mentee. We should use questioning and recapping to become as clear as possible about the allegations. Although, we should not disbelieve the mentee, we should not assume that the mentee has given a full and accurate account. We are only hearing one side of the story and should not rush to judgment. In fairness to the accused we should recognise that we are not in a position to decide the rights and wrongs of the situation.

Our duty is to support mentees to the best of our ability but it is important to recognise that making unsubstantiated accusations in public may not be in the best interests of the mentee. If the accusations turn out to be inaccurate or to be a misunderstanding, the position of the mentee could be severely damaged among friends or colleagues.

The most sensible course of action is to discuss the accusation with the coordinator or supervisor of the mentoring scheme. Together, you may decide to report the accusation to the proper authorities and allow them to investigate. Depending on the situation, the proper authority could be for example school or college Principal, an employer, the police, or the government department charged with social work responsibilities. We will look further at accusations in the workplace in a subsequent chapter.

Discrimination and harassment are immoral and are illegal in many countries. Obviously as mentors we should not discriminate against a mentee on grounds such as age, gender, sexual orientation, pregnancy, race, ethnicity, marital status or disability. Often such discrimination is unintentional. For example, making mentoring available only at times when a parent caring for young children cannot attend or arranging mentoring at a location that is very awkward for a person with a disability to access.

At this point let us clarify a few terms. Prejudice refers to a set of attitudes which sees the members of a particular group as inferior or judges them negatively without good reason. No doubt we all have our prejudices and it would be pointless to make prejudice illegal. Since they are attitudes, they are in the mind and can be kept concealed. In contrast, when people act on their prejudices to treat others unfairly, we call this discrimination which is sometimes accompanied by harassment. Discrimination and harassment can be outlawed by law because they can be observed and evidence of them can be produced in court.

Prejudice can be tackled by education and persuasion. Discrimination can be tackled by the law and by procedures within organisations, including the dissemination and implementation of codes of conduct.

A particularly pernicious form of discrimination is racism. A problem that we face here is defining race. Race could simply be defined as a group of people with a common ancestry that share certain biological characteristics. However, this is rather unsatisfactory. This definition could fit a family, most of whom were well above average height and had sticking out ears. Clearly there are genetic differences between individuals and between family groups. However, the physical characteristics usually attributed to races are superficial ones, based on outward appearance such as skin colour which has no proven genetic impact on mental ability, on moral character or on the ability to interbreed. The usually unspoken definition of race held by those who are racially prejudiced implies that some races are biologically superior and hence that races are biologically distinct subspecies. There is no scientific evidence to support such an assumption. We are all the same species. It seems that human groups have been interbreeding throughout history and to divide us into biologically separate sub species called 'races' is to perpetuate a myth.

Ethnicity is sometimes treated as an acceptable shorthand for race. That is a pity since ethnicity is a valuable concept referring to non biological differences between groups. An ethnic group refers to a group of people who share a common history and culture. Such a group may share a language, a belief system, a set of customs, ceremonies and way of life. Members will often pass on histories, myths and stories down the generations. Ethnicity can be a positive source of identity and pride. In a multicultural society the differing traditions in areas such as food, music, art, dress and festivals can enrich the lives of everyone. 'Ethnics' are not alien others, we are all members of an ethnic group.

Race does exist however, as an idea in our minds. Since people act on their ideas, true or not, we have to face up to the reality of racial prejudice and discrimination. The reason for discussing this here is that we may find ourselves supporting a mentee who is racist or is experiencing racism. The mentee may believe that they are not succeeding because others are discriminating against them. This may be true or it may be a way of justifying their own poor behaviour or poor performance to themselves. As mentors we may not be able to discover the truth. If we have some evidence of discrimination we should report it to our scheme coordinator.

What we should always do is to try to raise mentees self esteem and encourage them to give of their best and to not give up. In the author's experience in education, most teachers do their very best to encourage and support students from minority communities. Because they come from different cultures, students can on occasion interpret poor marks or the demands of their teachers as discriminatory. Mentors can help students think through these issues. They could of course, approach teachers on the student's behalf. However, it is much better to support students to speak for themselves. Any discussions with teachers should only happen with the consent of the student.

Stereotyping occurs where a group in society comes to have a particular reputation which is crude, unfair and oversimplified. For example a particular housing estate may gain the reputation of being home to criminal gangs and drug pushers. Whilst it may have more than its share of these problems most of its residents may not be involved in them. If we automatically distrust residents of that estate we are guilty of falsely labelling them. It is basic social justice not to condemn others on the basis of an oversimplified image that we have of the group or place that they come from.

We should avoid patronising our mentees by acting in a condescending way towards them and implying that we are better than they are. It is easy to fall into the trap of topping. Topping means that when the mentee reveals something that they have experienced, the mentor jumps in to relate a personal experience that is more serious or more dramatic. Hence the mentee is always made to feel inferior. This can happen for the best of motives as the mentor seeks to reassure the mentee that his or her troubles can be overcome by finding an example where the mentor triumphed over greater adversity.

Rather than reassuring the mentee, this can appear as one-upmanship which denies the seriousness of the mentee's experience. Mentors can usefully share their own experiences from time to time but should beware of continually topping.

We should, of course, always show respect for our mentees even if we profoundly disagree with them or disapprove of their behaviour. This links to the principle of being non-judgmental. This principle is sometimes interpreted as accepting the mentees behaviour and values without challenging them, whatever they are. The author believes this to be a fundamental misinterpretation of the principle. To be non-judgmental is to avoid condemning the person as a person. It is to avoid implying or accusing the mentee of wickedness, immorality, stupidity or inferiority. However, it does not mean that we abandon our values or hide them. It is perfectly reasonable and sometimes essential that we voice our concern about a mentee's actions, as long as we do so in a way which does not denigrate them as a person. For example as a mentor and a role model, you might want to voice your disagreement with a mentee's racist comments, or their regular use of illegal drugs, or question their aggressive attitudes to a partner.

The objective is not to condemn but to encourage the mentee to think things through. We respect our mentees but where we have concerns, we should support them to consider carefully the likely consequences for themselves and others of their proposed actions. If despite our best efforts the mentee appears to be considering action which would be illegal and potentially damaging to themselves and others what should we do?

This brings us to the principle of confidentiality. It is essential that we are absolutely clear about our responsibilities here. If our mentees reveal something that is illegal or significantly puts themselves or others at risk we must pass this information on. This is usually required by law in respect of children and young people and is known as mandatory reporting. Even if it is not legally required it is wise to share your concerns with the coordinator of your mentoring scheme. Having the support of a properly structured mentoring scheme with an organiser and a code of practice is a huge advantage in circumstances such as these.

You might object that this breaks the confidentiality of mentor and mentee. Some books on mentoring insist that confidentiality must not be broken under any circumstances. Look back at the basic ethical principles. We must put the welfare of the mentee first but must also keep our promises. If for example your mentee insists on your discussions being confidential and you judge that your mentee is extremely emotionally disturbed and in real danger of suicide, what do you do?

This situation can be avoided if the mentee is informed at or before the first meeting that:

"As your mentor I have a responsibility to report to the scheme coordinator anything you tell me which involves any serious breaches of the law and anything which is putting yourself or others at significant risk of harm".

In Australia for example, child protection legislation requires mentors to report any suspicion of child abuse to the relevant Government Department or agency. Other countries have similar requirements. It would usually be sensible to make such a report through the mentoring scheme coordinator so that you are able to get the advice of another experienced person.

This does not mean that we ignore confidentiality. Any reports made must themselves be kept confidential to those who need to know. They must not be gossiped about to family, friends or colleagues. For example, an accusation of violence could be made which turns out to be completely unfounded. To reveal the accusation to friends would soon lead to its spread and the assertion that "there is no smoke without fire" which could seriously and permanently damage the reputation of the falsely accused person. It should be stressed here that, as mentors, we do not judge the truth or falsity of any statements made by our mentee. That is usually the responsibility of those authorities to whom we pass the information.

Any non-reportable conversations that a mentor has with a mentee must be kept confidential unless the agreement of the mentee is obtained to share it with someone else or to record it. Usually this is not a problem. For example, during mentoring an unemployed mentee expresses a wish to do some work experience. The mentee is happy to agree to the mentor using a network of contacts to seek suitable opportunities. No confidentiality is breached when the mentor explains to an employer friend that the mentee might be interested in spending a few days working in his business to see how it operates.

Potentially, confidentiality could be breached if the mentor makes written notes on the mentoring session and files them away where someone else has access to them. A sensible precaution is to always ask a mentee's permission before taking notes and to explain to the mentee where they will be kept and who will have access to them. A mentor should not take notes that he or she is unwilling to share with the mentee. Some schemes ask for a brief written record of the progress of mentoring. This need not represent a problem. Mentor and mentee can usually agree a form of words which broadly indicates the areas of discussion without revealing any confidential details.

Other than the major exceptions of reportable information and where the mentee agrees to share information, mentoring conversations should be confidential. Clearly it is not acceptable for the mentor to chat to friends, colleagues or partner giving details of the conversations. In some schemes revealing the identity of the mentee is not an issue. In an educational setting the mentor/mentee pairings may be common knowledge since mentoring is a normal activity which many people take part in at some point. However, there are other schemes where mentoring is of a sensitive nature, such as mentoring an ex offender, where the scheme code of conduct requires the mentee's identity to remain confidential.

Having a sexual relationship with your mentee is strictly forbidden. If a mentee and mentor are both adults, they are of course free to have a sexual relationship by mutual consent. However, they should stop being mentor and mentee before that occurs. If they both want a physically intimate relationship they should ask the scheme organiser to terminate their mentoring and if necessary allocate an alternative mentor. By a sexual relationship we do not just mean physical intimacy. It can involve suggestive remarks or deliberately provocative body language. It can also involve grooming where the mentor prepares the mentee for intimacy by presents, complements or personal revelations. Mentoring is not a dating agency. If you have any indication of a fellow mentor misusing his or her position in this way, particularly if the mentee is a young person, you must report it.

The code of conduct may specify other boundaries to protect both mentor and mentee from misusing the relationship. Such misuse could include making false accusations or simply making excessive demands on the mentor's time. This can be an issue when the mentees are vulnerable young people or where the scheme is designed to support emotionally vulnerable individuals. The scheme may wish to protect the mentor's family from receiving visits or telephone calls from a mentee. Hence the code could specify the conditions under which mentoring must take place. It could also suggest that mentors do not give their home address, home telephone number or home email address to mentees. Contact using social networking internet sites should also be treated with great caution.

Not all electronic contact need be discouraged. Indeed, distance mentoring using email, telephone or video conferencing could be the main means of contact where the mentee lives in a remote location. In industry or the public service mentor and mentee may work in different locations, perhaps even in different countries. In higher education it is now quite common for students to be enrolled in courses in other countries as external students. Being able to contact a mentor electronically, could be an extremely useful source of support but it should be organised or authorised by the scheme coordinator and be within the scheme guidelines.

Trustworthiness is absolutely fundamental to the mentoring relationship. It can be hard to win in some cases. The main reason for a person seeking a mentor may be because there is no one else that they can trust. Hence they may be predisposed to suspicion. The best way to gain trust is to demonstrate trustworthiness by using your mentoring skills, particularly active listening, and to following the above principles. If you turn up on time, listen carefully, ask supportive questions, show respect, are non-judgmental, non directive and keep confidentiality, you will be well on the way.

A range of other issues peculiar to individual schemes may also be included in a code. It could for example require the mentee to abide by other rules that already exist within an organisation. It could impose restrictions on contacts with the media, the taking of photographs or specify procedures for the giving of references. There may well be a set of scheme guidelines within which the code of conduct is just one component.

Some Ethical Dilemmas

When faced with an ethical dilemma. Look at each possible course of action and ask yourself:

If I were the mentee how would I feel about this?

If I were one of the other people closely involved in this situation how would I feel about it?

This won't always solve the problem for you but thinking about the situation with empathy, from another person's point of view, should help you to deal with it in a sensitive manner.

Being non-directive

A manipulative mentor could use the wording of suggestions and questions to subtly steer the mentee in a particular direction. This would be unethical but it could be a consequence of the aims of the scheme. For example imagine that the aims of a government funded scheme were identified as:

'To increase the percentage of young people staying on at school after the compulsory leaving age.'

In such a case the success of the scheme would obviously be evaluated according to the numbers deciding to stay on. If this does not significantly increase, the scheme funding may be cut. There would be a strong temptation on the part of mentors to use all their skills to emphasise the advantages of staying on at High School and to denigrate alternatives such as seeking a full time job.

The ethical mentor should research the options with the mentee; looking at all the alternatives. Questioning should then be used to help the mentee sort out his or her preferences. If the aims of the scheme had been written differently and the scheme evaluated differently the ethical dilemma would be less acute. What if the mentee says the following?

"I don't want to spend my time stuck in school doing stuff that bores me silly. I want to grow up, get out into the world, earn some cash and have some fun. I can get some work at the meat processing factory. You don't have to do any qualifications and the money is good. I will be able to afford my own car in no time."

This is a real enough situation that the author has experienced. It might not seem to be in the long term interests of the young person to settle for an unskilled labouring job. Yet, to persuade him otherwise seems to contradict the principle of being non directive. What can you do?

The mentor should aim to explore all the alternatives carefully with the mentee and look at the long term as well as their short term consequences. In later chapters some techniques for doing this will be discussed. However, after all the consequences have been reviewed the mentee may still insist on leaving education.

Is it ethical to try to persuade the mentee into a different course of action? For the author the answer must be no because we cannot decide for someone else how they should live their lives. In a free society they must make their own choices. In the above case the mentee is hardly likely to pursue school study successfully even if he was manipulated into it since he lacks any commitment.

Law Breaking and Confidentiality

Your mentee casually mentions that she is a regular soft drug user. Here we should be careful not to be rejecting and critical of the person (being non judgmental). However you may wish to explain that you do not take drugs and explain why. You may also use questioning to satisfy yourself that your mentee understands the dangers and consequences of continuing to be a user.

If your mentee is of school age, this should be reported to the scheme coordinator. If the mentoring is in a school the report should be made to the school Principal.

If the mentee is an adult, the mentor has a fine judgment to make. If the mentee is using illegal drugs a in a workplace such as a hospital, the mentor would be wise to report it even though the mentee's job could be at risk, since the mentor's responsibility to the hospital's patients and staff surely outweighs confidentiality to the mentee. A report may well end the mentoring relationship but that is a price which has to be paid.

If however a mentee is an occasional leisure time user, apparently well in control and is not supplying others, the calculation may become a different one. Even if the mentee is reported to the police they may be disinclined to take action. In some jurisdictions drug use is so widespread that the police turn a blind eye to private personal use and concentrate their efforts on traffickers. Moreover, as a mentor you may be able to help your mentee to tackle a situation that is causing them great anxiety. Your support may reduce the likelihood of their drug use getting out of control.

A Traumatic Session

Occasionally a mentee may reveal some appalling event that has happened or is happening to them. The mentee may reveal personal details that shock you and that you find extremely distressing and difficult to cope with.

This may not be something which you have to report and the mentee may insist on your confidentiality. You can't just turn off your feelings when you part. At home the situation may be praying on your mind as you try to work out what you should say or do at your next meeting. Your partner wonders what the problem is. Can you share it?

If your partner already knows the person whom you are mentoring, you must not discuss it. If however the person and name of your mentee is unknown to your partner, you should be able to explain that you have been told something which had really distressed you and you are struggling to work out how to respond. You would not go into details of course, but hopefully your partner would be supportive and understand why you are distressed.

This situation also shows why, in some types of mentoring scheme, it is better not to mentor a personal friend or someone well known to your family.

A Fellow Mentor

Imagine being at a social event where a fellow mentor, George, is present and starts to talk about his mentee to a group of friends. You immediately realise that he is breaking confidentiality and breaching the code of conduct. What do you do? Should you report him to the scheme coordinator?

This is another judgment call. If possible interrupt the conversation with a comment such as:

"Of course George can't tell you all the details because we are bound by confidentiality but I find mentoring to be a really interesting experience. I am learning a lot. Don't you agree George?"

Hopefully George will take the hint and realise that he has dropped a clanger. If you feel that this is a one off aberration that he will not repeat, you might leave it there. If however you feel that he is an incorrigible gossip who will not be able to resist the temptation to do this again, you have a duty to report him to the scheme coordinator.

Do You Intervene?

You are out late on a Saturday evening. When walking through the centre of town you see your mentee, Angelina, emerge from a bar on the other side of the street with a group of friends. She has not seen you. They are having a fierce argument, with abusive language and threatening gestures. A young man pushes Angelina and she starts to cry. Do you intervene or do you pass by on the other side?

Your options include

1. Rush across to defend Angelina against the people who have upset her.
2. Cross the street to say hello pretending that you have not witnessed the row.
3. Observe the incident from a distance before deciding what to do.
4. Telephone the police.
5. Ignore the whole incident as none of your business.
6. Resolve to ask her about it when you next see her.

To make a judgment you will probably want more information. How old is she? Does she seem to be drunk? Is the entire group threatening her or is she part of one group which is arguing with another group? Does she seem to be at risk of further violence?

Ask yourself: if I was in her position what would I want my mentor to do?

Ask yourself: if I were not her mentor what would I do?

If this is simply an argument with her boyfriend she is likely to be very embarrassed at your intervention. On the other hand if she is a lone female being harassed by a group of men she would probably welcome your support.

One strategy would be to observe at a distance for a few moments to assess the situation. If you suspect that she is at risk—call the police, as you would for any young women you saw in that situation.

If you intervened would you simply make the situation worse and put yourself at risk? If it becomes clear that it is simply an emotional argument between two groups and is not descending into violence; walk away. When you meet her give her the opportunity to talk about the incident, perhaps by mentioning your evening out and asking her if she enjoyed her weekend. Do not press her if she does not talk about the incident. She has a right to privacy.

ACTIVITY: Create a Code of Conduct for Your Scheme

Here are examples of items which could be covered.

- Abide by the law and by the rules of the organisation that you are working in (even if you are a volunteer).
- You have a duty of care to your mentee and other people who may be involved.
- Show respect to your mentee, earn trust.
- Respect privacy—do not probe into matters that your mentee does not wish to discuss.
- Strive to be a positive role model.
- Show empathy.
- Be reliable, be punctual.
- Be non judgmental but do not abandon your own values.

- Be non-directive; support your mentee to reach his or her own decisions.
- Support your mentee to develop the self confidence to act independently—do not create a relationship of dependency.
- Be fair and equitable to mentees and others.
- Do not stereotype or discriminate unfairly.
- Maintain the boundaries appropriate to your scheme (e.g. do not give your home address or phone number).
- Do not have a sexual relationship with your mentee.
- Do not patronise or engage in topping.
- Never be sarcastic or belittle your mentee's achievements.
- Maintain confidentiality except where you are required to report possible law breaking or where your mentee, or another person, could be in danger of harm.
- Regularly liaise with the scheme coordinator.

CHAPTER FOUR

Self, and Self Esteem

When supporting mentees, we need to recognise both the common experiences that human beings face and the unique characteristics of each person. Whist some experiences, needs and characteristics may be almost universal, the range of human personalities, circumstances and wants is obviously enormous. Hence it is crucial that mentors take time to get to know their mentees and do not assume that what would be right for them is also right for the mentee. We have already discussed the importance of being non directive. In this and subsequent chapters some of the ways in which we are alike and are at the same time unique will be explored.

To be aware of 'oneself' implies being conscious of our own characteristics, capabilities, responses and attitudes. Having a 'self' is not just how we think and behave differently from everyone else. It is also being aware of our own separateness as a unique individual. It involves the ability to stand back from ourselves and have a mental picture of what we are like.

We have self consciousness. In other words, we each have a self image in our minds of what we are like and what makes us distinctive. Generally this will include both positive (e.g. I am likeable) and negative (e.g. I am not very patient) qualities. How do we acquire this self image? The self is not something that we simply biologically inherit from our parents although our genetic inheritance may influence it. To a large extent it seems to come from interactions, from birth, with the people around us. It is the quality of our personal relationships which seems to be crucial to our self image. If we get lots of positive feedback from others we will usually have a positive self image and this in turn should give us the self esteem which is essential for mental health.

Some people seem to have much greater insight into themselves than others. Moreover our self image may not be an accurate picture. For example a father may see himself as being fair minded to his children whereas they may see him as over strict and unjust. Although we may occasionally misread the reactions of others to us, it is our interpretations of these reactions that tell us what sort of person we are.

It is often assumed that there is a 'true' or inner self at the core of our being; which is the essence of what we are. For the religious this might be seen as an aspect of our spirit or soul. Others may take it for granted that it is built into our own unique genetic code. A strand of research in psychology takes a very different approach stressing the ways in which the self develops and changes through relationships with other people. Here the self is very plastic. Although we are all strongly shaped by our genetic inheritance, recent research suggests that we are all conceived with the potential to be many different selves. Our life experiences will determine which self we become.

Our early childhood and adolescent experiences are particularly important in the formation of our self and self image. Neurological research in the last few years indicates that his developing self image creates pathways in the brain which in turn affect our overall physical and mental development. If we have negative thoughts about ourselves when we are young, this produces high levels of stress which can damage our physical and mental development; triggering serious illness later in life.

If we feel constricted by an empty, dull or boringly predictable life, we might dream of breaking away and seek new experiences, relationships, challenges, and adventures. This has been described as 'finding oneself'—implying that a repressed, true, inner self is waiting to be discovered. However, embarking on a radically different life might be more accurately seen as recreating oneself. If you act differently people see you differently and treat you differently. As a result you see yourself differently. If you develop relationships with a very different group of people in a new setting they will have no knowledge of your previous history and will respond to what they see of you. Hence, your self image can change and you can feel yourself developing as a person.

The author has seen this process at work many times in adult education. The supermarket checkout 'chick' who went on to a get a first class degree in philosophy, growing in confidence and poise at each step in the process. The housewife and mother (her own description) who after years of part time study became a social worker presenting evidence in court with confidence and aplomb; the joiner who became a professional musician; the labourer who became a local councillor.

The message is clear.

We all have undeveloped potential. We can all change and develop ourselves.

A crucial part of doing so can be to change how we present ourselves to other people.

How does all this relate to mentoring? It is important because mentoring is usually about supporting someone through a transition in their lives. These transitions challenge people and can change them. It may be at work, taking up new responsibilities. It may be embarking on a new college course. It could be overcoming some traumatic personal event. It may even be moving countries as a refugee. How we cope with challenges of this kind shapes our self image, impacts upon our self confidence and can lead to personal growth.

If we don't manage the transition well it can of course have a very damaging effect on the self. In some cases it can trigger depression and mental disorder. Around one in five of us will suffer some form of mental disorder at some point in our lives. As we shall discuss in chapter nine, some of this may have a genetic base but much of it appears to be triggered by damaging events and relationships in our lives (i.e. it is situational).

As a mentor, if you help your mentee to develop a positive self image and self esteem you will have done them a really valuable service. You may even be able to help someone to recreate themselves as a more positive and confident person.

A person who has some insight into her or his own emotions and who is sensitive to the feelings of others is likely to be more successful in the transition process. Daniel Goleman has described this ability as 'emotional intelligence' (E.I.). It is importance for the development of self awareness, self esteem and self confidence.

Emotional intelligence involves knowing yourself and understanding your feelings. This helps you to understand the relationships that you have with others. It is being able to use, understand, and manage your own emotions; controlling anger, stress, and negative thoughts. In turn this enables you to think more clearly. People who have E.I. are less depressed, healthier, more employable, and have better relationships. People with high level of emotional intelligence are able to use techniques such as self talk (being able to reason with yourself to create a positive attitude), and relaxation techniques (such as controlled breathing).

Unfortunately, in the past we often saw emotions as being in the way— keeping us from making rational decisions. Research is now suggesting the opposite.

Social intelligence takes things a step further by stressing our use of intelligence in social relationships and social situations. It has two aspects. The first one is 'social awareness' in which we become attuned to others and can develop empathy (being able to put yourself in the position of someone else and see things from their viewpoint). The second is 'social facility' where we can present ourselves well to others, interact successfully with them, influence them, and show concern for them. Goleman examines recent research on the brain to argue that we are "wired to connect". This refers to the research finding that during interactions with others lots of brain activity is stimulated which affects our body as well as our mind. Social contact affects our immune system, triggers the release of hormones, stimulates the heart, and affects our breathing. Some relationships are healthy, enhancing our self esteem and having positive effects on our physical health. Other relationships can be toxic; depressing us, stressing our bodies, and making us more vulnerable to ill health. In effect relationships mould our biology and are vital for our wellbeing.

Clearly this form of intelligence is crucial to success in virtually every area of life including marriage, parenting, friendships, and in the workplace. Hence it is probably more important that other forms of intelligence for our success at work and for our personal happiness. If we are socially intelligent we can 'read' the emotions of others and develop a rapport with them. We intuitively know how they are feeling and what response they need from us. We are able to respond to them in ways that make us trusted, accepted and popular. We become an effective team player and perhaps a leader. Goleman describes Social intelligence as

"being intelligent, not just about our relationships, but also in them"

For Goleman altruism towards others is natural to us. When we have a relationship, social intelligence involves thinking about the best interests of the other person rather than just focusing upon ourselves. This is a pretty good description of the mentoring relationship.

The following example, contrasts the two approaches of Halim and Erica to the same situation. It will help us to understand the importance of using emotional intelligence.

Halim and Erica

Imagine Halim, a shy person, with a poor self image. His employer has sent him to an event where a new product is to be launched by a supplier. He knows no one else there. Since Halim lacks self confidence, he dresses in a dull and conservative fashion and makes little effort with his appearance.

Lots of people have already arrived and are talking animatedly in small groups. Halim enters feeling nervous and unsure. His body language immediately shows this. He does not approach any of the groups. Seeking the security of a quiet corner he pretends to study the view from a window, turning away from others in the room. Another guest, on his own, approaches and starts a conversation. Halim is tongue tied and does not make eye contact. Not wanting to appear stupid he can't really think of anything useful to say. The other person soon gives up and moves away when he recognises an old friend at the other side of the room. Halim is pretty much ignored throughout the event and can't wait to get away. An observer of Halim would see him as a rather awkward, dull person behaving rather strangely and avoiding others. The whole episode has confirmed Halim's negative view of himself. "Everyone else seemed to make friends so easily but they didn't want to know me. What is wrong with me?"

OR

Erica feels shy and awkward but she makes a real effort to be positive when meeting new people. She realises that if she can present herself positively as outwardly confident and friendly (however anxious she feels inside), her chances of making new friends will be greatly increased. Her employer has sent her to an event where a new product is to be launched by a supplier. She knows no one else there. Erica sees this as an opportunity to meet a wider range of people in her industry and make some new contacts. She makes a real effort with her appearance to present herself in a professional manner.

Lots of people have already arrived and are talking animatedly in small groups. Erica enters feeling rather nervous. However she is determined to make the effort to get to know people. She realises the importance of making a good first impression so she takes a deep breath holds her head up and walks confidently into the room. Approaching a mixed group of men and women she waits for a lull in the conversation before introducing herself to the woman next to her. She freely admits that this is her first experience of this kind of event. The people in the group are happy to explain the format. One woman is particularly friendly and later introduces her to several people from companies that deal with her own.

After the event Erica felt that most people there were very happy to chat to her and she had made some contacts that might be useful in the future. "I got on much better than I thought I would. What was I so nervous about?"

Clearly the above scenario is an oversimplification to make a point. When we meet someone for the first time they have little choice but to accept us as what they see. When a stranger offers to shake your hand you cannot afford to spend a few minutes logically working out whether it is a good idea to offer your hand in return. Nor can you read his inner intentions. You must make an instant decision. Can you trust this person? Are they a threat to you?

Recent psychological evidence suggests that our brains operate on a number of levels, most of which are subconscious. As we saw in Chapter two, one level of your brain will immediately warn you to be cautious if the person is showing unusual body language or appears strange. By ensuring that we appear to others as 'normal' and friendly, we can usually get an immediate positive response from them in a social situation such as the one described above. Moreover, once we get positive feedback from others, our self confidence starts to build. If this positive feedback continues we will develop a more positive self image and self belief. In turn this makes it easier to project ourselves positively to others in a self reinforcing process.

Self esteem can spiral upwards or downwards depending on the response that we get from the people around us.

If a mentee is shy, nervous and lacking in confidence the mentor can help just by being there, listening, taking an interest in the mentee and treating him or her as an equal. Here we are giving positive feedback and trying to encourage confidence and a more positive outlook.

Of course our efforts as mentors are likely to be overshadowed by the mentee's close personal relationships such as parent to young person, teacher to student, employer to employee, colleague to colleague. If these are giving very negative feedback what can we do? We can talk to the mentee about emotional intelligence and help them to stand back and see the relationship in a more objective light. We can help them to practice relating to others in less negative fashion. It may be entrenched negativity in the other person that is the source of the problem. If our mentee can come to see that the problem could be the other person's lack of social skills, they may begin to be less negative about themselves.

A skill that we are trying to encourage here is self talk. When faced with decision to make in a challenging situation we may try to think it through rationally. However, where self esteem is low we may get into the habit of negative thinking. Our internal talk may emphasise the dangers of failure or embarrassment, leading us to avoid situations by taking a day off sick, bunking off school, or turning down an opportunity. We can break this pattern by consciously being aware of the dangers of negativity and deciding to take a more positive line with ourselves. We can inwardly talk ourselves in to depression but positive self talk can help to ward it off.

Here again a mentor can help by raising the issue of self talk and giving illustrations of positive thinking to the mentee that can change the way that that he or she looks at the self and relationships. Ask "what can you say to yourself before meeting . . . . ?" Practising a social situation and the self talk that the mentee could use leading up to it, can be a useful exercise for mentor and mentee to do together.

The Basis Model

Alistair Smith* has developed the BASIS model to identify key factors that underlie self esteem and self belief (it has similarities to Maslow's hierarchy of needs). This model was developed in the context of accelerated learning but can have a much wider applicability. It can help to remind us of the conditions that we ought to put in place to support our mentee. The five elements within the model are:

- BELONGING

According to Smith, this concerns being "approved of and respected by others". Trust, loyalty, and a sense of well being, can grow when we feel that we are a fully accepted and valued member of a group. As mentors we can show approval and acceptance of our mentees to give them a sense of belonging.

It is interesting to consider whether the damage done by bullying is as much about being excluded and isolated as it is about being threatened.

- ASPIRATIONS

We need something to strive for in order to give us a sense of purpose. Smith claims "Aspirations provide motivation".

Mentoring involves support through a personal transition. That transition is likely to be accomplished much more successfully if we can help our mentee to develop realistic and achievable goals. Once the mentee has these goals, the mentor can offer support in identifying pathways to achieve them. Often this process will motive the mentee and gradually change his or her attitudes. Developing goals and identifying pathways together, transforms mentoring into a much more positive and purposeful experience for both parties. We are making progress together rather than churning through problems and anxieties.

- SAFETY

It is very difficult for a learner to learn, an employee to take on responsibility, or an excluded person to step out into the social world, if they feel unsafe and deeply insecure. Smith asserts that "students who are secure can take risks". This also applies to those seeking work and people in work. How many capable people have been too insecure to apply for promotion to a position that they could have filled much more effectively than the person who was actually appointed? Research evidence suggests that students who feel unsafe become highly stressed and tend to underperform in examinations. Some stress can stimulate and motivate us but excessive stress damages our ability to concentrate and remember. Clearly individuals differ in the degree to which they can accommodate insecurity and stress. Some people thrive on levels of stress, danger and risk taking that would drive others into high levels of anxiety. Effective mentoring should help mentees to be more resilient when faced with the day to day insecurities and stresses of their everyday lives.

Mentors can also help here by creating a safe environment in which to mentor, giving reassurance and showing confidence in the mentee.

- IDENTITY

Here we return to the notion of self with which we began this chapter. Identity is about having a good understanding of oneself including "strengths and weaknesses, values and beliefs". A strong positive sense of self identity leads to greater resilience in the face of the difficulties and setbacks that we all face from time to time. Hence, such a person will persist and show greater determination to succeed. A positive sense of 'who we are' should help us avoid depression and negative, destructive thoughts. However, some people can experience a deeply entrenched negative identity. If they have had multiple experiences of failure, a sense of their own inadequacy can become part of their self image. The mentor can help by encouraging the mentee to use self talk to reflect on his or her life, and identify achievements, positive qualities and skills. The mentor can give the mentee the great gift of experiencing a successful relationship.

Moreover, the mentor can help to bring some feelings of success to the mentee, which leads us into the next point.

- SUCCESS

It is not only important to be successful at some activity; our success also needs to be acknowledged by others. Far too often as: parents, friends, partners, colleagues and teachers, we take for granted the tasks completed by others and yet we are quick to criticise when they make errors. Giving recognition, such as a few words of praise (when deserved), makes the recipient feel good. It promotes in them, the sense that they have control over their own lives strengthening their self esteem and identity. How often are marriages undermined by frequent criticisms and complaints which are not balanced by thanks and praise when the partner is supportive and helpful? It is a good rule to try to ensure that deserved praise outnumbers criticism by a large margin. If the dominant pattern is one of praise and encouragement, occasional criticism can be taken on board without damage to self esteem. A four to one ratio is favour of praise is suggested by Smith.

Mentors should try to make opportunities for their mentees to do something positive. The way forward here is by a series of small steps. Agreeing on very achievable short term tasks, gives opportunities for praise which can gradually build up a sense of self worth. For example it might be suggested that the mentee looks up some information for the next meeting. If he does so, deserved praise can be given. It can also be given if the mentee makes an insightful comment during conversation or even if the mentee is always punctual.

Don't just take positive behaviour for granted. Show that you appreciate it and it will be more likely to continue. Never be sarcastic.

Try to make mentoring: *a no 'put down's' zone*.

Note that Smith's Book 'Accelerated Learning in the Classroom' published in 1996 contains much that is valuable but some of the material has been overtaken by more recent research on Brain Development. Smith discusses this in his later 2004 publication 'The Brain's Behind it".

We have stressed the importance of praise. But there are a range of other techniques that we can use to encourage a positive self image, self confidence, and personal aspirations, which we will explore in later chapters.

Mind Sets

Closely related to the notion of self, is that of mind set.

A person's 'mind set' is the way that he or she typically looks at the world and his/her place in it. It is a set of attitudes that people habitually use to respond to events, opportunities and challenges in life. Psychologist Carol Dweck (2006) contrasts two fundamental mind sets:

- THE FIXED MINDSET

This is the feeling that you are born with a fixed amount of talent and ability which cannot be changed. Hence you do not accept tough challenges because you fear failure. Change is viewed as a threat rather than an opportunity. The fixed mindset is a protection against disappointment and a way of avoiding tough challenges.

- THE GROWTH MINDSET:

This is the feeling that you can develop yourself—your skills, abilities and talents—over time, if you work hard and persist. People with the growth mind set have much less fear of failure and can see obstacles as interesting and stimulating challenges to be overcome. They are more resilient.

It seems likely that a person's mind set reflects their family background and early experiences. However, it is also possible to change a mind set as a result of mature reflection or new experiences. On the whole, people with a growth mindset will be more confident and are more likely to set themselves challenging goals and to reach them. Consequently those achieving promotion at work and success in education tend to have growth mindsets.

See chapter 11 for illustrations of other mind sets.

Resilience

Resilience is being able to face difficult and challenging circumstances and to continue to work through them without giving up. It means not allowing these circumstances to distort your development; for example not becoming resentful and negative, not abusing alcohol or drugs, not becoming violent or criminal, and not withdrawing into a private fantasy world.

The factors that influence resilience are now quite well known. It is based upon a positive mind set and upon maintaining your self esteem despite setbacks and difficulties. The factors involved are very similar to those found in the BASIS model outlined above, together with social and emotional intelligence. Also important is a strong set of personal values.

Material poverty, family disorganisation and conflict, social isolation, together with negative experiences of schooling, can undermine resilience. Having strong support from family, friends and the wider community plays a crucial part in maintaining it. To build resilience in the young we need to build a positive and protective environment which will sustain them through crises and difficulties. Without such an environment, difficulties can come to be seen as insurmountable barriers rather than challenges to overcome.

A relationship with a mentor role model can be a very valuable feature of that environment of community support. Accessing a mentor at a crucial turning point in your life could be the difference between maintaining a resilient attitude or retreating into negativity, depression and withdrawal.

Daniel and Wassell have produced a valuable series of workbooks which can be used to help build resilience in children and young people (see reading list).

Realism

Some self help guru's would have us believe that you can achieve anything if you set your mind to it—if you believe in yourself enough and are determined enough. In the author's experience this is nonsense (I could never now achieve my childhood ambition of being a professional footballer for Preston North End).

As mentors we work with our mentees to help them to build their self esteem, encourage a growth mind set and attempt to develop resilience. However, we should not build them up to fail by encouraging totally unrealistic aspirations. Our job is not to set goals for our mentees but to help them to become aware of opportunities and talk through with them the advantages and disadvantages of the alternatives open to them. If our mentee, in ignorance, considers setting a goal without appreciating the extent of the challenge which is ahead, it is surely our duty to ensure that they fully understand what faces them. As we shall see in chapter seven we can support our mentees to set their sights high without promoting an impossible fantasy. The best policy is often a step by step one which does not close off long term exceptional achievement but not guarantee it.

CHAPTER FIVE

Younger and Older

In this chapter some features of mentoring different age groups will be examined. Potentially, mentoring can be used with primary school children and any adult age group. Each age group has characteristics which influence the mentoring relationship.

Mentoring Children

Psychologists have long recognised the importance of young children bonding to adults and, as they grow, having role models to look up to and copy. Of course bonding usually takes place with parents, grandparents or other close relatives and family friends. Alternatively adoptive or foster parents may take on that role.

Unfortunately, some children fail to bond effectively with an adult. Others may bond with a parent of the opposite sex but lack a role model of their own sex. Single parenthood is common in many western countries but it is clear that having a single parent does not in itself cause developmental damage to children. Most children of a single parent grow into adulthood very successfully. However, some single parents do not become so by choice and may lack the support of other adults. They may be too young and too immature to cope well as a parent, finding it difficult to bond with their growing child. The child may become insecure and angry, growing up to reject authority. Sometimes mum or dad has a new partner who is unwilling or unable to bond with the child.

It might be thought that mentors could step into the breach to provide bonding and role modelling. However, this can be very dangerous. Boundaries are particularly difficult to maintain with children and closing the relationship could bring psychological distress to the child with negative long term consequences. It should only be undertaken by people who are fully aware of the long term consequences for themselves and the child. Mentoring the parent might be a better option.

There are dangers in using mentoring as a general emotional support mechanism for young children.

- Children will seek to bond emotionally with significant adults in their lives who they come to like and trust and who encourage them to share their fears and feelings.
- They may not understand the boundaries to this relationship and may feel rejected if the mentoring is limited to a particular time and place.
- Children may feel that they are second best if a mentor goes home to their own children or grandchildren and they are excluded.
- Children may make demands that seem reasonable to them but which the mentor is reluctant to take on. Are you able to take your mentee to sports training each week and then watch them play in competitions each weekend. Are you able to take him or her to your home or away on holiday?
- Mentoring is generally time limited. Ending the relationship after a few months will seem like rejection to the child.
- The child may expect the mentor to engage with his/her family. Doing so may lead the mentee to having to support a parent or other family member, or having to withdraw altogether.

- The code of conduct and rules of the mentoring scheme may limit mentors contact to protect both parties from the consequences of any accusations of abuse e.g. no home visits or outside trips. How do you explain this to young children.

It will be seen that there are a whole series of boundary issues here. Young children need to develop long term bonding within a family or surrogate family. Short term mentoring is no substitute for this and could potentially increase a child's distress when the inevitable separation occurs. Hence, in the above circumstances, a long term emotionally committed relationship is required which falls outside our initial definition of mentoring.

Mentoring should be about helping to empower people to be independent rather than entering a long term dependency relationship. People who are willing to take on the latter with emotionally needy children should consider fostering or becoming a professional social, or community worker. They could also consider becoming a volunteer, supporting professional care workers by, for example, running recreational activities for these children.

Where younger children do need additional support, the most effective approach may be to work with a group through a homework club, sporting club, drama or music. Here the child will not feel rejected if the mentor imposes boundaries to the relationship. However, the equality that characterises adult mentoring must be modified as the mentor leads activities and takes on a duty of care. In this situation, to involve older children as peer mentors or 'buddies' can be very useful. The adult is them the supporter of the peer mentor. The adult has a dual role as a coach and a mentor. The mentoring element involves being a good role model, being an active listener, asking the right questions in a sensitive manner and being ready to refer on to professionals if there are any serious causes for concern

Mentoring can be very successful in the field education of where children can benefit from some support in addition to that of a teacher. Again peer mentoring can also be used. We will explore mentoring in education in the next chapter.

Adolescence

The age groups that appear to give particular concern to mentors are those of adolescence and early adulthood. Mentoring tackles transitions and challenges. So does adolescence which could be said to begin with the onset of puberty and end with adulthood. Hence it is the transition from being a child to becoming an adult. This delineation is not quite as straightforward as it at first seems.

- The onset of puberty varies considerably between individuals but is usually around the ages of 11 to 13.
- Physical changes may begin earlier and proceed faster than psychological changes.
- Emotional maturity can lag far behind sexual maturity.
- Most girls mature physically before most boys.
- At what age does adulthood typically begin? 'Rites of passage' such as an 18th birthday, a 21st birthday, or leaving school, can mark a change in social and legal status but they do not necessarily bring psychological adulthood.

Recent research suggests that the frontal lobe of the brain which is thought to be the location of judgement and to regulate risk taking, does not fully mature until the mid twenties. Therefore it might be helpful to see adolescence ending for most young people at around eighteen years and being followed by a period of early immature adulthood lasting until around twenty two to twenty four years.

Mentoring schemes targeted at mainstream young people are often focussed on progress in education, training or career choice, all of which will be explored in the next few chapters. These can be interesting and enjoyable for both the mentee and mentor since observable progress is often possible within a matter of weeks or months. Such mentoring may not require the mentor to confront young people with behavioural or emotional problems. Hence it should not demand exceptional interpersonal skills.

Most young people move through the challenges of adolescence quite successfully. This is often because they have a strong family base, a set of caring friends and neighbours around them and a range of life opportunities. Unfortunately some adolescents and emotionally immature young adults can be found taking risks without thinking through the consequences and can become embroiled in binge alcohol drinking and other substance abuse. This group are particularly prone to thoughtlessly taking decisions which can damage themselves and others for many years to come. These include having children whilst not being in a position to support them, making ill considered marriages and abandoning good jobs, courses or apprenticeships rather than seeing them through. They are more prone to car crashes and are much more likely to be found committing violent and other criminal acts than older generations.

Sadly, the small minority of adolescents who regularly consume alcohol and or other drugs to excess can suffer serious damage to their brain development. In particular they can damage frontal lobe development and consequently develop a long term inability to make good judgement calls or to plan ahead sensibly. This is often combined with low self esteem, an early exit from education, poor literacy levels and petty crime. For a small minority, in later life these characteristics can lead into mental disorders and/or long term criminality. A high proportion of prison inmates have a history of drug/alcohol abuse, mental illness and illiteracy. Imprisonment is almost guaranteed to make the situation worse. Therefore in some countries every effort is made to avoid custodial sentences.

If we can keep them out of prison, most young offenders will grow out of crime. Probation and juvenile justice professionals supported by mentors can play an enormously valuable role in this process.

As they get older most young people reduce their alcohol consumption, and take fewer risks—some do not. Most young offenders grow out of crime—some do not. The right kind of support, at the right time in their development, could have made a real difference to the minority who get into trouble. Mentoring them is very challenging and should only be undertaken by trained and experienced mentors who are prepared to make a major commitment to the task.

Volunteers can be used here but people with a background in teaching, youth work, counselling or community work are likely to be particularly suitable. The author has experience of professional people in these fields taking up unpaid voluntary mentoring after retirement or alongside a part-time job and doing excellent work. Some of the most effective volunteer mentors lack this kind of professional background but have plenty of life experience, commitment and a full range of interpersonal skills. These people are wonderful unsung heroes whose achievements are by their very nature confidential. They give so much of themselves to others without any material reward. The point to be emphasised here is that mentoring an emotionally disturbed young person is not something to be tried on as a fad. It must be a serious commitment that is properly prepared for and supported.

A frequently noted characteristic of adolescents is self centeredness. Psychologists such as Erik Erikson have pointed out that adolescence is crucial for the development of the self concept. Hence, during this ego centric formative period, young people can be less sensitive to the feelings and needs of others as they struggle with their own identity. Parents often feel unappreciated and taken for granted which can generate family conflict.

Adolescents typically choose their friends from their own age group. For the sixteen year old, a fourteen year old may be impossibly young whilst someone in their twenties is of a different generation which is out of reach. For many teenagers an impenetrable barrier may arise with other age groups which lasts for several years. This simply reflects the process of becoming an adult during which the young person feels most comfortable with others at the same stage of development. They have passed childhood but are still practicing adult behaviour and are not yet ready for full adult responsibilities.

Teenagers who withdraw to some degree from relationships with parents and younger siblings may not be comfortable doing things 'as a family', preferring the company of their mates. Parents may get upset at the apparently bored and resentful teenager who is no longer interested in visiting granny on Sunday for a family picnic. The teenager feels that he or she is being treated as a child and lacks the experience or the emotional or financial resources to be independent. Tension in this relationship is common and normal. It is part of the process of the young person working towards the establishment of a separate adult identity which involves some separation from parents and the ability to make one's own choices.

Despite earlier physical maturity, adolescence is now more prolonged because formal education has been extended and adult life is more complex.

Teenage 'withdrawal' or 'rebellion' is often accompanied by the adoption of particular styles of dress, language, musical tastes, fads and pastimes that together form a distinctive youth culture. Each generation tends to have several contrasting youth cultures which reflect different social groups, social classes, and ethnic groups within the teenage world. For most young people the youth culture is adopted in a relative modest form and they do not become a major embarrassment to their parents. A group of friends sharing a youth culture is not a 'gang' but potentially they could become one. Gangs tend to have leaders who dominate by intimidation, lay down rules, can be in conflict with other gangs, be drawn into vandalism or more serious crime, and often engage in extreme risk taking. Only a very small minority of youngsters become gang members of this type but they can become dominant forces in the lives of young people in run down, disadvantaged neighbourhoods, where they can graduate into adult criminal gangs.

It is important to remember that despite outward appearances the underlying value systems of most young people reaching adulthood turn out to be remarkably like those of their parents.

It might be thought that the development of single age friendship patterns and youth cultures would create an impenetrable barrier between the young person and a mentor. However, the opposite is often the case. Tensions can develop between some young people and authority figures, such as parents and teachers, as young people push the boundaries of social rules. A consequence of this tension and of the faster pace of life, when both parents are working, can be that the young person has few extended conversations with an adult. A teenager may go for weeks without sitting down, one to one with a parent and discussing the youngster's concerns. In some families it never happens since meals are not taken together or are always accompanied by television programmes. A teacher with, say, twenty five youngsters in a class and a syllabus to get through, may only have individual one to one conversations with students when they get into trouble which is hardly the most appropriate time for relaxed friendly discussion. Yet young people need discussions with adults to talk over any concerns that they have and to think about their futures.

The mentor can play a really valuable role here. The mentor does not have authority over the teenager and the mentor has the time to spend in friendly conversation. The mentor will listen and not judge but will point out opportunities that can be considered and warn about pitfalls. Having the opportunity to practice adult conversation, being taken seriously as an independent person and being able to try out ideas on a sympathetic adult in confidence, are all features of a mentoring relationship that benefits the young person. The mentor can feel that little progress is being made but to the teenager this can be their first real experience of an 'adult like' relationship. That in itself breeds self esteem and self confidence.

We must not forget that a minority of young people fail to make effective relationships with their peers and can become social isolates. They may withdraw into their own fantasy world as a kind of protection for a self that feels rejected and lost. Day dreaming and fantasy computer games may become central to their lives. Day dreaming is of course normal and healthy within limits but when it becomes a substitute for friendships and real life experiences, we need to become concerned. Social isolates can also be tempted into the use of illegal drugs. Mentoring can be very helpful to these young people. They may be seen as weird or as a nerd by other youngsters but mentors can accept them and treat them with respect. The mentor can gently turn the conversation to the challenges facing the mentee in the real world and start to have conversations about issues that the young person has previously been trying to avoid.

Mentors often find that young people's thoughts are dominated by immediate concerns and that they have put off thinking about longer term issues such as career or continuing education. An important role for the mentor with the post fourteen age group is to raise these career issues. Some techniques for doing so are explored in chapter seven.

Mentors can be particularly valuable in supporting young people to stay in education or to access employment. At the time of writing, in Australia 19% of fifteen to twenty four year olds are unemployed or not in fulltime work, study or a combination of the two. This is over 560,000 young people. In Britain over a million people in this age group are unemployed. This is not a new problem solely due to global economic conditions. This figure has been high for over a decade as the economy needs fewer unskilled labourers and more skilled workers (often recruited from overseas to fill labour shortages). Many long term unemployed young people come from low income neighbourhoods, having dropped out early from school, with low literacy levels, few academic qualifications and no post school vocational study or qualifications. If only effective mentoring had been offered to them whilst they were still at school to support them to access and persist with opportunities, the picture might have been rather different. Sadly in 2009 the New South Wales Government withdrew financial support for 'Plan it Youth', a very cost effective mentoring scheme using volunteers, presumably to save money in the short term (see case study in Chapter 11).

Around 20% of youngsters experience a mental disorder of some kind during adolescence. If a mentor sees any evidence of this in a mentee, particularly if there is any mention of suicide, it should be reported to the scheme coordinator and professional help should be sought. We will return to this issue in chapter nine.

Challenges facing adolescents that mentors might encounter

1. Physical Development

- Uneven physical development occurs which may include an unattractive physical appearance for a while such as spots, braces, short stature.
- Poor nutrition from unstable or thoughtless family backgrounds is a major issue. Obesity and anorexia are increasing.
- Friends may be dramatically different in their rates of physical development.
- Physical development may be much faster than emotional and intellectual development.
- If sexual changes are not understood they may cause great anxiety, embarrassment and distress.
- Body image is crucial for young people.
  All of the above impact upon emotional development— self confidence and self image.

2. Emotional Development

- Establishing own identity as being different from parents.
- A changing and in some cases an unstable self image.
- A demand for more adult treatment, sometimes coupled with a lack of adult skills and resources to carry it off. A safe environment is needed in which to practice being an adult and to learn from inevitable mistakes—usually the peer group of friends of the same age.
- Accepting own sexuality.
- Can experience high levels of anxiety about themselves and their future.
- Often experience major swings in mood and confidence levels.
- Reciprocity is being reinforced—how to treat others well in order to be treated well. There is a gradual acquisition of emotional intelligence and social skills i.e. knowing how to behave, how to treat adults and peers to gain acceptance. This varies greatly between individuals.

- Becoming increasingly emotionally independent from family which can bring separation stresses.
- A desire for the symbols of adult/independent status, e.g. boy/girl friends, car, alcohol, cigarettes, able to stay out late. Some gain these before they are mature enough to deal with them safely.
- Occasional regression to child like behaviour in response to daunting challenges.
- Sometimes show resentment towards those who seem to be enforcing child status (parents, teachers). This may lead to rudeness and apparent rejection. Some resent and undermine school uniform.
- Preparing themselves for adult partnerships and possible parenthood.
- Some young people may have long, intense conversations about themselves and their relationships (particularly but not exclusively girls).
- Some young people lack the communication skills and attitudes to explain their concerns. Some boys may think it is a sign of weakness and effeminacy to reflect upon and talk about feelings and relationships.
- Some young people cope with change by withdrawal and become social isolates.
- Many lack insight into the changes that they are experiencing which leaves them anxious and confused.
- Vulnerability to emotional disorders.

3. *Intellectual Development*
- This is much debated and researched among psychologists—no consensus yet about the concept of stages in mental development
- The brain keeps developing throughout life. However it develops unevenly, in bursts, during childhood and adolescence with individual differences in the timing of development.
- The more we work it, the more the brain improves by reorganising itself and generating a denser network of connections between brain cells.

- Lack of motivation and effort slows development. Therefore parental attitudes towards education and emotional development are crucial
- There may be some gender differences in brain development. Females tend to develop better verbal and social skills. Males tend to be more proficient at visual/spatial tasks such as reading maps and understanding technology. How far this is learned and how far genetically inherited, is an issue that is still being debated. However, it is clear that there is a great overlap between the sexes, with many females being very spatially aware and many men being highly talented socially.
- Intellectual development includes the development of moral values which takes longer in some people than others. Is this due to rates of brain maturation or to varying child rearing skills by parents?
- Recent research suggests that the brain is programmed to learn languages, musical and physical skills in childhood. The brain seems to reorganise itself around the age of 12, after which it devotes more of its capacity to social, emotional and moral development. The brain is not fully mature until the early twenties.
  Therefore, we can grow our abilities. Effort plus good teaching = ability gain.

4. *Social Development*
- The change in social status from child to adult is very prolonged in humans. This takes six years or more. Perhaps between ages 12 to 18+?
- The great majority are moving towards employment and economic independence.
- It involves a dramatic change in adult expectations of young people; the rights they acquire and how they are treated.
- Varies between individuals, cultures, social classes and between historical periods.

- Withdrawal into single age friendship groupings is virtually universal around the world. But some young people lack the skills or social status to be accepted and become social isolates. The latter may include some high achievers at school, school drop outs, or school phobics. Some isolates may be bullied, rejected, humiliated, and laughed at. Sadly some consider, and even commit, suicide.
- Includes very sudden, dramatic changes of status which are potentially exciting and threatening—leaving school, starting work, etc.
- There is ambivalence about accepting responsibility for self. There is a desire for independence but a fear not being able to handle it—hence avoidance mechanisms e.g. start a row, escape into fantasy, feign illness, bunk off school.
- Conflict with parents is common but not universal.
- It is difficult for parents—could treat the adolescent as a child or alternatively, push adult status too early. This is a matter of judgment and opinion. No single right answer.
- Ideas and values are acquired about the world based on own experiences, aspirations, social position and sub-culture—these can conflict with parents values but usually follow them.
- Youth Culture. Apparent rebellion often masks conventional values derived from family/community but some suffer genuine cultural conflict and explore alternative values. Features can include: music, clothes, language, movements/causes (for a minority), gang culture (for some), drug use (particularly alcohol), pub and clubbing (some girls as young as 12/13 can pass for 18).
- Conflict between youth groups is common. Young people with different statuses may follow different youth cultures (neighbourhood based, class based, ethnic based; interest based). This conflict can be seen between schools or within school—often between bands/sets/ streams.

- A significant minority of young people experience family instability, lack emotional and physical support and have no positive role models at home.
- For members of ethnic and religious minorities there may be conflicting roles and value systems to be resolved. Conflict with parents may be a particular problem for those from ethnic/cultural minorities—pulled away by peer groups and the dominant culture.

Most of us go through adolescence very successfully despite all these challenges which is tribute to the strengths of our families, our communities and the adaptability of our brains.

But in adulthood, do we retain some immature adolescent attitudes and behaviour?

Working with children and young people brings us back to boundary issues. As we indicated in chapter 2 there is a danger that accusations of an inappropriate relationship could be made if the mentee has private meetings with the mentee in an unsuitable place or takes the mentee out on one to one excursions. This is particularly the case if a man is mentoring a girl.

A solution to this dilemma is for mentoring to take place in a public space such as a library or common room where the mentoring conversation can be seen by other adults. The space should be large enough so that the conversation cannot be overheard, to maintain confidentiality. If it has to take place in a separate room the door should be left open. Sometimes the mentor may wish to take the mentee on a visit, to a careers exhibition for example or to an employer to talk about an apprenticeship. In these circumstances someone else should be taken along. This could be another mentor or another mentee. Remember to always get written parental visit permission for a young person under 16. It is also a good idea to sit children or young people in the back of your car if you are driving them.

Adult Mentoring

Much adult mentoring takes place in the workplace. We shall look at this in chapter eight. Issues of careers, mental health and personal relationship problems will also be examined in later chapters. An example of where mentoring regularly takes place and an example of where mentoring could help are set out below.

Sometimes mentoring occurs as a natural spin off from some shared activity. We have no space here to look at a wide range of these but the following example illustrates how an organised mentoring environment can be relaxed and appear to be very informal.

Mens Sheds

In Australia the Men's Shed movement has grown rapidly with over 300 local sheds now in existence. A men's shed is a workshop environment where men can meet and work on individual or group projects. Often the shed members will make or repair things for the community. For example they might make some new picnic tables for the local park or repair donated furniture which can be sold at a charity shop. The underlying purpose of many sheds is to promote men's' wellbeing. They will aim to attract men who are seeking new friends and at the same time do useful and enjoyable tasks. Men who might derive particular benefit from such a shed are the divorced, separated or single, the unemployed, the retired and those with health issues. The depressed, the lonely and the socially isolated can find friendship and an emotional refuge here. Men with distressing or embarrassing health problems can often find someone trustworthy to confide in. A good shed will have an area where a couple of blokes can have a break and a private chat over a tea or coffee.

The older man who no longer has the regular job where he had the companionship of workmates, can lose a sense of purpose and gradually slip into depression particularly if he has health problems. Such a man is often reluctant to seek help from mental health professionals since this seems to be a sign of weakness and is itself emotionally challenging. However, joining the shed and finding new mates to work with, side by side at a bench, provides a non threatening place to talk things through. Being able to pass on your skills and experience gives a sense of well being and self esteem. Being able to learn new skills keeps the mind alert and positive.

Once established by older men, the shed can also offer a supportive environment and role models to younger men. Particularly those without a father figure in their lives.

Sheds have been used to help young unemployed by the older members passing on their skills and using their networks of contacts to help job seeking. They have also been used to help rehabilitate offenders by giving them a new network of mates who are not involved in a criminal subculture. Some sheds have given their key members training as mentors and formally recognise mentoring as part of their purpose. Others may never have used the term 'mentoring' but in practice are being mentors to shed members in need.

A development of the men's shed is the community shed which is also open to women. Membership can be mixed or separate days can be set aside for men and women. A Mens shed on some days and a 'Sheila's shed' on others.

A workplace environment can be a great antidote to a sense of worthlessness, loneliness and negative thinking.

Older Adults

There are some issues which are characteristic of older adults which we need to consider. Think about the cumulative implications of the following trends:

- smaller family size,
- more geographical and social mobility—hence a greater likelihood of sons and daughters living at a distance from parents,
- longer life expectancy,
- an increasing proportion of the population in older age groups,
- earlier retirement in some occupations,
- many more older people living alone,
- more older people living with long term illness,
- more fit, healthy, well educated, skilled and experienced people who have retired from full-time employment,
- Increasing numbers of people will spend 25 years or more retired—some will have more years in retirement than they did at work.

Clearly, the great majority of older people have much to contribute to society and will have many years of life to fill. How will they use them? Let us look at two extreme but by no means rare examples.

ACTIVITY: Betty And Ellen

Which organisations might be able to set up a mentoring scheme for the Betty's and Ellen's of their community? What would its aim be? How could it work?

Betty is 61 and is recently retired from a tiring and repetitive job in an insurance company which in later years she did not enjoy. She lives alone in what was her family home for 28 years. Having lost her husband to a heart attack three years ago, she has never fully adjusted to being left alone. He had looked after the finances, insisted on always driving their car and made most of the major decisions. Her only son Jeremy works in a demanding job in a city which is four hours travelling time away. He brings his son Damon, Betty's grandson, to see her for a weekend once every three or four months. Damon is not too happy at missing his weekend sport.

She had looked forward to retirement as a long relaxing holiday—a reward for years of employment. She had not given a lot of thought to filling the long days after the initial holiday mood had passed.

Betty lacks any ambition. She is not striving towards any goals and her life feels empty and pointless. She has come to feel that her best years are past and that she is useless and unwanted. Each day she worries about what will become of her when she is too old to care for herself even though that could be 20 years away. Her health worries have led to frequent visits to the doctor and a full range of medical tests but no significant health problems have been identified. She is becoming increasingly prone to depression and even has suicidal thoughts. Former friends and neighbours have begun to avoid her since conversations with her usually revolve around her health problems, her former husband and complaints about her son. She does not seem to want to go on holiday or outings, even though she is able to afford them. Much of the day is spent in front of the television. Her lack of exercise and fondness for sweet things are leading to obesity.

These days she often has a little cry to herself without really understanding why. The doctor has given her some pills which he says will help.

Ellen is 73 and an ex nursing sister. She lives alone after the death of her second husband. Her son and his family live 300 km away but she regularly hops on the train to go to visit them; making sure that she does not outstay her welcome.

Ellen leads a full and active life, regularly meeting new people and learning new things. She always seems to have several personal projects on the go. One of the goals that she set herself was to explore her family history and visit the villages in Eastern Europe where her grandparents had been brought up.

She discovered some long lost cousins on the internet whilst doing her family research and accepted their invitation to visit them with her son. Subsequently the cousins came to visit her. She learned a great deal about the life of her great grandparents during this process and is now writing it up for her grandchildren, complete with photographs taken on her trip.

Ellen has a wide range of other interests including acting as secretary to the Friends of the Public Library and going to the local scrabble club each week. On Friday lunchtimes she works as a volunteer mentor at the local high school, supporting a young student who has become demotivated at school after the breakup of her parent's marriage. Next year she is planning to learn how to use her digital camera more skilfully by joining an adult education class. Despite a creaky knee and needing to use a hearing aid she is determined to enjoy life to the full.

Perhaps if Ellen were able to befriend and mentor Betty, both would benefit. There would be no need to use the term mentor or to make Betty feel inadequate. The key would be to help Betty to find something positive to contribute where she could develop a sense of usefulness and pride in herself. Who knows she might be able to throw away those pills.

CHAPTER SIX

Mentoring in Education and Training

Please note that the term 'student' also includes apprentices and trainees. The term teacher also includes college/university lecturers and vocational trainers.

Mentors work in primary schools, high schools, colleges, universities and training organisations. They are sometimes described as 'Learning Mentors'.

A person taking on the role of a mentor in education may wish to focus on educational issues by supporting students learning. However, it is important to realise that mentors are often asked to work with underachieving students. This underachievement is often exacerbated by a lack of study skills. The mentor can be trained to help with such skills but frequently the issues lie much deeper. It might be for example, that the student lacks motivation due to personal relationship problems with a teacher, fellow students or parents. Being willing to talk through issues of this kind with mentees is an important part of the role.

Let us start with the educational aspects of the role and deal with other issues later in the chapter and in other chapters.

The terms mentor and tutor are sometimes used interchangeably to refer to teachers who are in fact teaching students one to one, or in small groups. Hence the distinctiveness of the term 'mentoring' can be lost. It is important to remember that the usual role of a mentor in education is to support the student's motivation and personal organisation rather than to teach or tutor a subject. In practice when teachers have tutorial groups they tend to combine some subject teaching with mentoring support. Teachers can also be asked to be personal tutors for students that they do not teach or assess. The student may be studying subjects that the teacher has no specialist knowledge of. In these circumstances the personal tutor can be acting more like a mentor than a teacher.

Where mentors in education are not teachers they should not try to direct, teach or assess the student. Moreover, the mentor must never complete student assignments for them. Any work that the students hand in must be their own.

Ideally mentors should liaise with subject teachers to clarify what legitimate help they are allowed to give on the course concerned. For example are they allowed to proof read and comment on the drafts of assignments or on developing pieces of practical work? Are they allowed to find and pass on learning resources such as internet sites?

Peer mentoring can also be tricky. Here a more experienced student supports a less experienced one. It can be tempting for the peer mentor to 'help' their mentee with their work. Some kinds of help may be quite legitimate but there is also the danger of plagiarism where the peer mentor does some of the mentee's work. Hence it is important that the peer mentors are properly trained and briefed on the boundaries of their role.

It can be seen that the dividing line between mentoring and teaching can easily become blurred especially if the mentor is also a qualified teacher or happens to have experience in the vocational area of a trainee. Therefore it is very important that the mentor clarifies the role and tries to bear in mind its boundaries. Remember that we are trying to help the mentee to become a more effective student who will be able to study independently when we are no longer there. Doing their assignments for them is cheating and creates dependency. We mentor for independence.

ACTIVITY: Reflect On These Statements Below. At the end of the chapter return to them and ask yourself if your views have changed.

Agree		Disagree
	Inborn intelligence determines success in education.	
	Understanding my own feelings will be a big help to me in becoming a better student.	
	You can't teach an old dog new tricks.	
	Making mistakes is an essential part of learning.	
	Anyone can succeed at school if they work hard enough.	
	School students don't need to know how to learn because the teachers plan all their work for them.	
	If your parents are unemployed and uneducated you don't stand a chance of becoming a lawyer or a doctor.	
	People learn best if they are put under a lot of pressure to succeed.	
	The more hours of study I put in, the more I will understand and remember.	
	Praising good work is more effective than criticising poor work.	
	Education is a competition between individuals to get the best grades and jobs.	
	I can improve my mental abilities by learning how to study.	

	Anyone can succeed at anything if they really want to.	
	We all have inborn genetic limits to what we can achieve.	
	My emotional state is crucial to how well I learn.	
	Success in education is irrelevant to success in the workplace.	
	If you know a child's I.Q. you can predict how well he/she will do at school.	
	You need to feel safe, alert and relaxed to learn effectively.	
	I work best when I am working towards a goal that is really important to me.	
	My brain is unintelligent because my mother smoked and drank heavily when she was carrying me.	

What is the Role of the Mentor in Education?

Teachers in their mentoring role and non teacher mentors can:

- ✓ support the student's self esteem and confidence—giving praise when deserved,
- ✓ support transition between schools, into colleges, universities, and training schemes,
- ✓ encourage regular attendance at school, college or training programme,
- ✓ listen to student concerns and provide reassurance,
- ✓ encourage persistence and resilience,
- ✓ discuss the selection of course and unit options,
- ✓ help keep the student on track with assignments,
- ✓ explain time management,
- ✓ encourage good study habits,
- ✓ discuss the planning of assignments,
- ✓ discuss methods of revising for tests and examinations,

- ✓ help the student to be assertive (not aggressive) and a self advocate—when necessary advocate for the student,
- ✓ demonstrate problem solving skills,
- ✓ support research skills, encourage the effective use of the library,
- ✓ explore the internet together but make sure that the school's internet use policy is followed—some sites are unsuitable (note that reproducing and submitting downloads as the student's own work is plagiarism—don't agree to it),
- ✓ support the student through personal problems and relationship issues,
- ✓ assist the student to access work experience placements,
- ✓ support the student to explore career options (see chapter seven).

Some Types of Mentoring in Education and Training

- • Employed specialist mentors.

We mentioned in chapter one that in the UK, paid mentors have been employed in so called 'under achieving schools' as part of the Excellence in Cities programme. They proved to be very successful. As valuable paid members of staff they got involved in a wide range of school activities not all of which were strictly mentoring. For example they have run homework clubs, excursions and sporting events. Such activities are of course valuable in themselves but they also provide informal opportunities to have conversations with mentees which can be followed up later in timetabled mentoring meetings.

- • Peer mentoring,

Here, fellow students act as mentors. See later.

- Teachers as mentors.

Teachers can be very effective mentors and mentoring can be seen as an aspect of a teacher's role. However, it involves adopting a style of relating to students which involves more listening than telling and invites the student to take more responsibility for his or her own learning. Some teachers love this approach, others find it frustrating. In practice, the staff student ratios in most schools make it very difficult to find the time for one to one or small group meetings with students.

- Community volunteers as mentors.

This can be very effective if the volunteers are trained, properly supervised and approach the task with the right attitudes and skills.

Starting Assumptions

There is a danger that volunteer mentors from the local community and peer mentors will come to education with outdated assumptions about ability and education. Sometimes teachers can also share such assumptions. Let us try to clarify and challenge them.

Mentors could be asked to work with students in a wide variety of situations from high flyers to those with learning difficulties. However, mentors are particularly valuable when they work with students who are turned off education, who for some reason are demotivated. Some such students may lack self esteem and self belief. Others may have a very short term orientation, preferring not to think of the future but instead concentrate on 'having a good time with their mates'. Others may be experiencing emotional or relationship problems which take precedence over studies that can seem boring and meaningless. If the mentor can help such students to develop self esteem and set personal goals, they will be doing the student an invaluable service. Experience suggests that self belief and the setting of targets to aim at, are important ingredients for success in education.

What counts as success can vary from student to student. Just turning up to class and managing to complete a course can be a great achievement for a student struggling with a disrupted home background.

The Intelligence Debate

Demotivated students can give the impression of lacking ability and not being very intelligent. In turn this can lead mentors and teachers to have low expectations of them. It is important to challenge the assumption that we are all born with a single, largely fixed level of intelligence which will impose strict limits on our future performance. This notion has its origins in Greek philosophy (Plato) and was taken up in the twentieth century by influential psychologists such as Binet, Birt and Eysenck. Out of their work developed the IQ test which could, supposedly, accurately measure our intelligence.

Birt and his followers propagated the idea of an 80-20 ratio of inherited intelligence to learned ability. If this were correct the intelligence test could provide an accurate measure of potential for use in employment selection and for admission to schools. In the UK the 11+ examination was widely used as part of the selection process for Grammar schools. Some contemporary research continues to support the notion that mental ability is strongly influenced by genetics whereas other research appears to show the opposite. Scientific studies have reached contrasting conclusions. Estimates of the contribution to IQ scores of genetics range from 40% to 80% (New Scientist magazine No 2754 p 81 2010).

Richard Nesbitt (2009) has studied the achievements of Americans from different ethnic groups and concludes that that it is a myth that success is simply the result of genetically determined intelligence. He stresses the malleability of human abilities and the huge scope for us to develop ourselves through a supportive home background and a commitment to learning. Sue Ramsden (2011) found that a person's IQ score can change considerably between the ages of twelve and sixteen.

The belief in the largely inherited nature of intelligence became a commonplace in the general population. It is not unusual for mentors to encounter students who to claim that they are unintelligent and lack any aptitudes or skills. Hence they can justify making little effort to attend or study and can justify dropping out of education as soon as they get the chance. As mentors we can challenge these assumptions by presenting an alternative way of looking at ability and intelligence.

Intelligence is sometimes presented as if it is a single magical ingredient that some possess and others do not. An alternative vision is to see human beings a having a large number of mental abilities. Precisely how many and how they work is still to be fully determined by brain scientists. Any complex task that we undertake, calls upon the brain to use a range of these mental abilities. To read this text you will need vision, word recognition, perhaps three types of memory, reasoning (which may itself require a number of processes to be in operation) and critical reflection (which again could involve complex processes). To play football intelligently, play a guitar, hunt a wild animal successfully, write a play, chair a meeting, negotiate a pay rise, perform well in job interview, or counsel a grieving relative, may each require us to integrate differing sets of mental abilities. One person may be outstanding at some mental tasks whilst another person may excel at other tasks.

Psychologists have pointed out that mental abilities tend to work together, rather than in isolation, and there is a tendency for some people to score consistently higher than others in paper or computer based tasks which involve solving logical problems. It is these scores than form the basis of IQ. However IQ tests measure performance at a point in time. They cannot tell us the extent to which the score is the result of genetically inherited ability. They are based on an observation of the results of thinking and do not directly observe or explain the process of thinking itself. For that we have to turn to brain science.

Among educationalists the work of Howard Gardner has been very influential. He argues for multiple intelligence theory, claiming that there are seven different intelligences: *Linguistic, Mathematical and logical, Visual and Spatial, Musical Interpersonal, Intrapersonal and Kinaesthetic.* Since individuals vary in their abilities across these different intelligences it follows that people vary in the ways in which they learn best. Some are visual learners, some learn most effectively through listening and questioning others best by having physical contact with the things that they are studying. This is the theory of 'learning styles' which has driven some teachers to distraction trying to develop individualised learning or to cater for all these styles within a single learning session.

Whilst Gardner's work can be seen as a great educational advance on crude IQ scores, brain science is helping us to look at human abilities in an even more sophisticated way.

This research still has a long way to go and there are many unanswered questions but our understanding has developed enormously in recent years and may well have developed further by the time you read this book. The essential point is that mental abilities are the outcome of a complex interaction between our genetic inheritance and our experiences. They both influence each other. If you interested, keep up to date using popular science publications such as New Scientist or Scientific American and their web sites.

What can mentors learn from brain research that we can pass on to our student mentees?

- Brain Power

Modern research shows that the normal brain in all humans has huge potential power. By the mid twenties we each have around 100 billion neurons (nerve cells). Each neuron can have up to 100,000 connections to other neurons. Hence we have a multi-trillion network of connections capable of performing twenty million billion calculations per second.

The human brain is the most complex object yet discovered in the universe and you and your mentee have each got one!

This is true for both sexes and all so called "races". Therefore educational failure is not due to lack of inborn 'intelligence' except where there are genetic abnormalities. At birth our brain is only one third the size of our adult brain (unlike other animals). Therefore we have a uniquely long childhood to allow the brain to develop. The great majority of our mentees have brains that are potentially powerful enough to learn very successfully. It is not the lack of innate 'intelligence' that is a barrier to their successful learning.

- Brain Development

Brain development is strongly influenced by what happens to us in the womb and in childhood. If the mother abuses her own body she damages her baby's brain development. To develop properly the brain needs to have stimulation. It needs to be challenged. This is particularly important in the first few years of life. Hence the quality of parenting is crucial for the development of intelligence. However, new brain connections are created throughout our lives. Mentees (and mentors of course) can continue to develop their brains at any age, unless struck by severe brain damage or dementia.

- Brain Plasticity

We now know that the human brain has a remarkable capacity to adapt to changing stimuli. It can reconfigure itself in the light of new experiences and the demands made upon it. Hence generations growing up with computer technology, mobile phones, I Pods and the like will have structured their own brains rather differently than earlier generations. We are only just beginning to understand the new ways in which electronic communication is changing the ways in which our mentees brain's perform.

- Ages and Skills

The brain appears to be programmed to learn certain skills more effectively at certain ages. In early childhood more of the brain is used to learn languages and body control skills. In later childhood the brain's focus moves towards social and moral development. The brain reacts more slowly as we age but our mentees and ourselves, remain very able to learn new skills and gain new knowledge. Experience helps a great deal.

- Use it or Lose it

The brain develops in response to stimulation, challenges and to solving problems. Therefore, if our mentees don't make the effort to work their brain hard, their mental abilities will decline or not develop as they could.

- Memory

Memory does not have a single location in the brain. It has been seen by psychologists as having three parts—short term memory, working memory and long term memory. Transfer to long term memory is closely tied to emotions and is probably one of the functions of sleep. Association (linking new knowledge to existing knowledge) is crucial. Hence, for our mentees, a good night's sleep is a vital part of successful learning.

- Learning and Motivation

Our brains evolved over millions of years. Over this time span we learned by doing and copying the actions of others not by sitting in classrooms, reading books or using computers. Learning how to learn abstract concepts is difficult. Some students imagine that if they find something difficult it means that they are unintelligent and they soon give up. They may have a fixed mindset and be distrustful of change. Successful students see difficulties as interesting challenges to overcome. They demonstrate a growth mind set with resilience, determination and commitment. Therefore, our mentees attitudes and emotions will play a big part in their learning.

To learn and remember effectively our mentees have to be experiencing positive emotions. They need to be in the right frame of mind—the right emotional state. They need motivation which brings positive attitudes and makes them attentive. Being able to produce this positive emotional state is part of emotional intelligence which was explained in chapter four (similar to Gardner's intra personal intelligence).

- Learning and Social Relationships

Also in chapter four we referred to Goleman's assertion that our brain is a social brain with a natural tendency towards cooperation and empathy. We are learning every day but most of our learning is not academic or vocational. Much of our mentees learning is about their place in the social world (Gardner's interpersonal intelligence). All their daily contact with others influences their brain development, which in turn can influence how their bodies react.

The brain and body are one and thoughts and emotions powerfully influence physical states and vice versa. For example, if our mentees are highly stressed they will find it difficult to learn.

Summary—Explanations of Educational Success and Failure

Nature—Inherited Ability

This view holds that we are born with a certain level of intelligence which largely determines our later success (perhaps an 80-20 ratio).

Modern research on learning and brain science suggests us that this view is too simplistic and can be very misleading.

Nurture—Social Environment

This view explains success by: social background (class, gender, ethnicity, neighbourhood) and how we are brought up (skills and attitudes of family/carers/neighbours)—these shape our attitudes to learning such as willingness to defer gratification, a belief that we can and will succeed, respect for the authority of teachers, and valuing educational qualifications.

Income and wealth are seen as important—money can buy a private education—students meet influential contacts for life.

Parenting—early bonding and the stimulation provided by parents is crucial for brain development, skills and attitudes including conversation, vocabulary, books, exploration of number, music, art and so on—some aware parents may be able to help their children to overcome the disadvantages of low socio economic position.

There is a correlation between background and success but many individuals do succeed despite a disadvantaged background.

Quality of Schools and Teachers

This includes preschools and nurseries. Students from a similar background can perform very differently in different schools. Commitment to a subject and chances of success are related to teacher skills and respect for the teacher.

However, even where teaching is of high quality many students still underachieve due to other factors.

Positive Attitudes—Hard Work and Determination

Here, anyone is seen as potentially successful, whatever their background, if sufficiently committed, determined and hard working.

Attitudes tend to come from social background anyway. We need the encouragement and guidance of others if we are to develop positive attitudes (parents, friends, teachers, mentors etc). Moreover, students need to be shown how to learn—to work smart not just hard.

What is the relevance of the intelligence debate for mentors?

The healthy human brain has huge potential for learning. Even if some are born with greater intellectual potential than others, the normal human brain is perfectly capable of performing well at school, college or in training programmes.

It is crucial that mentors do not label students as unintelligent or incapable. There is a strong temptation to massage a student's aspirations down to what we might see as realistic levels. BUT highly motivated students with clear goals, who learn how to learn, can make remarkable and unexpected progress. *Don't write them off.*

It is remarkable how students who find classroom learning difficult can have an encyclopedic knowledge of current musical trends or football clubs. Students who are apparently of low intellect can master highly complex computer games. They are demonstrating learning, memory and intelligence because they are motivated, safe and alert.

Social and emotional intelligence can be learned and is a great aid to success in education. It is vital for teamwork, happiness in life and success in career. Mentors can help their mentees to understand and develop it. Having a successful and rewarding relationship with your mentee is a great way to start.

We are not all equally good at everything. Mentors can help students identify their strengths and areas for improvement. Mentors can support students to form course and career goals and select educational options.

Students need to learn how to learn. As we shall see, mentors can be a great help here, even though they are not teachers and do not have subject knowledge.

LEARNING TOP 20—Thoughts to share with our mentees

1. Motivation is the key. A topic may be interesting in itself (positive emotion) or it may aid us to reach a goal (qualification? job?).

---

2. Curiosity—we need to be interested and curious to direct our attention to something—if we don't give something our full attention we won't learn or remember it very well.

3. Diet and exercise aid learning and emotional health. Eat a balanced diet to feed the brain. Eat breakfast. Avoid frequent fizzy drinks. Control alcohol. Try walking daily.

4. The more we learn, the easier new learning becomes (we learn how to learn).

5. Understanding aids accurate memory.

6. We learn best in a state of relaxed alertness with some, appropriate, stress.

7. Fear, anxiety, insecurity and low self esteem make learning much more difficult

8. Memory and emotion are linked. If we have no feelings for something, it is harder to learn it. If our feelings are too powerful, our learning can be distorted or suppressed.

9. We learn by associating (linking) new information with what we already know.

10. The more senses we use (sight, hearing, touch, bodily movement, smell and taste) the more associations we make and the more we retain (i.e. use both brain hemispheres).

11. Applying knowledge to a practical task, aids understanding & memory.

12. Returning to a topic regularly refreshes our understanding and memory of it. Creating our own notes & diagrams is a big help. Filing them in order and updating them regularly, helps to refresh memory.

13. Reinforce knowledge and understanding by using it to solve problems.

14. Teaching is a great way to learn.

15. For adults—our ability to learn new things from the same activity can start to tail off after about 40 minutes. We need a change of activity. Young children's concentration span can be even shorter.

16. A good night's sleep is crucial. Moving information to long term memory requires time for consolidation. This appears to be one of the main functions of sleep.
17. If we are allowed to make mistakes without fear, we can learn from them.
18. We are more likely to remember something that we find out for ourselves.
19. Some people like to see the big picture before exploring the detail. Others prefer to build up to the big picture by working through the detail. Try both.
20. Some types of music could aid alertness, relaxation and concentration.

Skills + Opportunity + Attitude → Success

Some Useful Techniques for Supporting Learning

If you are supporting a senior high school or college student, the first thing to recognise is that they have to be shown how to organise their time and their work. They may need help to make sense of the assignments that they have been set, to find sources of information, and to plan their answers. Frequently, students will have little idea how to plan and tackle revision for tests or examinations. Of course it is highly likely that in class they have had these things explained to them by their teacher. Unfortunately an explanation about how to organise your notes and plan your work is not the most riveting experience. Its importance may not hit home until the student is faced with several assignments due all at the same time with little idea where the relevant handout and notes from class are to be found. One to one help from a mentor can be invaluable.

Teachers may well find that their students bring a file and notebooks to class which gradually fill up to the point where the file is overflowing with material from several different subjects. A heavy bag is dragged around school or college, perhaps one day to fall over and spill the contents (usually on a wet and windy day!). Notes are hurriedly stuffed back into the bag to be sorted later (but later may not arrive).

How can the mentor help? It is important to offer to help but do not try to insist if your mentee refuses. She will probably remember your offer and may well ask for help later when she gets worried about her progress. We do not have space here to go into all the details of study skills. There are many books on the market that cover such skills. However, we will take an initial look at some of the key issues that a struggling student might need help with.

Amy's Scenario Illustrates a typical situation in education mentoring

Amy is 17 years old and attends Rockcliffe College. She is preparing for examinations starting in five weeks time in: English, Mathematics, History, and Economics. Her fifth subject is I.T. where she has to complete coursework by the end of next week involving the creation of a website for visitors to her region of the country.

She broke up with her boyfriend a few weeks ago and felt emotionally devastated. Hence, she has done little work since then. Now she has realised that she must get over it and get some work done if she is to get decent results to get onto the Travel and Tourism course at college that she has set her heart on

You are her mentor and she has come to you in a panic asking for help. She has been worrying all weekend about the sheer volume of work that she has to revise and she has no idea where to start or how to go about it. One of the teachers ran a session the previous week, with all the year group, to suggest strategies for revision but she was still too upset to take it in and daydreamed her way through it.

Amy's parents both left school at 16 and have no experience in further education or examination preparation. They are worried about her and pressure her each evening to go to her room and revise. This makes her feel guilty and stressed. She finds herself snapping at them which only makes them more anxious and insistent that she gets on with some work rather than go out with friends. Relationships between them have never been so bad tempered and distant.

She bursts into tears as she asks you "What can I do? I am going to fail, I know I am".

QUESTIONS

What help would it be unethical to give her?

What could do you do if you are unclear about how much help you can legitimately give?

As her mentor, what support and suggestions can you give to Amy?

See Amy's revision timetable later in this chapter.

1. Identify regular study times

Start with a blank 'My Week' timetable as shown at the end of this section. Suggest to your mentee that the essential things that must be done each week are entered on it, such as going to school/college, part time job, chores at home, sports training and so on. Then add some leisure time with friends. If the mentee is reluctant to fill it in, you could do so whilst discussing it together.

It is likely that much of the timetable in the evenings and at weekends will still remain blank. Ask your mentee to identify several 2 ½ hour slots during the week, which would be best for private study (homework, coursework, or revision), in addition to classes. Three or four slots might be a reasonable minimum for full time pre university study but an undergraduate will have less time in class and will require much more private study time. An example might be to have evening study slots on Monday, Tuesday and Thursday with a further slot on Sunday afternoon, leaving Saturday and three evenings free from study each week. Once this pattern is established it might be possible to slip in additional slots for assignments that are almost due.

Suggest that your mentee, in any one session, works for an hour or so followed by a break of half an hour and then works for another hour. In practice it may take 15 minutes to get started e.g. to decide what work needs doing, collect notes and books, or switch on and find the right files on a computer. Therefore the first session may only be about 45 minutes. That is ok.

If you try to concentrate for too long on a task, your performance starts to flag—particularly if you don't find the topic intrinsically interesting. Suggesting that after each session of study "you can give yourself a little reward" such as watching TV, or phoning a friend, also helps.

When faced with hours of slog, tackling work that is seen as boring or demanding, a student can easily find excuses not to begin and the work piles up. Setting a reasonable limit to the hours of work and seeing a reward at the end makes it more palatable. You should not stress how tough it is going to be or how hard your mentee must work. Instead say something like:

"I know you can do this. I have faith in you. You need to study but it does not need to take over your whole life. If you just work steadily and stick to your timetable you will be fine."

Being highly stressed and anxious is a major barrier to learning. Mentors can usually give reassurance that the course is well within the student's capability. Education establishments are usually careful to place students on courses at the right level for them. Teachers do not wish to set students up to fail, not least because that would reflect badly on the teachers.

Of course the mentor should not pretend that study is easy. It will be difficult at times but the more study you do the easier it gets, because with help, you develop the skills to study effectively.

My Timetable Date

Time	Mon	Tues	Wed	Thur	Fri	Sat	Sun
8.00 9.00 10.00 11.00 12.00							
1.00 2.00 3.00 4.00 5.00							
6.00 7.00 8.00 9.00 10.00							

2. Get a Filing System

When starting a class it is not uncommon for teachers to hear moans such as:

"Where were we up to? I can't find the work I was doing last week."
"Has someone nicked my work?"
"I did this on the computer last week—where has it gone?"

One approach to suggest to your mentee is to have a ring binder to take to school/college with sections for each subject or have a separate file and/or notebook for each subject. Many students neglect to separate their subjects in their files or folders producing a dreadful jumble. Paper in 'two ring' binders often splits at the rings and falls out. Hence work on a topic can get separated and individual pages can become meaningless. Four ring binders or the use of plastic sleeves can help.

Suggest that it is a good idea to add the date and a page number to each page. Where separate sheets of paper are used, a brief heading is also a good idea on each page. This will help students to keep work in order and to be able to find where they were up to in a topic when the next class comes round. When doing assignments on the computer, suggest that the student always starts by saving the file to a folder. They should then add a footer giving the students name, the filename, the date and page numbering. If you don't know how to do this, suggest to the mentee that you jump on computer together and find out how to do it or get someone else to show you.

To prevent bag and file overload it is a good idea to keep subject files at home that work can be transferred into, once a topic has been completed. This need not be expensive. Cheap card files in a cardboard box are usually adequate but they should be labeled and material be kept in subject and date order. It is also a good idea to keep your own copies of work produced on school or college computers. Thumb drives with masses of memory are cheap and a very good investment. They can also be used to keep a backup of any work done on your own computer at home.

It can't be stressed too strongly that helping a mentee to be systemic and organised is immensely valuable for successful study. For young students it is also a great preparation for the world of work to come. However, this is not the same as obsessive tidiness. A desk and floor covered in papers can be a sign of creative thinking taking place, of ideas from different sources coming together.

Some students, particularly in further and higher education now use laptop/notebook computers instead of paper and pen for note taking. This is fine but presents the danger of loss of notes if the machine is damaged, stolen or infected by a virus. The author has had students who lost a whole term's work stored on their machine. It is a good idea to advise students to print out their notes after class or to back them up to an external hard drive. Lazy or disorganised students can also fail to manage their computer files properly. They can lose notes or assignments within their own machine because they have not created appropriate folders for their files and have not named their files sensibly.

3. Schedule Assignments/Assessments

Most students will be tackling a course composed of several subjects or modules leading to a qualification. The assessment may well be a mixture of practical work, written coursework and end of unit tests or examinations.

Note that: the term 'module' often means a chunk of teaching and learning within a course. In contrast a 'unit' is an assessed component of a qualification. Today most qualifications are built up from units. It is quite possible that one module of learning may cover more than one unit of a qualification. For example a module on mentoring might prepare students to be assessed on three units: one on the principles of mentoring, another unit on listening and questioning skills and a third on dealing with conflict. This is a useful way for teachers to reduce the assessment workload on students but it can leave the disorganised student feeling confused.

A major issue for students is balancing the various demands of the units being assessed. Each unit may have several assessment tasks plus a written examination. Once they have been following the course for a few weeks the assessments may start to pile up. Students who are not used to taking responsibility for their own study can easily get confused about how many assignments are due, when each assignment is due and what to do first.

If your mentee has a range of assignments across several modules it is a good idea to use an assignment schedule such as the one below, to record assignments as soon as they as set. The mentee can then see at a glance what is required by when. The assignment details from the teacher will usually be in writing and should be placed in a separate file which can also be used for any material that the student accumulates to help complete the work (such as notes from a book or a download from the internet). Undergraduate assignments are usually posted on the university intranet and written assignments are also submitted on it. Hence a laptop computer has become as essential to the modern university student as pen and paper were to previous generations.

Name .... Assignment Schedule for term ....

Date set	For Teacher	Assignment (title or brief summary)	Date due	Done

A diary becomes an invaluable tool at this point. Many students prefer to use a mobile phone as an electronic diary but often they do not use a diary effectively to plan their study. A paper diary still has advantages. A mentor can demonstrate its use to record the dates on which assignments are due. Working back from submission dates the diary can be used to identify the weeks or specific dates on which work will be done on particular assignments. This will enable the mentee to plan course work across a period of weeks. When this is not done, the work piles up and the student misses deadlines or has to cram in the work immediately before submission with no time to produce quality.

4.   Plan Assignments

Often it is not possible to work on just one assignment at a time. Several assignments may be due in on that date. Information may have to be gathered or practical work completed over several weeks. Hence it is really useful if the student sets aside a little time each week to decide what they are going to concentrate on during the coming seven days. A meeting with a mentor is a good opportunity to do this weekly planning with the mentor's assistance.

The first priority is to be absolutely clear what the assignment requires your mentee to do. One way to clarify this is for your mentee to write out the assignment instructions (e.g. essay title, or task specification) in her or his own words. Some assignments require primary research such as experiments, observations, or interviewing. Others will require the student to undertake vocational tasks under supervision. Yet others will involve designing and making. The mentor could use questioning to ensure that the mentee is absolutely clear what is required.

Unfortunately, teachers can occasionally word assignments ambiguously or in insufficient detail, leading students to be unclear about the task that they are required to complete. Where this happens the mentor can suggest that the student returns to the teacher to ask for clarification. There is a danger that if this is done in a rude or aggressive way, a busy teacher might conclude that the student is just being awkward to avoid doing the work. As a mentor you might want to suggest that you and your mentee practice what will be said to the teacher and how it will be said. Show your mentee a polite way of approaching the teacher.

Secondly, make a plan together of how the assignment can be tackled. This will depend very much on the level and type of assignment. A good next step is to write down a set of questions that need to be answered in order to tackle the assignment. For written assignments this is turn leads to research using class notes, handouts, textbooks libraries, or the internet. Remind the students to make a note of the author, title, date and page numbers of any information that they use.

The structure of an assignment will usually be laid down by the teacher. Essays will require an introduction, a body and a conclusion. The introduction explains what the assignment will cover and is often best written last, which is easy enough to do if the assignment is word processed.

The body presents evidence and arguments in paragraphs and in a logical order. The conclusion refers back to the question set and summarizes the main arguments presented in the body. No new evidence should be given in the conclusion. The student should include a list of references and/ or a bibliography at the end. Reports have a more complex structure and will usually include a summary at the beginning. The teacher should specify the report structure required.

5.   Examination Revision

If your mentee asks for advice on how to revise, what could you suggest? Again the diary is vital for recording exam dates. Work backwards from these dates to plan revision. For a long course (a year or a semester) with an examination at the end, several weeks may be needed for revision. A good strategy is to start by making a list of topics that need to be covered. Syllabuses, textbooks, questions from previous years, and guidance from the teacher should give a full picture of the topics to consider including in a revision plan.

A useful next step is to go back to the timetable and allocate revision time for each unit, each week. A really well organised student will allocate topics to each revision session to make sure that all are covered. Remind your mentee not to try to revise for too long at any one sitting. After an hour or so it will get progressively harder to retain what is being revised. It makes sense to stick with the format of $2^{1/2}$ hours at a time with a break half way through. Stress the importance of sleep to consolidate learning. Studying very late at night can disrupt sleep and can be counterproductive.

What does your mentee do in a revision session? Just reading through notes or a textbook does not work! The student should do something active with the material. Answering past questions in note form is one option. Another is the revision card system. The idea here is to put the essential facts needed for each topic on one or more cards that can be carried round in a pocket (postcard size at most). Each card should look different—to aid memory. Use bullet points, shapes, diagrams, arrows, colour, underlining or highlighters. Use single, memory jogging words or phrases rather than sentences. Don't cram too much information onto one card. There should be white space around each point so that it stands out. Your mentee could spend several weeks of revision creating these cards, completing them at least one week before the assessment. During that final week the cards should be taken everywhere and gone over time after time. Taking blank cards and using them to try to copy out existing cards from memory is a good technique. Alternatively the mentee can give the cards to someone else and ask to be tested on them.

As a mentor are you allowed to help with revision in the above way? You will need to check this with the teacher. For some programs it will be perfectly acceptable since it is your mentee that is sitting the exam not you. Remember that one of our aims is to promote mentee independence. By showing your mentee study and revision techniques you are helping them to become an independent learner. Therefore don't do the study for them—give them techniques so that they can do it for themselves when you are not there.

Advice to Amy

Week 1 complete your IT coursework.
Weeks 2-5 create and use a revision timetable, similar to this:

	Mon	Tue	Wed	Thurs	Fri	Sat	Sun
9:30 – 12:00	English 1	Econ1	History 2	Econ 2	History 3	Off	Maths 4
1.30 – 4:00 pm	Maths 1	English 2	Time off	English 3	Econ 3	Off	History 4
6:00 – 8:30 pm	History 1	Maths 2	Time off	Maths 3	English 4	Off	Econ 4

Over the first three weeks each subject has 12 revision sessions. Each subject is divided into 12 topics. A timetable for each week has a topic in each session (Larger sections of the course be can split to get 12 topics).

Use three weeks to produce several revision cards for each topic during each session. Take a short break half way through each session to move around. Give yourself a reward for completing each day's sessions. Do not OVERWORK. You must build in leisure time and get plenty of sleep to consolidate your learning.

During the fourth week and up to each exam, go over the cards as often as possible—doing something ACTIVE with them. Take the cards with you wherever you go and use spare time to go over them BUT give yourself some down time. Cover all subjects not just your favourites.

Since exams will be spread out, you will need a new timetable after the first 3 weeks to ensure that each subject is revised in the days immediately before its exam.

Supporting Student Mentees from Minority Ethnic Groups

As we saw in chapter three, ethnicity refers to membership of a group that shares common features such as: a common way of life, family ties, history, language, beliefs, stories and myths. It was explained that the term race is often used to refer to an ethnic group. Race implies physical difference. It assumes that all the group members have a common genetic heritage which distinguishes them from other groups. It also carries with it implications of superiority and inferiority between groups. Since these assumptions are very questionable, the term ethnicity is less prejudicial and more accurate.

Some members of ethnic minority groups will be relatively recent immigrants. Indeed some may be refugees who have survived appalling experiences. Others may be descended from earlier inhabitants (such as Australian Aboriginal peoples or North American Indians) whose cultures have been largely swamped by waves of migrants.

Australian Aboriginal people were treated as a sub-human species in the 1901 Constitution which established Australia and were not granted full citizenship until 1967. Until 1972 Aboriginal children could be excluded from school by the Principal at the request of white parents. However, since 1975 racial discrimination has been illegal in Australia and racial vilification has been illegal since 1989. Hence, many Aboriginal adults do not have the experience of a completed, high quality, secondary education which makes it hard for them to support the current generation through the education and training system.

Some mentees from ethnic minorities in education and training will not share all the characteristics of mainstream culture. They will attempt to maintain and develop their cultural heritage including their own language and beliefs. If we are to mentor them successfully we must be sensitive to their backgrounds and circumstances.

It is important not to stereotype your mentee or to assume that a particular mentee shares the characteristics that you have been told are typical of that group. There are a wide variety of personalities, family circumstances, attitudes, talents and aspirations among every ethnic group. However it is useful to be aware of some possible influences upon these students.

Some mentees may not wish to identify themselves as a member of an ethnic minority or to discuss their background. That is their choice and mentors should not press students to discuss their background if they do not wish to do so.

Many mentees come from families with both ethnic minority and mainstream ethnic majority roots. Therefore they may be torn between different identities and unsure about the extent to which they should claim minority group status. They may switch from one identity to another as they move from group to group.

Some ethnic minorities have above average educational performance e.g. Sikh students in the UK or Jewish students in the USA. In Australia, students from ethnic minorities form a disproportionately high percentage of the top performers at the highest performing private schools. These students are mainly of South East Asian origin with parents from business or professional backgrounds who push their children hard.

In contrast, some Aboriginal students have low educational and career aspirations, low levels of knowledge about the education system and have little understanding of the world of paid employment. Therefore they lack confidence in their own ability to compete successfully in education and the workplace. These seem alien environments to them. When the work starts to get hard, as it does for all students, they may interpret this as a lack of ability on their part and give up too easily. Helping them to set goals and building their resilience are crucial tasks for mentors.

Some ethnic minority students come from families with no history of educational success. Moreover parents may not speak the dominant language and may not know how the educational system works. Therefore they do not have people at home who know how to get the best out of the available opportunities. There may not be anyone who can help with school assignments. They may not have the networks of people within the community that they can call upon to help with educational and career issues e.g. with gaining an apprenticeship.

Some of these students are part of well established families and communities which retain a strong sense of cultural identity. Others have been separated from their roots and know little about them.

In Australia, rather than there being a single Aboriginal culture there are several hundred Aboriginal language groups and nations, each of which has its own particular, territory, beliefs and traditions. Students from different groups may be in the same school. In some schools relationships between groups are amicable. In other schools these different groups keep separate from each other and may not cooperate well together.

It is easy for mentors to misinterpret the body language of mentees with different backgrounds from themselves. As we saw in chapter two, in some Aboriginal cultures eye contact is seen as threatening and to be avoided.

Mentors should remember that reluctance to make eye contact may not imply disinterest. It may simply reflect community norms e.g. showing respect. However it can be disconcerting for the mentor and leave the mentor feeling uneasy and that rapport, trust and empathy have not been achieved.

It might be thought that only mentors of the same ethnicity as the mentee should be used. This is not necessarily the case. Mentees of the same group are valuable since they may be particularly good role models and find it easier to empathise. However, sufficient suitable mentors of the same ethnic group may be hard to find.

Moreover mentees sometimes prefer mentors outside their own group as a way of reaching out to the wider society. Such a mentor may have a more extensive network of contacts to support educational progress and career aspirations. In the author's experience the personality of the mentor is much more important than their ethnicity. An exception to this generalisation can be the use of male mentors with female mentees from some ethnic minority groups. Muslim families in particular may well be reluctant to have white males mentoring their wives and daughters.

For people with strong family and community ties, maintaining these links is a high priority. Hence it is not uncommon for Australian Aboriginal families to visit relatives in other towns for extended periods, perhaps for major events such as marriages. This can mean that students are away from school and get behind with their work. In some subject areas, such as mathematics, English and science, later work builds on earlier work and gaps in a student's knowledge can handicap future learning. The same problem has been experienced in the UK with students from the Indian subcontinent returning home on family visits.

Traditionally some cultures have been oral i.e. the community's knowledge was passed on by word of mouth, from memory and by example. Much of it was communicated by group activities including stories, songs, music and dance. Consequently there is no tradition of reading written accounts. For a European style of education, exposing small children to books and reading stories to them from books, gives them a head start at school. In some ethnic minority communities, their own languages are still used and hence their children's command of English may be very limited. Moreover, they may speak their own version of English with a vocabulary and grammatical structure which is rather different from standard English. Some Bangladeshi immigrants from the rural areas of the Sylhet region and some Aboriginal communities are examples.

Where mentoring schemes are being established which cater for ethnic minorities, it is very helpful to give mentors specific training which outlines the culture of the minority group and prepares mentors for issues that might arise.

An Example of a Culturally Sensitive Issue

When mentoring adolescent students from Hindu and Sikh backgrounds the author found that families are particularly sensitive to any indication that boyfriend/girlfriend relationships are developing. Study can come a very distant second if a female student is conscious that her cousin in the same college has been deputed to watch her to ensure that she does not talk to any boys. If she is seen talking to a boy her family might withdraw her from college.

If she is successful and wishes to go to another town to further her studies this may be blocked by her family who fear for her safety. Does she insist on going at the risk of causing a terrible breach with her family or does she suppress her ambitions out of love for her parents and family loyalty?

Generally such families are very supportive of education and very caring towards their young people but sometimes they see the wider society as a corrupting influence and a potential threat to their children, culture, family traditions and religious beliefs.

Clearly this is an area where the mentor must go very carefully and not try to push the young person in a particular direction. The important thing is to use listening and questioning skills to help the mentee get the situation clear and examine the advantages and disadvantages of all the possible causes of action. What may be right for one person may be disastrous for another. Postponing a decision until the mentee is older is an option for her to consider but that may in turn lead to further issues surrounding a potential arranged marriage.

Ultimately the mentee must decide.

Peer Mentoring In Education

Peer mentoring involves one student mentoring another. Perhaps the most common form that this takes is in secondary education where an older student mentors one or more younger ones.

The Big Brother Big sister organization mentioned earlier, has been concentrating on school-based mentoring since the late 1990's and most of its schemes are school based. It has commissioned a number of evaluations which have shown that properly run mentoring schemes can develop more positive attitudes to school and improved self confidence together with better relationships with adults and other students. These lead in turn to improved grades in examinations and assessment tasks.

Peer Mentoring

This example of Peer Mentoring is a composite based on actual schools. A fictional name has been used.

Foxenhall High school was concerned that its intake of students from local primary schools was falling whilst that of a High school at the other side of town was growing. To try to understand why this was happening, the school surveyed local parents and held discussions with primary school staff. It discovered that Foxenhall had a reputation of being too large and impersonal. New students were reporting back to their parents and friends that they found it hard to fit in and feared bullying by students in the year above.

As part of its response to these findings, Foxenhall decided to use older students (15 and 16 year olds), as mentors to support the transition to secondary and to be available for their mentees during their first High school term. The school recognised that becoming a mentor would also benefit their older students by enabling them to develop their social skills and their sense of responsibility for others. A teacher agreed to take on the role of coordinating the programme.

The peer mentors used were all volunteers. They were carefully vetted to ensure that only students with the empathy to become effective mentors were chosen.

The next step was to train the prospective peer mentors using an outside facilitator and an existing well tried programme. They opted to use the Kids Help Line Peer Skills Programme which includes five modules: *Really Listen, Values, Problem Solving, Self Care,* and *Who Else Can Help.*

Foxenhall worked with students at its feeder schools during their last two terms of primary schooling. Initially the peer mentors went to primary schools to meet their mentees. This was followed up by visits to Foxenhall during the final term where the peer mentors took their mentees around the school. Then they enjoyed a choice of fun activities together, supervised by teachers, including sports, artwork and making electronic music.

When the mentees started at Foxenhall as High school students they were welcomed by their peer mentor and shown to their form room. Over the first few weeks the mentors checked up regularly with their mentees to ensure that no bullying was taking place and any worries that their mentees had were discussed and dealt with. The coordinating teacher held briefing sessions with the peer mentors to check that they were seeing their mentees and that all was well.

Feedback from both peer mentors and mentees was good and the school decided to make peer mentoring a regular feature of its transition arrangements. It is also intended to use peer mentoring to support students joining the school during the year into all year groups.

Bullying

Bullying is a problem across the world and has been extensively studied. It damages both the victims and the perpetrator. Victims are often socially isolated. The isolated become victims and bullying increases their isolation. The resulting high levels of anxiety, damages their ability to study successfully. At the extreme it can lead to depression, mental illness, and suicide.

Bullies themselves have often previously been bullied. They also tend to suffer depression and low academic performance. Hence the problem tends to be self perpetuating from generation to generation unless it is tackled. In each generation large numbers of students have their lives blighted by it.

Unfortunately bulling remains very persistent and the bully finds new ways of harassing victims. Cyber bullying is a particular problem where the bully uses mobile phones and the internet (including social networking sites and email) to undermine and frighten the victim. Critical denigrating messages may be sent and false rumours spread to humiliate the victim. In 2007 NetAlert and ninemsn undertook an online survey which found that 16% of young people said they had been bullied online and 14% had been bullied via their mobile phone.

These problems have been widely recognised by education authorities and anti bullying policies are usually in place in schools.

Again social isolation, low self esteem and loneliness make the victim vulnerable and may have been a major initial motivation for posting personal details on a public website. As we saw in chapter two, low self esteem can lead to a passive style of communication. Hence the victim is not assertive enough to seek help. However, sometimes the victim is pushed to the point of responding with aggression. In the USA 71% of school shooting incidents have been linked to bullying (see edmentoring.org).

The key to combating the bullying is to tell someone in authority who will do something about it. It is not uncommon for complaints from the victim to parents or teachers to be brushed aside—perhaps because the adults concerned do not know how to respond or because they can't distinguish bullying from the inevitable conflicts and disputes that young people experience.

Mentoring can be an effective way of tackling bulling (see for example the Team Mates programme in Nebraska USA). It can break into the social isolation and passivity of the victim. The mentor can act as an advocate for the mentee to school authorities and can build self confidence and greater assertiveness in the mentee which supports her or him to be a self advocate and 'blow the whistle on the bullies'. Remember from chapter two that it is assertiveness not aggression that mentors should be trying to encourage.

What advice should the mentor give the victim of cyberbullying? ReachOut. com suggests the following tactics.

- **Keep a record** (including time and date). This may help to find out who is sending the messages.
- **Tell someone.** Talk to someone you trust.
- **Contact your service provider and report what is happening.** They can help you block messages or calls from certain senders.

- **If messages are threatening or serious get in touch with the police.**
- Cyber bullying, if it's threatening, is **illegal**. You don't need to put up with that!
- **Don't reply to bullying messages.** It'll only get worse if you do. By replying the bully gets what he or she wants. Often if you don't reply the bully will leave you alone.
- **Change your contact details.** Get a new user name for the internet, a new e-mail account, a new mobile phone number and only give them out to your closest friends.
- **Keep your username and passwords secret.** Keep your personal information private so it doesn't fall into the hands of someone who'll misuse it.

Higher and Further Education

In the University sector there is a long tradition of one to one personal tutoring which has sometimes been called mentoring. Historically much of this has been informal. It has involved two way discussion rather than the didactic teaching of the lecture hall. More recently Universities have developed sophisticated formal mentoring schemes for both staff and students. The traditional approach of the older universities involved much one to one contact between staff and students but most modern universities have to deliver mass higher education alongside their research work. Hence peer mentoring, student to student, has mushroomed to fill the void. University students have of course always supported each other but we are now at the stage where more formal schemes of peer mentoring have been introduced.

A typical example of mentoring in a small regional university can be found at Southern Cross University in New South Wales where students who have "survived" their first year are invited to become mentors for next year's incoming students. The volunteer mentors are given free training and an opportunity to get a mentoring certificate to add to their CV (resume). They are offered staff support and an opportunity to further develop their social and communication skills. These mentors offer personal support, can explain university processes and procedures, and can refer on to specialist support services when needed.

A significant feature of higher education today is distance learning where many students are part-time, combining study with employment or raising a family (or both!). Mentoring has enormous potential here since contract with staff may be limited to residential vacation schools and/or the occasional email. Peer mentors may use email, telephones, or network using university intranet sites. Former part time students who have successfully completed their courses can be particularly valuable mentors. They must of course be very careful to avoid plagiarism.

In other further education colleges generalisation is more difficult since colleges vary greatly in their specialisms and clientele. Usually in Further Education (TAFE and Community Colleges in Australia) the great majority of students will be part time, many will only attend for one year or less and many will be adults. In these circumstances the FE teachers, many of whom are themselves part-time, often become the defacto mentors of their students, although in some courses mentoring is part of the curriculum and is formally timetabled.

CHAPTER SEVEN

Mentoring to Aid Career Choice

The focus in this chapter is on initial career choice and support for career change. Career progression and promotion within the workplace will be commented upon in the next chapter.

This is about decision making. We know from psychological research that conscious decision making is often an intuitive, emotional reaction to alternatives. Whilst this often works well in day to day familiar situations, when making major life decisions about unfamiliar options it can lead us astray. Therefore as mentors we should urge caution upon a mentee who seems to be jumping into an instant choice. We should encourage our mentees to take their time and think things through more carefully and systematically.

There are a range of specialist careers advice services available in most western countries. As mentors, our aim should not be to supplant these services but to work in partnership with them. Career professionals may simply not have the time that a mentor has available to fully get to know the mentee and explore alternatives. We can have preliminary discussions with the mentee so that they have their thoughts clear when they meet professional careers counsellors. We can also help them to reflect upon the ideas discussed with the professionals and support them to put their decisions into action.

For school students, it is the author's experience that some careers teachers are overstretched and often take on that role as an add-on to their main teaching subject. Actual careers lessons and courses are often a low priority in a crowded curriculum and sadly they tend to be timetabled mainly for lower achieving students. Where the careers brief has been given to the ex physical education teacher who developed 'dodgy knees', the outcome can be great for both teacher and students as long as the teacher approaches the task with skill and enthusiasm. Unfortunately that is not always the case. Hence, sometimes volunteer mentors may be called upon to help an overloaded careers teacher or even compensate for a poor one.

For us, as mentors, 'career" should not just mean employment. It should be about supporting our mentee to make the big decisions about how to spend the next phase of life. To take an obvious example, it is pointless for a person living in a country town who wishes to remain there, to select a career that involves moving to a large city. Similarly someone for whom playing sport at the weekends is of central importance needs to look carefully at the working week required by potential employers. You may be surprised by the number of people who latch onto a career choice without thinking through the negative impact that that choice would have on some cherished aspect of their lives.

The realistic career options available will be influenced by the age and experience of the mentee. To work with them effectively we need to identify the unique characteristics of each person, including their values and attitudes.

Contrary to what we might at first assume, most people do not place 'earning as much money as possible' as their highest career priority. Psychologists of motivation have suggested that work fulfills a range of human needs and wants. Obviously we want it to give us sufficient income to meet our physical needs and most of us also want to be in a safe environment, although some people get a thrill from risk taking. We also look to work to give us a social experience where we make friends and gain the respect of others. This in turn helps our self respect and sense of belonging. Do we also have a need to do some creative or fulfilling work? No doubt this need is stronger in some people than others but without it work can be a very impoverished experience.

Clearly attitudes vary towards promotion and assuming responsibilities including leading and managing others. We will find it useful to know whether our mentee has shown leadership skills and is attracted to jobs that provide that opportunity.

For those about to complete compulsory schooling, issues such as continuing education, staying or leaving home, training, gap years and travel may need to be considered. Therefore:

Career is about making lifestyle as well as job choices.

One approach that the author has developed and used successfully is the six question strategy which fits quite closely the Mentoring Stages outlined in chapter one. This strategy, set out below, takes mentor and mentee through a process of discussion and research based on set of questions and supporting activities.

Mentors will need to adapt the process to the mentee's background and situation. It is important to remember that the process is not likely to be a simple progression through these six questions. Everything will depend on the personal circumstances, wishes and characteristics of the mentee. The mentee may have ideas about how to proceed. But when you start to discuss career together, if you don't know how to begin or if you get stuck, you can go back to these six questions and their supporting activities.

If your mentees are experienced adults wishing to change career and have some ideas about the direction they wish to take, some of the stages below may be skipped over and the activities suggested may not be needed. However, you should look at them carefully because, used selectively, they could be very valuable. For example the Record of Achievement applies to all of us. In the case of a young person with no idea of which direction to pursue, systematically going through the six questions and some of the suggested activities, can be a great help. Many young people will find the prospect of seeking work to be very daunting. They may have avoided thinking too much about it until a mentor came along to help them. New mentors may also feel lost; not knowing where to start. If so try the six questions.

Mentors should not be surprised or upset if the mentee has sudden changes of heart and overturns the discussions of the previous week. False starts and back tracking are part of the process. Be patient and go again.

QUESTION 1. What is my mentee's SITUATION?

Here we identify factors that will influence career choice and career accessibility such as:

- values and life style preferences,
- personality and personal qualities,
- circumstances and commitments,
- interests,
- education, skills and qualifications,
- experiences,
- health issues,
- willingness to train,
- willingness to make short term sacrifices for long term gain,
- attitude to risk taking
- and any networks of useful contacts of the mentee.

Our purpose is not to probe into private matters out of vicarious curiosity but to make explicit any factors that the mentee might want to take into account when making decisions and which will open up opportunities or impose limits on what is possible. The idea is to make sure that nothing important is missed.

Careers guidance professionals are likely to have some psychological tests and sophisticated software that can generate career options. As lay mentors we can take a different and complementary approach.

As mentors our key starting point, as always, is to be a listener and questioner. We should be an active listener who is alert for hidden messages. For example, is the mentee thinking of a career which meets the aspirations of a parent or partner rather than their own? Statements such as:

"Dad thinks I should go to agricultural college and then work on the family farm. How do I go about getting in?"

should immediate raise alarms. The first sentence is strong hint that your mentee is not fully committed to this course but feels obliged to pursue it.

It is not our job to persuade the mentee to defy the father. Instead we should ask questions to ensure that the mentee has fully thought through the implications of any decision and is aware of alternatives and their likely consequences. Perhaps your mentee really wants to challenge the parent but fears a row and parental anger. Here a discussion of assertiveness rather than passivity or aggression might be needed. Alternatively the mentee may decide that family loyalty is more important than personal ambition. That is the mentee's choice. We should try to ensure that it is genuinely the mentee's own.

One way of doing so is to ask challenging questions to encourage our mentee to see things from a different angle. We are trying to widen their thinking by asking "what if . . . . ?"

Record of Achievement (RoA) and Career Portfolio

As you proceed, your mentees will collect lots of information and, if you follow the advice given here, will create some more documents themselves. They are strongly advised to create a portfolio (let's call it *My Career*) where they can keep all relevant material. In due course some of this material can be transferred into an attractive presentation folder which we can call a 'Record of Achievement' (RoA).

The *My Career* portfolio is always a work in progress. It can exist in a variety of formats. It may simply be a set of files in both paper and electronic formats. The electronic format, on a computer, enables the mentee to update information quickly but remember to make sure the printed version does not contain outdated documents. A portfolio can also include a wide range of larger items and objects. These would be included as examples of work produced in training, in previous employment or in your mentees own time.

What could the *My Career* portfolio contain?

- Thoughts about ambitions, goals and lifestyle preferences
- Details of work and educational history.
- Summary of skills and personal qualities possessed,
- Reports e.g. from school or work.
- Awards, certificates and qualifications.
- Letters of appreciate and testimonials.
- Examples of work produced (could be photographs or video).
- Details of personal experiences and achievements.
- Details of any short courses and training.
- Details of any community service and personal interests.
- Any other material that presents the mentee in a positive manner.

All the above should be summarised in an up to date Curriculum Vitae (C.V. or resume).

Some adults may still have an RoA, or equivalent, from school days, a C.V. (resume) that was submitted for a previous job application and other personal records. Mentors are strongly recommended to ask their mentee to bring any material that they can muster, to a session where it can be discussed, placed in the *My Career* file and later used to put together an up to date RoA. It is well worth while your mentee spending a little money on an attractive presentation folder with pockets to store documents. It can be used to assist with the completion of application forms and can be taken to present at interviews. An attractively presented RoA can create a very favourable impression. Your mentee will come across as a well organised and well prepared candidate.

In New South Wales, schools were issued with an 'Employment Related Skills Logbook' that fulfills a similar purpose. Unfortunately, in the author's experience many of them stayed in careers teacher's cupboards rather than being used creatively with students.

The *My Career* portfolio is not only a source for the RoA. Actually creating it together, enables the mentor and mentee to review what the mentee has been through in life and what has been achieved. As you go through the material it is sensible to organise it under side headings in a logical order and add a contents page at the front. Going through this process will help you to work together to answer this first question.

Stress to your mentee that once they are in work they will find it helpful to maintain a *My Career* portfolio to help with job reviews at work and any applications for promotion. Since changes of job are likely to be more frequent in the future economy, it makes sense to keep the *My Career* portfolio ongoing rather than having to create a fresh one when job hunting begins again.

Let us look at some further activities that mentor and mentee can do together to identify factors that could impact on career choice, starting with personality and personal interests.

Personality

The 'Big Five' model, (frequently used by psychologists) identifies five key aspects of personality. Most people can identify their own characteristics by making use of these aspects. These are: extraversion (being lively, sociable and outward looking), agreeableness, conscientiousness, emotional stability and openness to experience. Reflecting upon these helps us to become more self aware and to match ourselves with the requirements of differing careers.

Look at the activity on the following page. Whilst not being a scientific psychological test it can help us to think about how extrovert or introvert we are. Go down the list and circle the appropriate number. For example if you enjoy playing team sports circle 1. If you dislike playing them circle 5 if you don't have strong feeling either way circle 3. If you enjoy them to some extent circle 2 and so on. Don't worry if your mentee has difficulties with a pair and claims that they are not alternatives. That response is great because it opens a topic for further discussion and gives you some insight into your mentee's self image.

Don't just give this to your mentee to do. You should both do it and then compare and contrast your responses. This activity is not a validated psychological test. It is merely a device to get you talking together and finding out more about each other.

When you have finished your discussion, one of you could write a brief summary of the mentee's positive characteristics and store it in the *My Career* portfolio to help with the creation or update of a C.V. later in the process. Try to avoid negative statements. Use positive words—'persistent and determined' rather than 'stubborn'.

ACTIVITY: My Personality—Try this yourself

Enjoy playing a team sport	1 2 3 4 5	Dislike playing team sports
Friendly	1 2 3 4 5	Reserved
Loud	1 2 3 4 5	Quiet
Lively	1 2 3 4 5	Calm
Impulsive	1 2 3 4 5	Thoughtful
Short tempered	1 2 3 4 5	Even tempered
Risk taker	1 2 3 4 5	Careful
Innovator	1 2 3 4 5	Traditionalist

Joker	1 2 3 4 5	Serious minded
Prefers watching TV	1 2 3 4 5	Prefers reading
Confident	1 2 3 4 5	Cautious
Acts without thought	1 2 3 4 5	Thinks before acts
Easily bored	1 2 3 4 5	Persistent
Prefers working in a team	1 2 3 4 5	Prefers working independently
Easy going	1 2 3 4 5	Disciplined
Affectionate	1 2 3 4 5	Cool
Prefers company	1 2 3 4 5	Happy alone
A Rebel	1 2 3 4 5	Respects authority
Ambitious	1 2 3 4 5	Content
Optimistic	1 2 3 4 5	Pessimistic
Lives for today	1 2 3 4 5	Plans for tomorrow
Spends spare cash	1 2 3 4 5	Saves spare cash
Trusting	1 2 3 4 5	Suspicious

Looking at skills

You may get some objective evidence of your mentee's skill levels from any qualifications that they have gained, or from any references, testimonials and reports that they are willing to show you. However it is important not to neglect the mentee's own assessment of their skill levels, even though this is very subjective. It may tell you that they have negative feelings about themselves or have an unrealistically high appreciation of their skill levels.

The set of general skills required by employers are not always the same as those required to gain a qualification or complete a course. A job may be a technical one requiring specialist knowledge and hence a technical qualification. However, qualifications are often used by employers as a cost effective way of narrowing down a field of applicants. The actual work may not need that qualification. Moreover once you start work no one may care very much what course or qualifications you have gained. The essential point is 'have you got the general skills that make you a good employee and good colleague'.

Employers have tried to define these skills. They are usually called 'generic', 'core', or 'key' skills and turn out to be very similar across different countries and employment sectors. If your mentee can demonstrate these skills and show some evidence of them in the RoA, it will stand them in good stead at interview and in work. The names given to these skills vary but they include skills such as:

- communication
- literacy
- numeracy
- information technology
- self management and organisation
- initiative
- leadership
- team working
- ability to adapt and learn
- problem solving
- licensed car/van driver
- cross cultural understanding
- additional language speaker

You may find your mentee severely deficient in some of these skills. If so, the question to ask yourself is, "is there any way that my mentee could improve in these areas?" If I.T., literacy or numeracy were a problem you could suggest a course at a local college or adult education centre and offer to provide backup support for work set by a tutor. Options which might help to develop other skills, such as self management and team working, could be a work experience placement or doing some voluntary work. Your own networks may enable you to introduce your mentee to an employer or organisation which could help.

ACTIVITY: How Good Are My Skills? Try this yourself

Skill	Dreadful	Poor	OK	Great
Speaking				
Listening				
Writing accurate sentences				
Mental arithmetic				
Using statistics				
Doing complex maths				
Working in a group				
Getting on with new people				
Leading groups				
Helping people in need				
Taking accurate notes				
Using Libraries				
Reading complex documents				
Report writing				
Sport				
Music				
Art				
Making & repairing				
Looking after animals				
Hard physical work				
Using machines/electronics				
Using computers				
Using the Internet				
Observing & Experimenting				
Interviewing				
Solving problems				
Organising and planning				
Remembering				
Discussing				
Cooking				
Managing money				
Controlling my temper				

Coping with a crisis				
Traveling to new places				
Punctuality				
Having fun				

Keep the completed chart in *My Career* Portfolio. You might want to review and revise it later.

Using a Questionnaire

A simple questionnaire that you both fill in is another option to discover your mentee's situation and compare it with your own. Below is an example for a recent school leaver. If this was a questionnaire for an adult we could add further sections e.g. on employment

Warning. Think about the likely impact on your particular mentee of these questions. You may want to amend them to fit a particular mentee and give more space for some answers. Don't try to force your mentee to answer the questionnaire or any individual questions where there is a reluctance to respond. You might not want use a written questionnaire like this if you know your mentee is a low achiever whose answers will be predominantly negative. Use general discussion instead.

Remember to use this as a trigger for discussion and to explore some answers in a lot more depth.

ACTIVITY: Questionnaire

Looking Back At School

	Question	Answer
1.	Did you enjoy learning?	
2.	What were your best subjects?	
3.	How well did you get on with your teachers?	

4	How well did you get on with other students?	
5.	Were you ever bullied?	
6.	Did you often skip school?	
7.	Did you ever get into trouble at school?	
8.	Did you get any awards at school?	
9.	Did you represent the school at anything?	

Looking at Leisure time and Health

10.	How do you spend your leisure time?	
11.	How much sport/exercise do you do?	
12.	Do you spend much time with your family?	
13.	Do you spend much time with friends?	
14.	Which type of TV programme do you prefer?	
15.	Are you a member of any social or sports clubs? If so which ones?	
16.	What kind of music do you like?	
17.	How much alcohol do you drink in a typical week?	
18.	Do you smoke? If so how much?	
19.	List any medical conditions that you have that could affect career choice.	
20.	How much time per week do you spend on electronic games?	
21.	How much use do you make of social networking sites?	

Looking at Other Experiences

22.	Where is your favourite holiday destination?	
23.	Do you have any really close mates?	
24.	Have you lived anywhere else? If so where?	
25.	What is your experience of religion?	
26.	Do you belong to any clubs or other organizations?	
27.	What causes do you feel strongly about?	
28.	Have you done any voluntary work? If so what?	

Commitments and Concerns

29.	What is the most important thing that has happened to you over the last few months?	
30.	Are there any things that are making life difficult for you at the moment?	
31.	Do you have anyone dependent upon you? If so who?	
32.	Do you have any commitments that would make it difficult for you to live elsewhere?	
33.	Do you have any conditions or impairments that impose limits upon what you can take on? If so what?	

Add this to the *My Career* portfolio.

Construct/rewrite a Curriculum Vitae (C.V.)—sometimes called a Resume

The material collected so far, in the *My Career* portfolio can be used to put together a new draft C.V. or to review an existing one. This process will also add more information, to enable mentor and mentee to reflect on strengths and achievements so far. Obviously, it is also a crucial element of a job application. At this stage the C.V. should be just a draft because it will need to be adjusted to fit the kind of post being applied for.

It is sensible to use a template here. A template is an existing layout with side headings and a professional looking style. You just type information into the spaces provided. A range of templates are provided in word processing programmes such as Microsoft word. However, others are available on career information websites such as: www.myfuture.edu.au

Don't go for anything too fancy. Stress simplicity and clarity. When it comes to an actual job application your mentee can choose another template if the first one is felt to be unsuitable.

C.V. side headings should include at least the following.

- Personal information: full name, address, telephone, email, date and place of birth, nationality if not a national of that country. Family information such as marital status and children is optional but can suggest personal stability if included.
- Education and training: list of schools, colleges and training programmes attended with dates and qualifications obtained. For some posts a list of short course and recent in service training attended is very valuable.
- Employment and self employment: list of positions held, most recent first with dates and correct job titles.
- Achievements.
- Community service: try to find something genuine that you have contributed to your locality or to a national charity.

- Interests: including sports, membership of organisations, hobbies, travel, positions held. Don't go overboard here but show you have some sensible interests outside work.
- Contact details for at least two referees.

By now you should have plenty of material to use to ANSWER QUESTION 1. What is my mentees situation?

If you review all this material together, you may want to produce a summary of any key points that will need to be borne in mind when identifying a preferred life style and selecting a career to pursue. You know where to save the summary!

QUESTION 2 What are my mentee's life style and work PREFERENCES?

So, you now know quite a bit about our mentee. Next, we should explore personal preferences including values, ambitions, and feelings about possible work environments. These include ambitions, subjects enjoyed, stay home or move away, values (e.g. serve others or seek high income), outdoor/indoor, travel, short term/long term, safe/adventurous, willingness to study, shift work.

Discussing the following questions together is a good start.

Hopes

| Is there any place that you have not been to yet but would like to visit? |
| Is there anything that you would like to do that you have not had the chance to try yet? |
| Is there any new skill that you would like to learn? |
| Can you imagine yourself in 10 years time? If things went well for you what might your life be like? |

Which of these places would you prefer to live in? • Where I live now, • a major city, • a country town, • a small village, • at the coast, • in another country, • another option
What other ambitions do you have that you have not mentioned so far?

ACTIVITY: My Values

Each try this questionnaire to get a sense of what matters most to mentor and mentee at the moment but remember that these can change over time. The answers here can be a real help later in finding a career option that would suit your mentees preferred life style. When job options are considered later, go back to these answers and ask if the job would be a barrier to any of these preferences.

	Very important for me	*Not a priority for me*
A high income		
Having children		
An exciting social life		
Self-respect		
Loving and being loved		
Good health		
Having a set of real friends		
Family		
A sport		
My girlfriend/boyfriend/partner		
A good night out		
Being respected by others		
Inner peace		
Religion		

Education		
Security		
The environment		
New experiences		
Helping others		
Books		
A sense of achievement		
Being my own boss		
Leisure		
Having fun		
Freedom		
Knowledge and understanding		
Wealth		
Music		
Qualifications		
Owning my own home		
My appearance—clothes etc		
Risk taking		
My car/bike		
My garden		
My animals		

Save in *My Career* portfolio.

ACTIVITY: Key Employment Issues

The following questionnaire should enable you to get to grips with some key issues.

Which of the following appeal to you most? Put Y in these boxes. Which would you hate? Put N in these boxes.

Rewards

| | a high paying job is essential for me

| | I will accept a reasonable wage if the job is decent

| | I don't care about the wage level as long as I enjoy the job

| | I want a career with promotion opportunities

| | I just want a decent job without a lot of responsibility or stress

I prefer working indoors:

| | in a workshop

| | in an office

| | in a shop

| | in a hotel, café or restaurant

| | in a salon

| | in a gym or sports centre

| | in a hospital or medical centre

| | in a school or college

| | in doors but none of the above

I prefer working outdoors

| | with animals

[ ] with trees, plants or crops

[ ] constructing

[ ] transporting

[ ] mining

[ ] at sea

[ ] outdoors but none of the above

I would like to work for

[ ] myself

[ ] government

[ ] a business

[ ] non-profit organization

[ ] medium/large organisation

[ ] small organisation

This type of work would suit me

[ ] physical work

[ ] work with machines and technology

[ ] work in an office organising and administering

[ ] work with money, figures or statistics

☐ selling products

☐ provide services for customers

☐ with children

☐ being self-employed

☐ scientific or technical work

☐ caring for those in need

<u>I prefer these working relationships</u>

☐ work alone

☐ be part of a team

☐ lead/supervise others

☐ work with customers

☐ work with people who need help

☐ having someone tell me what work I should do

<u>My attitude to education and training</u>

☐ want to study/train full time before starting my working life

☐ willing to study/train part time whilst I am employed

☐ prefer that no further study or training needed

☐ would like to be an expert or specialist that others turn to

<u>My attitudes to conditions are</u>

☐ willing to do overtime

☐ willing to work night shifts

☐ willing to do weekend work

☐ willing to work where there is noise and dirt if required

☐ willing to cope with extreme environments if properly protected

☐ willing to clean up after others

☐ a pleasant and comfortable workplace is essential for me

Save in *My Career* portfolio.

For mentees who find it hard to think long term and who look for immediate gratification the next two activities might be useful to get them thinking.

ACTIVITY: In Three Year's Time. Try this yourself

Where I want to be living	
Things I want to have done	
Places I want to have visited	
Things I would like to own	
Things I want to avoid	

Save in My Career portfolio.

For those who find it difficult to express themselves in words, drawing a couple of cartoons might help.

Draw yourself as you are now with your favourite possessions.

Draw yourself as you would like to be in a few years time

Remember that all these activities should stimulate discussion. If some answers are contradictory that is good because it picks up some issues that need to be thought through.

By now you should be able to answer question 2 about life style and work preferences. Again, writing a summary of the answers to this question (saved it the *My Career* portfolio) will be very helpful when discussing the next question.

QUESTION 3. What ALTERNATIVES would fit my situation and preferences?

By now our mentee should have done quite a bit of thinking and have a clearer idea of their preferred career requirements. We have reached the stage where we can identify a number of possible jobs, education or training routes, and career paths that would match with the situation (Q.1) and preferences (Q.2) of our mentee. The idea is that we create a long list of possibilities which we can later narrow down to a short list for more detailed investigation. It is important not to jump to a quick decision. Let us leave the actual choosing to QUESTION 4 and, for the time being, concentrate on finding possibilities for our long list.

What is the difference between a job and a career? A job involves immediate paid employment which may not have any long term prospects for personal advancement or self development. This may suit people who are not ready for a longer term commitment or who shy away from training and responsibilities. Whereas a job which is also a career implies some long term commitment to and planning for, an occupation that enables you to develop over time. Almost invariably this involves gaining qualifications and being willing to take on new tasks as knowledge and experience grows. Careers are also more likely to open the door to self employment than are low skill, low responsibility jobs.

If you take a career path that you later find unsatisfactory, you may feel that you have wastefully invested a lot of time and effort. On the other hand it is important to realise that people move much more between jobs and careers today as opportunities, technology and the demands of employers change with increasing rapidity. Most of us will move jobs and careers several times during our working lives. Skills and experiences gained in one career are likely to be very valuable when you train for the next one.

We are now faced with the massive range of possible occupations. There are thousands of them. The best way to start is with a process of elimination. Decision making is very difficult when there are a large number of alternatives. If we can narrow the choice down to two or three comparing the advantages and disadvantages of each of them is much easier. Therefore a good strategy for your mentee is to start by eliminating: the unattractive, those for which she cannot see herself ever becoming qualified or those which clash with her preferred life style i.e. use a process of elimination.

As a starting point to tackle this question look at the following activity using career segments. The range of career types has been compressed into eight segments.

Ask your mentee to select or reject segments. This is not a final decision merely a place to begin. It helps to narrow down the initial search.

Selecting more than one segment is good. It enables you to seek occupations using the shared characteristics of two or three segments.

ACTIVITY: *Career Segments*

Eliminate the impossible—investigate what remains

8. Make Construct Build Repair Mine, Technology

1. Grow & Nurture Plants Animals Farm Garden

7. Help others Health Education, Welfare Children

2. Manage Administer Business Finance Government

6. Provide Services, Travel, Leisure, Sport, Hospitality Fitness, Hair Beauty.

3. Communicate Entertain Sell Advertise Market Media

5. Protect Law Armed Forces Police Security

4. Design Research Develop Create

Put a tick in each of the segments where you think there are some possibilities that could interest you. Put a cross in each of the segments which refer to work that you would never wish to do. Put a question mark in any remaining boxes. Place in *My Career* portfolio.

By combining ideas from two or more boxes you can come up with some great possibilities to investigate e.g. Jo ticked 2, 7 and 6 which got Jo thinking about managing a gym or sports centre.

Use Career Planning Resources

We now need to do some research using all the information that we have identified so far. Remember, at this stage we are trying to create a list of possible job/career options, courses and training opportunities. As you create the list it is a good idea to write down key information about each option as you come across it and file it safely (guess where). In the following box is a template for a record sheet that mentor and mentee could complete together for each serious possibility. Where possible, encourage the mentee to take responsibility for writing record sheets and filing them—to encourage independence.

- Professional advisors

Having done lots of preparatory work in answer to questions 1 and 2, this would be a good time to make use of professional careers services if they are available. Careers advisers (sometimes called careers counsellors), will be aware of career opportunities that your mentee might never otherwise consider. They should have a good knowledge of local employers and current vacancies. They should also be able to give advice on local training providers and the opportunities that they offer.

You mentee's situation, preferences, and an initial elimination using the above segments, will give a careers adviser lots of good information to work with. Taking along the *My Career* file should also be really helpful. Often advisors will have access to sophisticated computer software that can generate career suggestions based on information that your mentee submits. This information may be typed directly into a computer or may involve the careers advisor asking questions and entering responses. However, some websites enable people to do this for themselves without consulting an advisor. What you get from an advisor or website will depend upon the accuracy of the information that they are given. The author used such a programme which suggested he become a prosthesis fitter. Not his ideal choice!

Professional careers advisors are usually very helpful and professional. However, it is important to remember that they usually work for businesses with contracts to fulfill and targets to meet. Hence, they have an interest in placing your mentee, within a limited time period, into an approved destination. Hopefully, the preliminary work you have already done together will expedite this process. Some employment services run their own training programmes and provide work experience opportunities. These can be very valuable but it is sensible to look at all the alternatives before signing up to one of these options.

If there is no professional advice available to your mentee or the advice has not been effective, there are other avenues to pursue.

Career Option Record	
Title of job/career	
Entry qualifications required	
Skills and qualities required	
Experience required	
Hours of work & Working conditions	
Location	
Remuneration (pay and other benefits)	
Type of contract (FT., PT., Casual etc)	

Type of work	
What specific tasks would I have to do?	
How much individual responsibility would I have?	
How much team working?	
Promotion prospects	
What kind of organisation would I work for? (govt. /private/charity etc)	
Training to be undertaken (once employed)	
Any other information	

Save in *My Career* portfolio. If a training course or continuing education is being considered a different recording sheet will be needed.

- School/ college subjects

These can be another useful source of career ideas particularly for young people who are about to leave education or have recently left. The internet site www.myfuture.edu.au has a wealth of useful information including subject wheels which show, for the main school subjects, an array of possible occupations that students who have an interest in that subject could explore. Each wheel sets out the occupations in bands according to the level of qualification required to enter them. Your mentee is likely to find some great options here to include in the long list.

- Colleges, universities and training providers

For the career minded, examining the prospectuses of colleges, universities and training providers is a worthwhile exercise. One of the great features of modern western societies is their second and third chance opportunities. Local colleges (e.g. TAFE in Australia, FE in the UK) usually offer a huge range of options for both school leavers and adults. Where they are not provided face to face on a local campus, many qualifications are available through distance learning. If your mentee is interested in distance learning, ask if any peer or learning mentoring support is available.

Look with your mentee for the level that might be appropriate and the department or faculty which fits the segments that you identified earlier.

Basic skills courses including literacy, numeracy, and IT are appropriate for those adults with deficiencies in these areas. For example, a high proportion of the prison population struggle with basic literacy and numeracy. Mentors supporting offenders and ex offenders may wish to encourage them take up these courses and could offer to work with colleges to give extra support.

There may well be purpose designed programmes at local colleges to support adults with disabilities and learning difficulties. The tutors of these courses may also be able to help people into employment.

There will be introductory level courses for the unqualified school leaver and unqualified adult returner to education. Courses at this level will be less likely to qualify fully your mentee but they may provide a stepping stone into more specialised higher level options. Some will be taster courses for a range of related occupations which will give your mentee a chance to try some alternatives. Intermediate level courses will provide marketable vocational qualifications in many occupational areas such as construction, administration, hospitality, horticulture, motor vehicle, retailing and caring. Higher level courses at diploma, degree or post graduate level could include higher level technical knowledge and skills, management, or preparation to enter the professions. Some diploma programmes at local TAFE colleges can be upgraded into degrees by progressing onto shortened university courses.

- Using the Internet

There are a wide range of internet sites that you can explore together. The problem here is not shortage of information but becoming overwhelmed by the sheer quantity of it. Therefore, think for a minute or two before you dive in. The type of site to go for depends upon the progress that you have already made.

❖ If your mentee is still struggling to identify possibilities for a long list, look for sites which will take you through software designed to help your mentee identify a range of career options, such as *Career builder*.

❖ If your mentee wishes to find out more about possibilities on the long list, look at sites which will give you detailed information about particular jobs/careers including: entry qualifications, employer expectations, working conditions, wages/salaries, training required, and promotion opportunities. These can be general sites covering a wide range of industries or they can be specialist sites for particular fields or employers.

❖ If your mentee has already chosen a job/career path or wishes to find out where opportunities would be available if they selected that option, look at sites which give information about current job vacancies, including employer details, job and person specifications (including specific employer requirements), locations, contract details (full-time, part-time, permanent, short term, casual?) and details of how to apply.

Remember that governments are major employers—try their sites including your local council.

If you or your mentee do not have internet access, try a library—almost all will enable you to get on line there.

Using Libraries

The old fashioned catalogue search of the careers section of the local, school or college library still has a useful place. Use the expertise of the librarian. If a particular item is not available in that library, ask your librarian who will probably be delighted to help. It may be accessible through inter library loan. Remember that libraries don't just give you books they can also stock useful newspapers, CD's and DVD's. They will have a range of magazines devoted to specialist topics which give an insight into what it is like to work in a particular occupation, what current issues are concerning people in that field, as well as job adverts, course adverts and references to internet sites that you can follow up.

Internet accessible computers are also generally available for public use in public and college libraries.

Find out on which days your local newspaper focuses on job opportunities and runs the most job and training advertisements. Again they should be available in your local library.

Labour markets

If your mentee wants to continue to live in the area, do you know what kinds of opportunities are, and are not, available there? Careers advisers should be able to give you a good overview. The internet will also enable you to access government sites which show statistics from the census for your area. These should show the numbers and percentages of jobs in different categories. In Australia you can look this information up on the site of the ABS (Australian Bureau of Statistics). The website of your local council is often a very useful source of information and may well have some links are worth exploring.

Apprenticeships

If your mentee shows interest in an apprenticeship, a good start in Australia is to look at www.australianapprenticeships.gov.au. From this site you will be able to obtain the address of your local Australian Apprenticeships Centre where your mentee can obtain detailed, up to date advice and support, including help with contracts. These centres are designed to be one stop shops for both employers and employees. It is likely that they will expand their role in the future to give advice on a wider range of skill and training opportunities. Other countries have similar sites.

It is now possible to start an apprenticeship whilst still at school. That option can be accessed through the school careers advisor.

ACTIVITY: Explore These Examples Of Australian Internet Resources.

Identify the purpose of each site. How useful do you think it would be to your mentees?
(Internet sites open and close quite often. Don't be surprised if some have closed or changed their address).

www.australianapprenticeships.gov.au
www.abs.gov.au
www.careerlink.net.au
www.careerone.com.au
www.centrelink.gov.au
www.dest.gov.au/careerdevelopment
www.futuremorph.org
www.goingtouni.gov.au
www.industrialrelations.nsw.gov.au
www.jobguide.dest.gov.au
www.joblinkplus.com.au
www.jobs.nsw.gov.au
www.jobsearch.gov.au
www.makeit.net.au
www.mycareer.com.au
www.myfuture.edu.au
www.necu.com.au/financiallit
www.seek.com.au
www.smartmoves.questacon.edu.au
www.training.com.au
www.workplace.gov.au
www.year12whatnext.gov.au
www.youthpathways.dest.gov.au
www.youth.gov.au

A particularly useful UK site for young people is www.connexions-direct. This site offers information and advice on careers together with a range of other topics that are important to young people.

For a fun activity—look in careerpath.com at the colour leadership activity but don't take the results too seriously.

QUESTION 4. Which alternative will I choose as my career GOAL?

From the long list that the mentee has compiled, the possibilities will need to be narrowed down to a single one or to just a few options that are the most attractive. How do we do this? Mentors can use questioning and discussion to ensure that the mentee understands as fully as possible the advantages and disadvantages of each of the alternatives.

At this stage it often comes down to a feeling; to an emotional response. Something will trigger enthusiasm on the part of your mentee.

"Yeah, I could really see myself doing this".

It is often about 'envisioning'. This means imagining yourself in that situation, doing that job. Imagining how it would feel. If it feels good, the response is positive. If the mentee envisions problems, fears and anxieties, it will not feel right. It is a good idea to encourage the envisioning but there is a danger that it could be based on false perceptions of the job. So first look back at the career option records and make sure that your mentee is as fully informed as possible.

It is important to remember that our decisions are not simply the result of rational calculation. They are based on our previous life experiences; often on parental attitudes and deep seated emotional events which we can no longer consciously recall but which continue to influence our feelings. When we make decisions in everyday life we do not usually go through a conscious rational process such as the one that we are following here. Usually we make quick decisions based on our previous experiences which trigger an emotional reaction. They are intuitive yet often soundly based on unconscious processing within our brains. However this can be dangerous for career choice because:

- There are a large number of factors to take into account which our intuition may not be very effective in processing.
- We may have no direct experience of the relevant career to base our feeling upon. Our emotional response may be a reaction to misinformation or false assumptions.

Hence the mentor's role here is to ensure that the mentee has really researched the favoured options, to ask questions and encourage the mentee to reflect deeply on the advantages and disadvantages of possible actions. We should try to inject a degree of rationality and realism without dampening positive hopes and aspirations.

As a mentor you might want to ask your mentee to spend a week reflecting on the options on the list and trying to imagine being each one (i.e. envisioning it). When you next meet you can discuss what conclusions were reached. A simple chart such as the example 'My Next Step,' which follows, might be a useful summary aide to use.

My Next Step. (an example for a 16 year old potential school leaver who is interested in working in tourism).

List of Options	I Like this Idea	Worth Considering	No chance
Stay at school until 18 to do more advanced study			
Get a short term job in a local motel to make some cash			
Go to college to get a vocational qualification in tourism			
Go on a short training scheme to develop hospitality skills			
Leave school & stay unemployed while I figure out what to do			

By this time one option may be the clear front runner but what if it has been narrowed down to two or three? How can we help our mentee identify a preferred goal?

It is important to stress to a mentee, particularly a school leaver, that it can be quite sensible to 'decide not to decide' on a longer term goal at this stage. The mentee may have insufficient life experience or maturity to make longer term commitments. Instead a shorter term goal could be chosen e.g. 'to obtain a broad based qualification leaving my options open' or to 'spend a year getting some work experience'.

Networks of people

As a mentor one of your great strengths could be your network of local contacts. Could you use it to arrange a visit to an employer in the chosen field? If so your mentee could prepare, in advance, some questions to ask. These could be based on the option record sheets that were referred to above. If your mentee shows some real interest in that option you could try to organise a work experience placement with that employer.

ACTIVITY: A SWOT analysis

If your mentee is still unsure about one or more options try a SWOT analysis. This is a technique widely used in industry to help to decide on a course of action. A blank SWOT follows. Use a separate SWOT sheet for each option. Ask your mentee to write in each box any points that they think will be relevant to that option. Strengths and weakness relate to the immediate situation whereas opportunities and threats require thought about the longer term.

SWOT ANALYSIS FOR OPTION: ....

Strengths	Weaknesses
Opportunities	Threats

Rate this option overall

Very good ☐   Good ☐   Poor ☐   Very Poor ☐

The Choice

Once the mentee has chosen a preferred option it becomes their goal. It is possible to choose more than one goal if they are compatible with each other e.g. obtaining a short term clerical job whilst trying to get bookings as a professional musician with the hope of turning this into a full time career. But, of course, choosing a goal does not automatically mean achieving it. What is clear is that setting an achievable goal can give motivation and direction. It can help the person to feel more optimistic and positive about herself or himself and gives more meaning to their life.

The dilemma faced by the mentor here is 'what is achievable and realistic'? The twin dangers are:

- The mentee sets a goal which is way beyond him or her and hence the mentee is set up to fail—which destroys confidence and motivation.

- The mentee lacks the ambition and confidence to set a challenging goal and settles for something well below potential.

It is not up to the mentor to persuade the mentee into a particular course of action. As has been emphasised a number of times, mentors should use discussion, questioning, warnings and encouragement to help the mentees to reach their own decisions. However, in the author's experience mentees often grow and develop gradually and eventually achieve goals way beyond what may have been predicted for them.

It is better to aim high. Even if you don't quite make it you may well have achieved more along the way than you would have done by aiming at something well within your previous capacity. This can be pointed out to a mentee but if the mentee does not feel ready for an ambitious goal don't show disappointment in them—accept their decision and support them to achieve it.

When a high goal is set your mentee should be advised to have a back-up alternative in the same vocational area, in case they don't quite make it. Someone who aims to get into university to study medicine might not get quite good enough grades to do so but still has a wide range of other professional careers in the medical field to choose from by doing a degree in medical science. If they had not stayed in education to do a post 16 course, these other options would not have been there.

Don't forget the second chance opportunities through local colleges and distance learning. Remember: that

- mentees may have several false starts before finding a goal that they can really commit to and they can always go back to the *My Career* portfolio and look again at their option list (or start afresh as a new idea comes to them),
- adults typically have several different careers in their life time,(these may involve developing new skills in the same broad field or using their existing skills in a different field).

QUESTION 5. What do I need to include in my Personal ACTION PLAN?

Your mentee has made the crucial step forward of identifying a personal goal. Where do we go from here? If the goal involves getting a formal academic entry qualification, the route may be relatively clear through an application for a course at school, college or university.

If the goal involves getting an apprenticeship, traineeship or immediate employment, a strategy will be needed to get there. Responding to a job advert, applying through an employment agency or using an apprenticeship centre are obvious routes. However, in the author's experience, many jobs are not filled by simply advertising a vacancy. Often applicants are already known to the employer. The job may never be advertised. Alternatively the employer may already have someone in mind but goes through the motions to follow the firm's equal opportunities policy by placing an advertisement anyway. Particularly in small businesses, networks of family and friends, using friends of friends, or calling in favours, are often the routes to getting jobs.

Perhaps your mentee comes from an underprivileged or minority culture background where they lack social networks to link them to employers. How could your mentee become known to a potential employer and have an opportunity to show their positive attitudes and qualities, before a post is even advertised?

- Visits to potential employers arranged through the mentor's network of contacts. If the mentor is part of a formal mentoring scheme, other mentors in the scheme or the coordinator, may be able to supply contacts.
- A work experience placement—working without pay for a few days to gain experience, gives a chance to show commitment and perhaps gain a useful reference.
- Door stopping likely employers and handing in a letter expressing interest and enclosing a CV.

Usually the route to achieve a career goal will involve a range of actions and could stretch over years; if gaining qualifications is involved. It is often useful to break down these actions into a set of steps, in chronological order. The one 'step at a time' approach can make achieving the goal rather less daunting. If the mentee wishes this can be written down as a personal action plan and of course added to the *My Career* portfolio. Also included in the action plan can be support to: complete C.V's, application forms, applying over the internet, letter writing, making telephone calls and interview preparation. We will look at some of these under the next question.

On the following page is a fictional example of an action plan completed by Sam a young person who has selected a career direction. Sam wishes to explore the career opportunities in more depth and to identify the right qualification and training course to undertake. Note that the plan is relatively simple and easy to understand. It is challenging but realistic. Moreover, it can easily be rewritten or added to if circumstances and preferences change.

My Action Plan   Sam Aldholm   Date 20 April 2010

My Goal	To work for a professional sporting club in administration or organising events.		
Steps towards my Goal	Action to be taken and sources of information/help that I will need	Time Scale	Done
Obtain more information about the work of professional sports administrators.	With support of mentor, use internet to discover more on qualifications, pay, conditions and responsibilities of admin staff in professional sport. Use the mentoring network to find a local sports administrator that I can talk to.	By end of May	

Gain some work experience with a professional sporting club.	Write to professional clubs in my region asking for a placement. With support of mentor identify people in my local community with contacts in professional support that I could approach as advocates for me. Undertake placement.	By end of August	
Obtain entry to a business studies qualification with a particular focus on sports admin and management.	Visit my local college to identify possible courses. Explore university websites and library resources to identify possible degree courses and their entry requirements. With support of mentor, select and apply for most suitable course.	By end June	
Be able to present myself as fit, healthy, and a regular participant in sport.	Join a gym; work hard at my own personal fitness. Train with my local cricket club and try to make their first II.	Ongoing	
Keep up to date on sporting issues.	Read newspapers and sporting magazines each week. Regularly look at key sporting internet sites.	Ongoing	
Prepare for applications and interviews	Update my ROA and CV With mentor practice application form and interview technique.	By end June	

QUESTION 6. What help does the mentee need to IMPLEMENT the plan?

Clearly this will depend upon the extent to which the mentee can now take independent action and what resources they have access to. Can the mentor now withdraw and let the mentee get on with it?

In some cases the answer is yes. The mentor's objective of encouraging independence in the mentee, may be best served by taking a backseat. If continuing support is needed it could be provided by other specialist helpers, perhaps already identified through the mentor's network of contacts, such as employment agencies or college tutors. However, some mentees will need continuing support from a mentor to implement their career action plan. This might involve support with:

- accessing and using internet sites,
- transport,
- visits to employers,
- visits to colleges or training organizations,
- accessing distance learning opportunities,
- arranging work experience placements,
- making telephone calls,
- writing letters,
- updating a c.v.
- completing application forms,
- electronic applications using the internet,
- interview preparation.

Continuing emotional support may also be crucial to maintain the self belief needed to continue with the application process. It may be needed to encourage persistence and resilience in the face of the rejections which are often part of the process. The techniques that can be used here are the staples of mentoring discussed in earlier chapters: active listening, questioning, showing trust and empathy to support self confidence and self esteem. Reassurance may be needed where the mentee finds that there are more competent applicants than positions available. Rejection does not mean that you are hopeless, it just means that, on the day, someone else had a little edge over you. On another day you could be the one with that 'edge'.

The mentor need not be alone in providing this emotional support. Where possible, the family and friends of your mentee should come into the picture to provide day to day encouragement. Yet there are potential problems here. Where they lack the skills to support effectively, family members can make matters worse. Partners or parents for example can show frustration where progress is slow and start to blame your mentee or urge totally unsuitable action. Can the mentor contact the family and advise on the best methods of support? This should only be done where the mentor has knowledge of the family and is very confident of a positive response. Any suggestion that the mentor is interfering in family matters could produce a very negative reaction which would be damaging to the mentee.

Let us now look at a few practical support activities that could be in an action plan.

It is a good idea to go back to the mentee's Record of Achievement and C.V. referred to earlier. Both of these should be prepared in an attractive, good quality format and they should be adapted to reflect the career goal or course that the mentee has decided upon.

If the mentee is intending to apply for a job rather than further training, carefully analysing the details of particular vacancies can make all the difference. Look at job advertisements, employers' websites, and at the details sent with application forms. They should contain a job description (JD) and a person specification (PS), although they might not use those terms. The JD and PS will tell you what the employer is looking for. Your mentee should make sure their ROA, CV, and application form bring out the fact that the mentee has, as far as possible, the qualifications, experience, personal qualities and skills that the PS specifies. They should also feel able to tackle the responsibilities stated in the JD.

Sometimes employers are overambitious in their documentation so don't be put off if your mentee cannot quite cover all the bases. It may be the nearest candidate rather than the, non—existent, perfect candidate that gets the job. Where there are a number of applicants, employers will often create a checklist to narrow them down. This will usually consist of a chart drawn from the JD and PS with essential and desirable qualities listed. Candidates' application forms will be compared to the list and given a score. Those with the essential qualities and highest scores will be invited for interview. Therefore, making sure that the requirements of the JD and PS are addressed on any letters of application, CV's and application forms is vital.

Some employers will just ask for a letter of application. Mentors should offer to check these before they are submitted. Other employers will require a completed application form. The mentee could usefully complete a practice form. The mentor could then go through it, looking at it from a prospective employer's viewpoint and suggest ways in which it could be improved. A frequent issue here is the mentee's reluctance to identify their positive qualities, skills, and achievements. Mentees often undersell themselves because they lack self confidence, do not wish to appear boastful or simply fail to recognize their strengths. Where they have followed the six question approach and created an ROA and *My Career* portfolio, this is less likely to happen.

For technical higher status jobs, aptitude tests, in-tray exercises or group interviews may be used. Mentors could try to find out if any of these might be used and if so discuss how to approach them with the mentee.

A mentor can also offer to pretend to be the employer, using the JD and PS, at a practice interview. The box which follows gives advice on conducting yourself at an interview which mentor and mentee could look at together prior to the practice and could look back on afterwards to review how it went. If the mentee does not want to practice, just talking about the points made in the box would be useful.

If your mentee does not get the job, have a debriefing session together. Explain that not getting the job is not a failure. Many more apply than get appointed. Many more interview well than are taken on. Most of us have to put lots of applications in before we make it. Use the whole experience as a means of learning how to improve for the next application.

THE INTERVIEW—suggested advice to mentee.

For every vacancy there may have been many applicants. An Interview, therefore, gives an opportunity for the interviewer to compare you with other applicants and to assess your suitability.

Prepare yourself thoroughly. Don't see the interview as a threat or someone trying to catch you out. Instead see it as your chance to show your positive attitudes, qualities and achievements. Remember that you are also interviewing them to see if the position will suit you. Ask questions and listen carefully to the answers.

First impressions are very important. What you look like and what you say in the first few minutes of an interview are vital. An interview is a first meeting; but with a purpose. Here are a few guidelines to a successful interview.

Before You Go

1. Find out as much as you can about your prospective employer/college. If you are applying to work for them or study with them, they will assume you made this decision after finding out key facts about them beforehand.

2. Work out well in advance how long it takes to get there. Make a trial journey if necessary. Don't arrive late. Be there are least 10 minutes before your interview.

3. How you look is even more important than what you say!! Attempt to look your best. A clean, tidy appearance will help you but make sure your clothes are comfortable. Casual clothes such as jeans and T shirts are generally frowned on at interviews.

Women should remember that they are not going to a party. They should dress smartly and avoid excessive use of make-up.

Be certain that:- hair is clean and combed; hands and nails are clean (for when you shake hands), teeth are well cleaned (for when you smile, talk and to guard against bad breath), you sit up straight in your chair and do not fidget; speak clearly and look at the person that you are talking to.

4. Try and assess the skills and abilities needed in the job you are being interviewed for. Look at any job description and person specification issued by the employer.

5. Consider Taking with you: your Record of Achievement, the name, address and telephone number of two people who will give you a reference (if not already supplied on an application form).

6. Practice the answers to likely questions before you go (see below). Do this with your mentor, a friend, or just in your head. This is not easy—many people don't bother but doing it will give you an advantage.

When You Get There

1. Be prepared to take an aptitude test or fill in forms.

2. Be polite to the receptionist or secretary on arrival. The interviewer may ask her/him for an impression of you.

3. Interviewers can be expected to concentrate on your:

    *   appearance, mannerisms and speech;
    *   experiences and achievements;
    *   ability to engage in friendly conversation;
    *   special abilities and aptitudes;
    *   interests and leisure activities;
    *   personality (try to be cheerful and bright);
    *   attitudes (be interested, willing to learn and keen to start).

4. If you feel very stressed, do a physical relaxation routine and deep slow breathing.

5. When you meet the interviewer, smile, say good morning etc, when introduced, be prepared to shake hands (it's a good idea to wipe your hand dry of perspiration before you go in).

6.

DON'T	DO
Sit until you are asked.	Be honest.
Smoke or chew gum.	Look at the questioner.
Fidget, slouch or mumble.	Answer fully and clearly.
Pretend to know the answer if you don't.	Be friendly and positive.
Criticise your school or your present employer.	Ask for clarification if you don't understand the question.

Remember - Yes and No answers are not good enough. Use the questions as an opportunity to sell yourself.

7. Be prepared to answer questions such as:-

*   What course/subjects have you studied or training undertaken\
*   What are your hobbies and interests?
*   Why do you want this job/ place on this course?
*   What do you know about this company/college?
*   What do you feel about further education and training?
*   What positions of responsibility have you had?
*   What do you see yourself doing in ten years from now?
*   What are your strongest qualities?
*   Tell me about your work experience?
*   Why should we employ you/ give you a place?
*   What is the biggest problem you have had to overcome?
*   What would you do if (think of possible emergencies)?
*   Outline a conflict situation that you have had to deal with.

8. Have questions ready to ask yourself, for example:

- Ask for more detail on the work that you will be doing.
- Will I get training? What kind? What qualifications will it leads to?
- What will the pay be? During training? After training?
- What are the employment prospects with this qualification (if college interview)?
- What are the days/hours of work/?
- Do I have to wear special clothing?
- What are the prospects of promotion?
- May I show you my RoA folder?

At the End of the Interview

1. Thank the interviewer for the interview. Be prepared to shake hands again.
2. If you are offered the job: Do clear up anything you are not sure about; Don't accept without being confident that the job/course suits you and that you suit it (unless you have no other prospects!). Ask when you can meet the people you will be working with and look around the place (if not already happened).
3. If you are not offered the job Ask them to bear you in mind if another vacancy arises and ask how you could improve your interview technique.

This item has drawn on a handout prepared by John Martin, Wood Green, Sandwell, England.

Summary of The Six Question Approach to Career Development—for the mentee

1. What is my SITUATION?

Such as: personal needs, commitments, circumstances, skills, qualifications, experiences, health, and network of useful contacts.

Creating a Record of Achievement and a draft Resume can help here.

2. What are my life style and work PREFERENCES?

Such as: ambitions, subjects enjoyed, stay home or move away, values (e.g. serve others or seek high income), outdoor/indoor, travel, short term/long term, safe/adventurous, willingness to study, shift work.

Completing a questionnaire can help here.

3. What ALTERNATIVES would fit my situation and preferences?

Explore possibilities, remove the less desirable to identify some options.

Using career segments and a subject wheel can help here.

4. Which alternative(s) will I choose as my career GOAL?

Investigate the advantages and disadvantages of the alternatives. Make sure that I really understand what would be involved. Select a long term or short term personal goals.

Using a SWOT analysis can help here.

5. What do I need to include in my Personal ACTION PLAN?

Using a template can help here.

6. What help do I need to IMPLEMENT my plan?

My mentor can help. I may get professionals to help. I may need to share this with my family, friends and contacts to ask for their support.

Some help with contacts, resume, application and interview preparation can be useful here.

CHAPTER EIGHT

Mentoring in the Workplace

The reader interested in workplace mentoring might come straight here. However this has not been written as a free standing chapter. To avoid excessive repetition it assumes the reader has at least, already looked at the first four chapters and chapter seven.

Workplace mentoring will usually be focused on one or more of the following:

- helping a new, promoted or transferred employee adjust to their new responsibilities, colleagues and working environment,
- giving additional support to women trying to break into management or traditionally male occupations,
- supporting employees who are recent immigrants— particularly if English is not their first language or if they come from a very different culture,
- supporting employees suffering excessive workplace stress,
- preparing an employee for promotion or new responsibilities,
- supporting an employee undergoing training or skill development,

- supporting employees who are introducing new technology or new management structures and procedures,
- supporting someone setting up or developing their own business,
- supporting someone who is experiencing a problem at work.

In a professionally run organisation, mentoring will be one strand of a comprehensive staff development programme. Where new systems are being introduced and where new skills need to be acquired, staff are often sent away on short courses or trainers are brought into the workplace. Online training is an increasingly used alternative. These can all be very valuable. However, when the newly acquired knowledge and skills are actually applied in the workplace, local complications can often arise and the employee can struggle. At this point a mentor can be of real value where mentor and mentee can look together at developing issues. Mentoring can also be more suitable and more cost effective than some formal personal development training programmes. It can be used when trainees are attending formal learning programmes, or working on distance learning packages, to reduce dropout rates and improve the quality of learning.

In the author's experience, senior executives within organisations can fail to appreciate the time and resources required to set up a high quality mentoring scheme. They might assume that a couple of hours to brief their staff, followed by attaching an experienced colleague to a less experienced one, is all that is required. A scheme that amounts to no more than this, is likely to be given low priority and soon slip off the agenda of busy people. Evaluations across the world have shown that it is crucial to recruit quality mentors and to train and support them properly. We can't just assume that anyone can do it or that the scheme will function well without effective planning, preparation and oversight.

Chapter 11 looks at the organisation of a mentoring scheme and identifies the key tasks that need to be undertaken.

In the workplace, the mentor is often a more experienced colleague. Alternatively, an outsider could be brought in to take on the role. Outsiders are particularly useful for small businesses or where specialist knowledge is involved. In the USA in particular, some companies offer mentoring for a fee. Reputable companies can offer a valuable service by employing highly trained and experienced staff, including professional psychologists, who can make use of sophisticated personality and aptitude test to support the mentee. However, it cannot be assumed that all companies operating in this field really understand mentoring.

Some caution is recommended. Sometimes what is on offer is expensive, poor quality training or internet coaching which should not be called mentoring.

Altruistic rather than commercial motives usually form the best basis for effective mentoring.

Some larger organisations use professional mentors or have staff whose formal duties involve a significant account of mentoring, although that might not be their official title. In major hospitals for example, some senior nurses may be appointed as nurse educators where mentoring is an important part of their work.

Some organisations deliberately encourage their staff to become mentors as a part of their professional development since mentoring skills are seen as transferrable to other relationships in the workplace.

Employees who have little knowledge of mentoring may fear that it is a technique by which management is seeking greater control over them and is reducing their autonomy by monitoring their work more closely. Hence it is helpful to have trade union, professional association or other employee representatives involved at the planning stage of the mentoring scheme to reassure them about its aims and operation. Employee representatives might also be invited to sit on a scheme management committee and to help with mentor training. Such input can be very valuable in designing an effective scheme and encouraging staff to participate

Workplace Culture

As we have already seen mentoring schemes develop a distinctive culture based upon their own particular circumstances. The same applies to workplaces. Workplace culture has been extensively studied by sociologists.

In addition to the obvious differences between governmental, non profit and private sector organisations, wide variations also exist within these sectors. Some workplace cultures are very conducive to mentoring but others are toxic to it. Mentoring tends to thrive in 'flatter' hierarchies where innovation is welcomed, decision making is open and collaborative, and where everyone's expertise is valued. Alternatively, where management is authoritarian, decision making centralised and employees tightly supervised, it may be much harder to get a developmental mentoring culture established although sponsorship mentoring may work in these circumstances.

An intriguing possibility would be consciously to use mentoring to change a workplace culture from an authoritarian to a more collaborative and participative form. This would of course require a range of other measures to sit alongside it.

Coaching

Writers on management, particularly from the USA, tend to group workplace mentoring with workplace coaching since both involve support being given to employees to develop themselves. Although they can often overlap we can distinguish between them.

Coaching usually aims to improve specific workplace skills. It is often a relationship where a more senior person who 'knows best' instructs or informs a less senior person in the correct way to do something. The coach often dictates the agenda rather than negotiating it. The coach will review the work being performed by the so called 'mentee' and give feedback which identifies correct and incorrect actions or level of skill acquisition.

To distinguish coaching from mentoring is not to denigrate it. Both of them can be included in a continuum of strategies to support and develop staff.

Sponsorship Mentoring

Sponsorship Mentoring, as identified by Meggison and Clutterbuck is a type of workplace mentoring where the person being mentored is described as a protégé rather than a mentee. Here the mentor acts as a champion of the protégé to aid his or her career progression. Hence the mentor is often the protégé's supervisor or a senior manager who spots talent and uses mentoring to support and develop it. When done properly, this approach can benefit both the organisation and the sponsored person. However, there may well be a price to pay if the aims of the scheme are not clear, matching is not done carefully and the relationship is not monitored and evaluated effectively.

The mentor could be using mentoring to create one or more loyal supporters in his or her own drive to succeed. The mentor may be involved in a power struggle for influence in the organisation where the protégé is expected to give loyal support. Moreover the sponsorship of a loyal protégé may be at the expense of a more independent minded individual and may not necessarily give the best outcome for the organisation or the individuals concerned.

Political affiliation can be the basis of sponsorship mentoring in governmental organisations—'jobs for the boys'. This can lead to less competent individuals being promoted to the detriment of the service. A properly organised formal mentoring scheme with high ethical standards is usually preferable to the ad hoc sponsorship of favoured staff by their managers. It is more effective and will help to reduce the negative aspects of sponsorship identified above.

Developmental Mentoring

In coaching and in sponsorship mentoring the focus tends to be mainly on the needs of the organisation. Developmental Mentoring tends to focus more on the needs of the mentee. It is a much more equal, side by side, relationship in which alternatives are discussed and where mentees are encouraged to take responsibility and make their own decisions. Mentoring is not so much about telling the mentee the right way to do things as: supporting the mentee's personal development, discussing problems, looking together at alternatives, encouraging mentees to take charge of their careers and make their own decisions. In this form of mentoring, the mentor does not operate as a line manager. Indeed it is preferable if a colleague who does not directly supervise the mentee's work, takes on the mentor's role.

Whilst the starting point is the mentee's needs, these will frequently coincide with benefits to the organisation since the person seeking a mentor is likely to wish to improve her or his work performance in order to be on top of the job, win the respect of colleagues and perhaps to gain promotion.

When and Where

Can you recall the example of Annette at the beginning of Chapter two? Mentoring which is confined to the mentor asking the mentee "how are you getting on?" when their paths happen to cross, is likely to be ineffective. Even an arrangement where mentee is invited to contact the mentor when a problem is encountered rarely works because the mentor may not be immediately available or the mentee does not want appear incompetent or to interrupt a busy colleague. Yet the author has found that workplace mentoring frequently degenerates into the above pattern simply because mentors are not properly briefed and are not required to report on their mentoring activity.

The conventional form of effective workplace mentoring is one to one, at a pre arranged regular time and at the workplace. This is fine but there are other options. Telephone mentoring can supplement the occasional face to face meeting as long as these calls are pre arranged and time is allocated for them. Mentoring can also take place at a distance through pre arranged teleconferences. Modern business laptop computers make such communication relatively straightforward.

Another option is group mentoring which can also take place at a distance using teleconference technology. This is sometimes called hub mentoring. It can be particularly useful where a group of employees are confronting similar issues in different locations such as a new sales team being supported whilst they 'bed in' to the organisation. Where a group of dispersed employees is following a common staff development programme, peer mentoring, supported by someone who has recently completed the programme, could be a useful hub mentoring relationship. It has also been used in the college sector. For example, several teachers, from geographically dispersed campuses of a college, were planning to introduce a new course which had previously been trialled in another college. A member of staff from the latter college peer mentored the group through a teleconferencing hub until they had successfully implemented the course.

Initiating a Workplace Mentoring Relationship

As explained above, to avoid favouritism or unhealthy sponsorship, it is often best to have someone other than the immediate supervisor acting as mentor. However, supervisor mentoring cannot be always avoided. The supervisor may be the only available mentor or the only one with the experience and knowledge that the mentee needs. If human resource specialists are coordinating the scheme and allocating mentors, they should be alert to the dangers referred to above. In practice much will depend upon the size of the organisation and the dynamics of personal relationships within it.

Recommendations for mentoring will often come from a staff appraisal, employee development or performance management scheme. Here mangers interview individual employees to review their performance and development at regular intervals. These interviews should result in some agreed action to support further improvement or to address problems and deficiencies. Clearly mentoring is a possible and appropriate action in these circumstances provided that the employee is a voluntary participant. Sometimes employees will agree to take part to get managers off their back. Equally, a manager might suggest mentoring because some action has to be identified and she can't think of anything else to offer. If mentoring is entered into without enthusiasm or commitment on either side, it is likely to fail and the mentoring scheme itself will be discredited. Going through the motions of mentoring to satisfy bureaucratic requirements is just a waste of the organisation's resources.

A particularly difficult situation can occur where an employee in an appraisal interview is told that some aspect of his performance is poor and that he will be allocated a mentor to help him improve. If the mentee genuinely wishes to have a mentor's support, this can be a very effective strategy. However, if the employee is coerced into becoming a mentee, particularly if he dislikes or distrust the selected mentor, the situation can deteriorate rather than improve.

Mentoring should never be used as a disciplinary action or punishment. An employee may require close supervision but this should not be mislabelled as mentoring.

The mentoring relationship should be a safe, trusting and confidential place not a threatening one.

It is up to the mentor to create a positive environment for mentoring but the issues covered should reflect the mentees issues and concerns

Selecting Mentors and Matching With Mentees

How do we know which manager, supervisor or employee will make a suitable mentor? Chapter two explores the qualities and skills possessed by effective mentors. It provides a basic checklist that can be used for self assessment by those considering becoming a mentor. Chapter 11 gives some advice on mentor selection and matching. The mentor selected will depend on the aims of mentoring. A new employee might best be mentored by someone doing the same or similar job, whereas mentoring someone to prepare for promotion should be done by someone at or above the level at which the mentee is aiming, perhaps from another department. Before the match is finalised both the proposed mentor and mentee should be consulted and agree to the arrangement.

Career Progression and Promotion

During our working lives we move through contrasting stages. For the person pursuing a career, as opposed to series of jobs, there are at least four of these. At first we seek to establish ourselves by: learning our new role, acquiring new knowledge and skills, and making new relationships. Hopefully we go on to, gain advancement and perhaps responsibility for the work of others. At some point we reach a stage of maintenance where we continue to work effectively at the same level and finally we withdraw from our working lives. Of course, for many of us who switch careers we may go through this process a number of times. As a mentor it is helpful to ask our mentee to reflect on which stage their career has reached and what implications this has for them. In the author's experience some mentees prematurely write off further career development and can become somewhat cynical and withdrawn. Yet when offered a new role with new opportunities, they can be re-energised. You could discuss this together.

It is part of the responsibility of senior managers to recognise and nurture talent. Mentoring is an important technique for doing so. In practice it is not always the most talented who reach the top. It can be the most ambitious and calculating. Sometimes the talented can be rather diffident. They may need someone, such as a mentor, to believe in them and encourage them to make the most of their abilities.

Some mentees will be not particularly interested in promotion. They may not want the stress of becoming a manager and leader of others but still want to develop their careers and take on new challenges. They may do so by moving sideways and by learning new skills.

For those seeking promotion, it is worth bearing in mind that if you wish to climb high you need to move fairly quickly. Research suggests that people who stay for many years in the same post before seeking promotion will find it much harder to get to the top. Yet too frequent changes of post can lead to accusations of unreliability. Moreover the higher you climb the broader the range of responsibilities you are likely to acquire. A technical expert who is promoted may well soon be floundering with budget management and human resource issues not previously encountered.

Discussing the speed and direction of career movement is important. Your mentee may have become too engrossed in day to day tasks to think through these issues.

- How long does your mentee need to stay in a position to gain the skills and experience needed and to establish personal credibility, without overstaying and losing career momentum?
- Does your mentee fully realise what promotion will bring?
- Does your mentee have the knowledge, skills and experience needed?
- Does your mentee have skills in financial management and the management of staff? If not how can these be gained?
- Is a sideways move to gain a broader range of experiences a good idea as a prelude to an application for promotion at a later date?

It should be crucial to demonstrate leadership skills if you wish to gain promotion. Leaders who dictate and operate on the basis of "Do it because I say so" are likely to be less effective than leaders who can convince their staff to follow them because the staff trust the leader and believe in what the leader is asking them to do. Having power is not enough, generating commitment and enthusiasm is what works. Yet, if organisations restricted themselves to employing highly gifted leaders we would not have enough to go around. Many people are promoted to senior positions who find leadership very difficult. Hence they have to learn how to lead.

Unfortunately many do not do so effectively. Mentoring can help, provided that the selected mentor is a good role model.

Leadership is a skill that can be learned. It can be explained on a course or in a book but actually observing it and discussing it with the leader concerned is a more powerful experience.

Status in the Organisation

The mentor does not have to be older or be in a more senior position than the mentee. Indeed a junior member of staff could mentor a senior manager in some situations. Perhaps new accounting software is being introduced. A junior from the accounts department who has good IT skills might mentor a line manager in sales, who needs to manage his budget using the new system, until the manager has fully mastered it. This is sometimes (not very accurately) called reverse mentoring.

Challenging Your Mentee

It is relatively easy to have a cosy relationship with a mentee where a pleasant conversation takes place and complements are exchanged. Yet, really to help that person develop, a challenge is needed. As explained in earlier chapters, both mentor and mentee will have a particular mindset, a characteristic way of looking at the world and of approaching issues that arise. Encourage your mentees to become aware of their own mindsets. Talk to them about social and emotional intelligence (see chapter two).

The key here is for the mentee to retain self respect and self esteem whilst being able to be self critical, to have enough insight to recognise where self improvement is needed and to have enough self belief and confidence to make that improvement. A mentor who is simply critical can undermine a mentee. One who does not challenge may do little good. Therefore the way in which the challenge is made is vitally important. Using questioning and active listening encourages the mentee to become more self aware and to recognise opportunities for improvement. An example can illustrate the point.

Alain

Alain has recently been appointed to the post of technical services manager at the corporate headquarters of a large insurance company. Although he has undertaken a management course he has little previous experience of leadership. He now heads a team of twelve staff.

The previous departmental head had a reputation for being eccentric and dictatorial. Alan is determined to be an effective leader and to have an efficient and responsive department. He recognises the importance of taking his staff with him in the development of the department. To facilitate this he organises a weekly team meeting where the staff have the opportunity to talk over any issues and to help shape the departmental development plan.

After a few weeks Alain becomes aware of some dissatisfaction in the team. He overhears one staff member calling him 'Mr decisive' with a heavy touch of sarcasm in her voice. In the meetings he is also conscious of a couple of people regularly arriving late and others always trying to leave early. One person ostentatiously yawns and stares out of the window at regular intervals. Others seem to enjoy the meetings and always contribute at length.

In line with corporate policy Alain has been offered a mentor from another department and decides to take up the offer.

He talks over his concerns with his mentor Rachel, at their second meeting. Since she has responsibility for a policy development which she wishes to share with a range of staff she suggests that she attends the next meeting to introduce her policy as an agenda item. This will give her a chance to observe Alain's relationship with his team and his leadership style. She also invites Alain to attend one of her team meetings.

They get together after both meetings and Rachel has some challenging questions to ask and comments to make. She starts by complementing Alain on his efforts to create a positive team ethos and a culture of consultation and consensus. Then she tries to get Alain to see things from his staff's point of view. Rachel asks questions such as:

- If you were a team member attending that meeting what would you like about it? What would irritate you about it?
- If you were a team member with a heavy workload, how much time would you think it reasonable to spend attending team meetings?
- Why do think the meeting kept drifting away from the agenda?
- What kind of decisions can you make alone and which should you consult on?
- Should you start by giving your own views or only introduce them in your summing up at the end of discussion?
- What is the best way of curtailing a speaker who is not offering any constructive comments?
- How might you change the way in which you run your team meetings?

These questions prompt some discussion and Alain invites Rachel to make some suggestions. He realises that a number of improvements are possible. He decides to make the meetings fortnightly instead of weekly, to impose a time limit and to stick more strictly to the agenda. Rather than consulting and having a lengthy discussion of every small point he is much more selective about the agenda, consulting on important and longer term issues whilst making day to day decisions himself. He will continue to encourage staff to put items of concern on the agenda but will not allow discussion to drift on unnecessarily and will curb the contributions of those who like to ramble on repetitively and at length.

After a couple of meetings with the more focused and decisive approach he finds a positive atmosphere is beginning to develop in the team and some valuable ideas coming forward for inclusion in the next development plan.

Rachel did not instruct her colleague Alain in how to run his meetings but she did get him to reflect upon them critically and to see the situation from a fresh angle; supporting him to develop his own strategy for improvement. She waited to offer suggestions until he invited her to do so. This gave him a sense of working constructively with an equal partner rather than being talked down to or dictated to.

Encouraging Talent into Senior Positions

Mentoring does not need to be confined to existing employees. The 'Lucy Programme' for example, is targeted at talented young women in New South Wales Universities studying business, finance, economics, accounting or law. These students are given an opportunity to explore career options in management with the support of an experienced mentor who is a working professional in a public or private sector organisation.

Developing Independence

Where a mentoring relationship degenerates into one of dependency, the mentee will run to the mentor whenever difficult situations have to be faced. Surely our aim should be that the manager develops the skills, confidence and personal maturity to be able to take decisions without this prop. The way to do so is to support the mentee through some initial situations and then gradually step back as they become confident and have developed the capacity to make decisions without the mentor's aid. The problem solving process outlined later in this chapter may help.

Independence does not mean isolation.

Stepping back does not mean that the mentee is left to tackle problems and make decisions alone. Mentors should be helping mentees to identify the key colleagues and stakeholders that they could consult and make use of in the future. Part of becoming an effective decision maker is knowing when and whom to consult.

Developing a Mentoring Plan

Even where mentoring is focused upon the needs of the employee there are likely to be spin offs for the organisation. Where an organisation is resourcing a mentoring scheme, whether it is in the private, public or voluntary sector, it is reasonable for it to expect mentors and mentees to be accountable for the time which they spend in mentoring activities. Moreover the management might expect to see evidence of a return on its expenditure. That return might be a mentee who is happier and hence makes more constructive relationships at work or is better equipped in some way at tackling work tasks. This might involve the acquisition of skills, developing more positive attitudes or an enhanced understanding of their present or a future role.

Hence it is reasonable for the organisation to ask mentor and mentee to develop a simple shared mentoring plan for their work together. Such a plan should go a long way to prevent mentoring just become an excuse for a break and a pleasant chat. It should include:

- An overall goal and specific objectives or targets for their time together.

A goal should be presented as brief general statement such as *'to be prepared for promotion opportunities'*. Objectives and targets are more precise, measurable statements such as *'to complete the Diploma in Marketing qualification by the end of this academic year'*. They often represent steps towards a goal. These goals and objectives should be agreed through discussion and might include personal (in effect, emotional) support in addition to support for the development of work competences. They should be based on the original purpose of the mentoring scheme and include the mentee's specific personal goals. Any benefits to the organisation should be identified. Specified goals act as motivators and give a sense of direction.

- Activities that they intend to carry out.

These will centre on focused discussions but they might also include practical tasks such as:

* ❖ work shadowing,
* ❖ sharing literature, manuals and other electronic or physical resources,
* ❖ visits to look at practice elsewhere including conferences and exhibitions,
* ❖ problem solving together,
* ❖ sharing research tasks or trialing new software or techniques,
* ❖ practicing workplace scenarios such as meeting customers or being interviewed,
* ❖ the mentor observing the mentee at work followed up by a discussion between them about what went well and what could have been done better (see example in previous box),
* ❖ introducing the mentee to experts and key people in the organisation to create a network of useful contacts.

* Time and other resources needed.
* How progress will be recorded, reported and evaluated. This is covered in chapter 11.

Some organisations use a mentoring schedule where all the dates of meetings and the meeting focus is identified in advance. It is a certainly a good idea to schedule regular meetings well in advance to ensure that they actually take place. Yet in practice, incidents, problems and opportunities are happening all the time. We need to be able to respond flexibly and not feel that we have to stick rigidly to an over planned programme. It is the mentees development that matters not ticking off sessions on a schedule. Hence some support may be simply taking advantage of openings that come along rather than being planned, such as recommending the mentee as cover for a colleague who will be away on extended leave; to extend the mentee's experience.

Supporting and Challenging Anna

Anna, a newly qualified technology teacher in her first high school post, has been matched with a more experienced colleague Maria, who has agreed to be her mentor. Before the start of term they discuss the classes that Anna will be taking and look at the draft schemes of work that Anna has produced. They look at teaching approaches, learning activities and the resources that Anna will need. Maria shows Anna some examples of assessment tasks that she has set students in the past which she thinks would be suitable for Anna's classes. Anna reviews these and adapts a couple of them to use in term one.

Once the term gets underway Anna finds that she has some disciplinary problems with a group of low achieving boys in one of her classes.

She consults Maria who offers to come and support her in the classroom for a couple of lessons. Maria approaches the Principal who agrees to cover Maria's classes to enable her to give this support. Maria does not want simply to sit at the back and observe since the students will think that Anna is being inspected. Neither does she wish to take over the class since the whole point is to see how Anna handles the disruptive group. To avoid undermining Anna's self confidence and authority with her class, Maria stays in the background but joins in to help a struggling student once they get down to work.

Maria quickly spots that Anna is using negative and critical language with the students that she is anxious about. She shows hesitancy with them and makes threats that she does not and cannot implement. After the class Maria complements Anna on her planning and learning activities but is also able to initiate discussion about some alternative strategies that Anna could consider trying. These include being clearer about classroom rules, taking an individual interest in students to establish a connection with them, using positive rather than negative language and using more opportunities to praise students when they do cooperate.

Maria realises that some class members are disruptive because their written English is poor for their age group. They find spelling and sentence construction difficult and are ashamed of their efforts. They fear ridicule from more capable students. Hence they disrupt the class whenever written work is required. She points this out to Anna and they discuss together how this issue could be dealt with. They decide to consult the Head of English who coordinates the school's literacy strategy.

Mentee/Mentor Boundary Issues

As a mentor in the workplace you will need to decide how available to make yourself to your mentee. Do you give your mentee your mobile phone and email address whilst inviting contact with you at any time? Do you limit contacts to working hours or just to a specified time each day? Do you restrict them to agreed mentoring meeting sessions only?

The key here is to agree together, at the first mentoring meeting, the appropriate level and method of contact. Regular scheduled meetings should provide the core of the process. However, where mentoring has been put in place to support someone experiencing ongoing problems, a very accessible mentor might be desirable who could be contacted by phone, email or face to face contact. For new employees contact could be more available and frequent in the first few weeks, tailing off later. Preparation for promotion might only require regular scheduled meetings.

Usually in an organisation, arrangements should be made to ensure that emails between mentor and mentee are kept confidential. However, where young people are being mentored it is perhaps best not to use email and to keep contacts face to face, except perhaps for telephone calls to make or change appointments.

The time demands of the relationship may also need to be negotiated with the scheme coordinator and the mentor's line manager. If the mentee is likely to be demanding, is the management prepared for the time demands of the relationship upon the mentor and her consequent unavailability for other duties?

Some Tips for Managers Acting as Mentors

- Make your mentee a coffee.
- Have regular but quite short mentoring sessions (30 to 40 minutes).
- Don't boast or talk down to your mentee. Don't pretend to be invulnerable or infallible.
- Asking the right questions is more important than giving the right answers (this should promote thinking and problem solving skills).
- Show a genuine interest in your mentee.
- Help your mentee do develop a wider awareness of the organisation and its objectives. Encourage your mentee to reflect on personal contributions to these objectives. Broaden your mentee's perspective.
- Admit and explain at least some of your mistakes, to assist your mentee to avoid making similar ones.
- Show faith in your mentee and look for opportunities to give deserved praise.
- Find out how your mentee works and manages time. Have a discussion about it.
- Discuss together the organisation's informal culture (if you don't know what this means—find out together).
- Try to replace moans and negative thoughts with positive proposals for improvement.
- Make sure that your mentee does not become socially isolated or too partisan, by building relationships, trust, and collaboration across departments.

Workplace Stress

If a worker has some control over his or her working environment and work tasks, a moderate amount of stress can be stimulating and even enjoyable. However, excessive stress can be extremely damaging to both physical and mental health. It can also poison workplace relationships. Where a worker is closely supervised, with little autonomy, the problem is compounded since the worker has little opportunity to change working practices to combat stress. Such workers tend to be the less skilled and to be at the bottom of the hierarchy. A casualised workforce is particularly vulnerable. The consequences are: high levels of anxiety, tension between colleagues, and the potential to become severely depressed.

We will discuss anxiety and depression in the next chapter. The important point to note here is that mentoring has the potential be a very valuable component within a strategy to tackle workplace stress. It is likely to be most effective in organisations with flatter hierarchics, where employees are able to have some individual or collective control over their work practices and where they can participate in making decisions affecting their immediate workplace. Mentoring coordinators might like to remind employers that health problems resulting from stress can add significantly to their costs.

It is tempting for employers to confine mentoring to managerial, technical or professional staff but it may be the least skilled, the least secure and those with fewest promotion opportunities, who are most in need of support.

Where the stress is the result of severe trauma at work, e.g. the death of a colleague in a workplace accident, it is usually advisable to seek professional support from a counsellor or psychologist.

Managing Problems

Where an employee is struggling to cope with a problem at work the support of a more experienced colleague who has tackled similar problems before, could be very valuable. Alternatively, there could be a personal problem that is causing an employee distress and interfering with their ability to do their job effectively. A line manager or human resources manager might propose mentoring as a way forward.

Whilst we might aim to remove problems, sometimes the best we can do is learn how to contain and manage them.

There are numerous books and articles offering general strategies for tackling problems. Each author has his or her own prescription to offer. However, most of them are quite similar in their approach. If you are looking for good, in depth, advice on problem management, Gerard Egan's *The Skilled Helper* is well worth reading. The seven question approach set out below is the author's attempt to summarise some well established approaches.

Tackling significant problems at work and making major decisions for the organisation are in some respects, similar to making personal life decisions. Yet there are also significant differences. Workplace decisions may well affect a large number of people and can have a crucial effect on the lives of others, not just the decision maker. They may be taken after advice from experts and after consultation with colleagues. The process is often well documented through the notes of meetings, emails, letters and even corporate plans or policy statements. Moreover, they will have to be justified to superiors and the decision maker will be held accountable for the outcome. In these circumstances using a systematic and open process such as the one below can be helpful.

Usually the problem solving process produces a choice between alternative courses of action. However, sometimes it is sensible to postpone a decision until the situation becomes clearer. As we pointed out in the chapter on careers, decision making is often a partly unconscious, intuitive process which manifests itself as an emotional response to the alternative courses of action. Sometimes a particular decision just feels right. Often such feelings turn out to be correct in high pressure situations demanding immediate action because the emotional responses are based on previous experience. However, when we are dealing with irreversible choices between several alternatives which have not been experienced before, the emotional response may be based on partial or inaccurate knowledge. It could be simply a fear of the unknown e.g. "I may not be able to cope", "What if

I don't have the skills to do this"? Here a more carefull systematic and conscious process is required.

ACTIVITY: The Seven Question Approach to Helping Your Mentee Tackle Problems

Imagine you are the mentee. Apply this approach to a problem that you are currently facing. Reflect on how useful it might be in mentoring.

Question 1. <u>How does the mentee see the situation?</u>

Get the mentee's story. Don't jump to conclusions. It is important to get a full and clear account rather than rush towards solutions. Are there obvious gaps that need to be explored? Listen actively and use questioning to clarify the mentee's understanding of events and relationships. Look for hidden messages.

Does the mentee show empathy for others? Is the mentee able to recognise his or her mistakes? Does the mentee unnecessarily blame himself or herself, or blame others. Is there a breakdown of any relationships? Is there any evidence of depression or excessive anxiety in the mentee? Is the mentee negative—arguing that nothing can be done?

Question 2. <u>What is the real problem?</u>

Sometimes the apparent problem is hiding a deeper issue. Is this the real problem? Do you have to tackle any blind spots or distorted views that the mentee has which are preventing her/him from seeing things as they really are? Is the mentee focusing on superficial manifestations of the problem rather than underlying causes?

Remember you only have the mentee's perspective. Don't assume that it is the full story. Although you have a duty towards your mentee you also need to be fair to anyone else who might be involved. Use questioning to help the mentee to identify the real issues that need to be resolved. Write a brief summary of the problem.

Question 3. <u>What are the needs, wants* and goals of the mentee, the organisation and the other people involved?</u>

Help the mentee to clarify personal needs, wants and goals—what outcomes would be practicable and acceptable? It is also important to look at the extent to which the personal goals of your mentee are congruent with the goals and needs of the organisation. Encourage your mentee to think of the needs and goals of any other people who are involved. Write a summary of the needs and the preferred outcomes of all those involved including the employer and fellow employees.

* needs and wants are distinguished in chapter 10

Question 4. <u>What additional information do we need?</u>

This can be crucial. The mentee may be making assumptions which turn out not to be true. The mentee may not be aware of all the facts. Is additional technical information needed? Has the mentee made assumptions that need to be checked? Does the mentee need to do further investigation of the attitudes and goals of others? The mentor might suggest some research that the mentee can do before they meet again. The mentor might also want to check some of the facts that the mentee has given—without breaching confidentiality.

Can we identify costs and benefits, including quantifying the financial implications?

Question 5. <u>What alternative courses of action are possible?</u>

Brainstorm the alternatives by making a list of all the possible solutions that you and your mentee can think of—however daft. Encourage the mentee to imagine solutions that would produce an outcome which might meet the needs and goals of others and as well as themselves. Do not choose or dismiss any alternatives at this stage. If necessary go back to question 3 if you need more information to complete your list.

Question 6. <u>Which alternative(s) offer the best prospect for tackling the problem?</u>

Take each alternative in turn and look together at the advantages and disadvantages of that possible solution. A SWOT analysis (see chapter seven) may help. Encourage your mentee to choose the solution that will best tackle the problem and come closest to achieving the goals of you all, including the organisation. Use discussion and questioning to help your mentee to choose solutions which are achievable and realistic whilst being genuine solutions to (or ways of effectively managing) the real problem. Remind your mentee of the importance of taking others along.

There may be more than one way to tackle the problem and your mentee may have to negotiate a solution with others. Hence it is important to remain open to other solutions.

Don't neglect your emotional and intuitive reactions. They are an important part of the calculation. Have they changed now that you are better informed? Are they a warning—pointing you to something that you have not taken fully into account?

Question 7. <u>How can the selected alternative(s) be implemented?</u>

- Make a plan together
- Support your mentee to implement it
- Monitor it and be willing to review and suggest changes to it, as necessary but encourage your mentee not to give up too easily.

Note: where the problem involves disputes with others, negotiation may be required. See chapter ten for advice on tackling a negotiation.

In practice we all know that tackling problems can be very messy. Usually other people are involved. They do not always share our approach or wish to cooperate with us. Sometimes in the workplace the seven question approach can be followed in a conscious, linear, step by step fashion. Often life is more complicated. Perhaps the mentee does not recognise that there is a problem. Alternatively, the mentee may not be able to give a full and accurate account of the problem; its full extent may only gradually emerge over time. This may well lead to backtracking and rethinking.

In the workplace, some problems are seen as interesting challenges to be tackled and solved. However, others will generate stress and anxiety. These are often problems involving difficult relationships with others such as colleagues, customers, superiors, subordinates, or suppliers. Moreover high stress situations may have knock on effects on family and other personal relationships. Even where the problem is a very technical or practical one it is likely to involve an emotional response on the part of the mentee. Where strong emotions are generated and a person's competence and status are threatened, it may be very difficult for them to approach the situation in a balanced and objective fashion. Talking things through carefully, in a calm atmosphere, with a mentor can help the mentee to get problems into perspective and to approach them more rationally. See chapter ten for more on tackling relationship conflict and dealing with aggression.

Much depends upon the mentee's level of emotional and social intelligence. Mentees who lack this kind of intelligence may find it difficult to develop empathy and may well lack insight into their own motivation and behavior. They may have a very false picture of how others see them. For example a manager's attempts to be decisive and show leadership may be interpreted by her staff as bullying and being unwilling to consult them. Therefore part of the role of the mentor can be to use listening and questioning to encourage the mentee to reflect on her or his own behavior, uncover blind spots and develop a more realistic self image.

Perhaps the best way to use the seven question approach is as a check list to make sure that something important is not being missed. It can also be turned to when your mentee gets stuck and is not sure how to proceed. Once you get used to asking these questions they become a natural ways of approaching problems. You no longer need a piece of paper to turn to for guidance.

Timing the point of decision and of action, is important. Poor problem solvers either tend to:

- jump at the first idea that come to mind without thinking through the implications or looking seriously for alternatives,
- OR avoid dealing with it for as long as possible in the hope that it will somehow go away or resolve itself (although sometimes, delay is the best option).

The starting point is to identify correctly, and fully understand, the real problem. This can often be obscured by superficial issues, conflicts between individuals or a reluctance to face up to reality.

Remember that the needs and goals of the mentee and any other people involved should be spelt out as clearly as possible. Once this is understood, the full range of possible strategies to solve or manage the problem can be identified. Some will be obvious from the start. However, other options tend to emerge over time and in consultation with colleagues. When we have to explain the issues to other people we are forced to get them clear in our own minds in order to do so. The very act of explanation often throws up alternatives that had not previously been considered.

Each option should be looked at seriously and be examined to decide the extent to which it solves the problem whilst meeting the needs and goals of the mentee and the other people involved. Solutions which may meet the goals of the mentee but which fail to satisfy others are likely to lead to more conflict and generate further problems down the track.

Complaints and Accusations Arising in Mentoring Conversations

Employers need to be aware that mentoring can reveal situations such as bullying, sexual harassment and unfair discrimination in the workplace. Clearly where the safety of employees or the public is at risk, any allegations must be taken seriously. Formal complaints or grievance procedures would be the preferred route for action rather than mentoring conversations. However, employees who would not make a formal complaint may reveal such situations to a mentor in confidence. What action should the mentor take?

There is an issue of confidentiality here and a moral dilemma. It could be argued that the complaint should not be brought to the attention of management unless the mentee agrees. The mentee may not agree, feeling that that there is insufficient evidence to substantiate the claim and fearing the recriminations that may follow, particularly if incidents took place in private and cannot be proved. The mentor might offer to act as advocate for the mentee and to support the mentee through the grievance process.

The danger for an organisation is that poisoned relationships can change its culture and undermine staff morale. Colleagues may be drawn into conflicts, siding with one party or the other. Where for example, a manager bullies and discriminates without challenge, impressionable members of staff may form cliques around the bully and copy this behaviour. An example might be where a laboratory technician reveals concerns to a mentor about the competence of a senior colleague. If a mentor becomes aware of a situation of this kind, the mentor could consider raising it as a general concern with the mentoring coordinator, without going into any specifics identified by the mentee. Clearly there is a danger of breaking confidentiality. However the mentor needs to balance a duty to the mentee with a duty to other colleagues and to the employer.

Much will depend on the mentoring coordinator having the confidence of mentors. Where a coordinator becomes aware of widespread concerns about a particular individual or department from a number of mentors, the coordinator may decide to raise the matter with more senior management without naming individual mentees. Obviously it is crucial to avoid gossiping and the spread of unsubstantiated allegations.

Confidentiality is less of an issue if it is pointed out at every first mentoring meeting that the mentor can consult the scheme coordinator whenever needed and that the mentor must report any evidence of illegality or misconduct at work, to the scheme coordinator or to senior managment.

Where a particular mentee complains that a supervisor at work has discriminated against him should we automatically believe everything that our mentee tells us? Should we, in our desire for justice and redress, immediately speak up on behalf of the mentee and accuse the supervisor? We have a particular responsibility to the mentee but we also need to recognise our duty to the accused. The mentor can listen empathetically to the mentee but cannot act as the judge, since only one side of the story has been heard.

If it is felt that the employer concerned is not taking the matter seriously, the mentor could discuss with the mentee the desirability of consulting a trade union representative. In some situations legal advice could be sought. In many countries legislation outlaws discrimination at work and a complaints can be made to a government agency which will investigate them. In Australia for example Federal and State laws make discrimination or harassment at work illegal. In NSW a complaint can be taken to the Anti Discrimination Board. However, it is also important to recognise the implications for the mentee of being seen to be a 'whistle blower'. Such a person can easily be labeled a troublemaker who needs to be sidelined or moved on. A career could be destroyed.

Much will depend upon the culture, policies and procedures of the organisation. Will complaints be seen as an implied criticism of senior management? Do they have the courage to tackle such issues or would they prefer to keep them quiet? A fine judgment and no little courage is called for here. All this emphasises the importance of organisations selecting appropriate and properly trained people to take on scheme management responsibilities

The Benefits of Workplace Mentoring

Effective mentoring in the workplace can benefit the mentor and the mentee by:

- enabling them to feel valued and recognised,

- enhancing their morale and commitment to the organisation,
- improving their communication skills
- creating networks of supportive colleagues,
- helping to develop their skills understanding and knowledge.

All of the above benefit the organisation and contribute to succession planning.

CHAPTER NINE

Mentoring People with Health Problems

There can be few people who have not experienced severe health problems or who have not seen them in a family member, friend or colleague. Most of us show concern and offer support but we are often unsure how best to help. Would opening up a discussion of the issue be welcome? Ill health generates uncertainty, anxiety and fear; not just in the patient but also in those closest to the patient. Sometimes when we know someone who has been diagnosed with a serious condition we wait for the ill person to raise the issue because we are not sure what to say. This can be interpreted as indifference.

Partners, relatives and close friends are potentially a strong support framework for the sick. Yet the partners and immediate family may be sharing the emotional distress of the patient and may themselves need emotional support. Hopefully they will receive it from their friends. Yet sadly we live in a society where many individuals have become socially isolated, lacking partners, close friends or a close family network. Clearly there is often a need for additional emotional support from outside.

Sharing a home with a partner, young person or parent who is struggling with a long term illness can produce high levels of stress and conflict between them. Sometimes the carer or supporter becomes emotionally worn down with work, worry and taking on the role of constant listener and reassurer of a sick person. Both need a break from each other and someone else to share their feelings with. Women often seem better able than men to reach out and admit their fears and feelings of distress. Men can find it harder to talk about their emotions, feeling that to do so is unmanly and a sign of weakness. It needs someone with particular social skills and experience to get them to open up.

Whilst there are a range of professional support services such as hospital social workers, these are in great demand and are often unable to meet all the needs of patients, their immediate families and carers. They may be stretched to support those who are referred to them and may not have the resources to seek out others who try to struggle on alone and are unable to or reluctant to, give voice to their needs. Mentoring can fill some of the gaps. Often the word mentor will not be used. That is unimportant as long as some of the lessons from mentoring programmes are learned and applied.

Ideally, the mentor chosen will be someone with personal experience and some knowledge of the medical condition that their mentee is experiencing. Mentor training is particularly important here where emotions are close to the surface and a thoughtless comment can cause great distress. There is real danger that a mentor with a little knowledge of a similar condition or who has been given information from a well meaning friend will give inappropriate or outdated advice.

Mentors might trawl the internet or read magazine articles giving advice on treatment which is at odds with the treating doctors. Sharing this unthinkingly with patients can undermine trust in their doctors, promote unnecessary fears or give unrealistic hopes. This is particularly true when complementary medicines and treatments are proposed. This is not to suggest that patients simply accept uncritically the judgements of their doctors. Asking for a second medical opinion may well be a sensible course of action. But it is important for mentors to be clear about their role and not to pretend at knowledge and expertise that they do not have or attempt to pressure their mentees into a particular course of action.

How do we overcome these dangers? One approach is to choose mentors from properly established support groups who work with medical social workers and the medical profession. Such groups usually have access to up to date information and have good networks of contacts. They know who to refer mentees onto for additional professional help, when necessary. They are also very keen to welcome additional volunteers to help support those in need.

A mentor has the great advantage of having empathy without being personally involved in the family. Whist mentors might feel some of the distress of the mentee, there are boundaries around their involvement and they can return to their other life. Hence they can be more objective and be more aware of the likely effect on their mentee of any comments that they make and of any questions that they ask. It is quite a difficult skill to show empathy and rapport whilst remaining calm, rational and objective. This means that mentees of the seriously ill are rather special people. Not all members of support groups can do this effectively. In some cases their own feelings from their own or a loved one's illness are too raw. Although they might not become mentors, these members can take on a range of other tasks to help the group such as fund raising and publicity.

Support groups can be very valuable when they offer group mentoring. Here a number of people can meet face to face or online to share experiences of successful recovery, treatment or management of the condition with one or more peer mentors. Support groups can also help the partners and children of patients deal with their own feelings. To be a mentor specifically for the seriously ill requires some specialist knowledge which we cannot address here but the general skills and ethical principles covered in our earlier chapters still apply. One example is the innovative peer mentoring using telephone support for individuals, or for groups which the cancer council has developed. This scheme operates for people with cancer, for the bereaved and for carers and family members.

Mental Health and Mentoring

In the British NHS the prescription of anti depressant drugs almost doubled in the first decade of the 21st century. Thirty nine million prescriptions were issued in 2009. The Royal College of General Practitioners has claimed that many of these are being prescribed unnecessarily. Most are relatively cheap but they can have significant side effects. More access is needed to psychological therapies which have good success rates with many conditions but which are more time consuming. There are long waiting lists for such treatments. (The Guardian Newspaper 14/6/2010).

Britain is not alone. In Australia mental health has long been a neglected and underfunded area.

Some specialist mentors may work for schemes which specifically serve the mentally ill. They should have specific training and experience in the field. However, mental health issues can arise in any setting and may surface whilst the mentoring is supposedly pursuing another goal such as career development or educational attainment. Therefore all mentors should have some awareness of mental health issues.

If your mentee appears to be suffering from severe depression or anxiety what do you do?

- Assess the risk of suicide or harm (see box below). If the risk is high, do not leave them alone—get immediate help, contact your mentoring scheme coordinator, take them to hospital emergency.
- Listen non-judgmentally. Be an active listener. Show concern.
- Give reassurance and information. Explain that however bad they feel now, these feelings are temporary. There is help available and with help they will feel much better.
- Encourage and assist the person to get professional help. Local sources of help should be explained in your training.

- Encourage self-help strategies (see the box at the end of this chapter).

(The material in this section is adapted from 'Mental Health First Aid' by Kitchiner and Jorm. If you intend to work with vulnerable people you will find it very helpful to take a mental health first aid course. See the Website: www.mhfa.com.)

ASSESSING THE RISK OF SUICIDE

Those most likely to commit suicide are: males in the fifteen to thirty four age group, adolescents, the retired, those suffering depression or other mental illnesses, excessive users of alcohol and other drugs, the socially isolated or lacking a partner, the long term chronic sick, and people experiencing a crisis or trauma which distorts their rational thinking. The latter can include people made redundant, bankrupt, who have lost a loved one, experienced the breakdown of a relationship, are a refugee, or have experienced war or terrorism.

Among young men, suicide rates have tripled over the last thirty years. Four times more men than women commit suicide but women are more likely to attempt suicide unsuccessfully. We should take these cries for help very seriously. If they are unsuccessful and do not receive help they may well try again and succeed.

In Australia Aboriginal people have particularly high suicide rates.

Remember your active listening skills and be alert for hidden messages. If you have any concerns do not be afraid to ask these questions directly.

- Are you having suicidal thoughts? If yes, continue.
- Have you ever tried to commit suicide?
- Do you have a plan to commit suicide?
- Have you got hold of the means to carry out your plan? (a gun, drugs, a rope).

If your mentee answers yes to these questions do not leave them alone. Get help. Inform your scheme coordinator. Take them to emergency at your local hospital.

Some Basic Background on Mental Disorders

The following notes are for the general information of mentors. As a mentor you are not expected to treat the mentally ill. However, you could play a very valuable role in encouraging them to seek professional help if they are reluctant to do so. With the agreement of the professionals treating them, you may wish to offer some practical and emotional support whilst they are receiving treatment; perhaps through a recognised support group.

Types include

- Clinical Depression. This usually prevents people carrying out their work and having normal relationships with others. It affects people in all age groups but is particularly common in adolescence and the elderly. Often overlaps with anxiety disorders.
- Anxiety Disorders. These can also prevent a person living a normal life. They include post traumatic stress, phobias, obsessions and compulsions. Panic attacks are common and can be very frightening. Some people also have generalised anxiety about many aspects of their lives. These are quite common experiences but most sufferers do not seek professional help.
- Psychosis—occurs where a person has lost touch with reality. Schizophrenia, bipolar disorder and drug induced psychosis come into this category. These conditions affect less than 1% of people each.
- Other Personality Disorders—occur when a person has characteristics and attitudes which are very inflexible and which make it very difficult for them to adapt to change and to make successful relationships with others. Hence some individuals may appear to be very odd and eccentric. Others may be very dramatic, emotional and erratic. Some may avoid social contact whilst others may be excessively dependent. There are overlapping symptoms between these disorders and the other categories of mental disorder. These

are severe for a very small proportion of the population. For the sufferers they can be extremely disabling.

How Much?

It is important to note that different countries classify mental disorders in different ways and have different views about what should count as an illness. Hence the above conditions may be classified and described differently in different countries. The World Health Organisation estimates that 25% of the world's population suffer mental illness at some point in their lives but this may well be an underestimate. Each year in the USA 26% of the population are identified with a mental disorder. In Britain it is 25% and Australia 20%. In Western Europe mental disorders are the leading cause of disability.

Six percent of Americans are classified as having a severe mental illness whereas the comparable figure in Australia is three percent. Therefore whilst severe mental disorders affect quite a small proportion of people, less severe disorders are a common experience. It is quite possible that one of your mentees could be a sufferer.

Diagnosis and Treatment

Controversy continues about how far we should use the term illness to describe mental disorders. Using the illness label can be useful in removing stigma and reassuring sufferers that it is not their fault. On the other hand it can lead the sufferer to conclude that they are victims of misfortune and that there is little that they can do about it except take medication.

It is clear that some conditions are the direct result of genetic factors, abnormal brain development and chemical imbalances in the brain. In other cases the disorder may be a response to extremely stressful and traumatic experiences. Alternatively, they can be a learned response or due to distorted thinking. We know that our thoughts affect our emotions and our physical state and vice versa. So it is often impossible to untangle the causes of particular symptoms.

Today, effective treatments are available for almost all of these conditions. Often these are not cures but they do control symptoms sufficiently well for people to live a reasonably normal life. Some conditions e.g. bipolar disorder, seem to be biological in origin and can often be treated with medication. In other cases successful treatment may depend on the active cooperation of the patient. Life style changes and changes in thought patterns may be needed.

Psychiatrists are medically trained and can prescribe medication whereas psychologists have studied human behaviour and treat people using techniques such as Cognitive Behavioural Therapy (CBT) which try to change the way people think and act. When treatment is delivered by skilled professionals, these techniques have a high success rate. It is a myth that we cannot treat mental disorders. However, some personality disorders are extremely difficult to treat.

Panic Attacks

These have symptoms similar to heart attacks and asthma attacks. The victim may have a raised heart rate coupled with perspiration, breathing difficulties and feeling faint which leads to a momentary loss of consciousness. If you can't be sure which is which—call an ambulance. These panic attacks are caused by a reduction in oxygen getting to the brain leading to mental confusion. Often they are triggered by rapid shallow breathing which does not oxygenate the blood properly.

If panic attacks take place what can be done? Move the person to a quiet place and keep bystanders well away. Calm the person giving reassurance— you can't die from a panic attack (at worst you black out briefly whilst your breathing returns to normal). Encourage him or her to control breathing by taking a deep breath whilst counting slowly to three, holding the breath briefly and letting the breath out whilst again counting slowly to three; until their thoughts become clearer. Once they are calmer, listen actively, be non-judgmental, and reassure them that you will stay with them until the attack is over.

Depression and Anxiety

The most likely conditions to be encountered when mentoring are depression and anxiety. As mentors, if in doubt we should ask ourselves if our mentee simply is feeling low and fed up, as we all do sometimes, or is suffering from severe (clinical) depression. See the box below for indicators of depression. Clinical depression is a serious condition which can be long lasting and can prevent a person leading a normal life. In extreme cases it can lead to self harm and suicide

- What causes depression?

It is often triggered by short term stressful or traumatic events. However, it is also strongly associated with longer term factors such as: a family history of depression, chronic illness, substance abuse, and sexual orientation (bisexual or homosexual). Moreover, rates of depression are higher in remote and rural communities than in the cities. Women have much higher rates of depression than men but men are much less likely to seek outside help; so the statistics may be flawed. Aboriginal communities often have very high rates of depression—at least twice as high as the general population with suicide rates running about four times higher. Mentors may find that bullying at school, at work, by a family member, or even cyber bullying, is a significant trigger for depression and anxiety in a mentee.

- Adolescence and depression

Teenage depression is fairly common but is often unrecognised because adults see the depressed youngster as just being a typical moody teenager. In adolescence it is particularly dangerous because the young person may be experiencing it for the first time and not realise that help is available and that it can be overcome. Around 1 in 5 adolescents will experience very serious and prolonged periods of depression.

- The Mentor's Role

People suffering depression will often benefit from being able to talk about their feelings with a sympathetic listener. As a mentor you may be able to help by being an active supportive listener but it is important to recognise that you are not a counsellor, psychologist or medical practitioner. If in any doubt—refer on to your scheme coordinator. Together you may offer to refer your mentee for professional help. Your coordinator should know who to contact. Sometimes that will be end of your involvement with that person but if you both wish to continue, you could be one element in a support network that is put in place. You may be able to use your mentoring skills and your scheme's network of contacts, to assist your mentee to find new opportunities and build a more positive life for themselves.

IDENTIFYING CLINICAL DEPRESSION

If your mentee experiences some of these symptoms for a fortnight or more, inform your mentoring scheme coordinator and strongly encourage your mentee to seek professional help (such as a doctor, qualified counsellor or clinical psychologist):

- increased moodiness irritability and frustration
- finding it hard to take minor personal criticisms
- spending less time with friends and family
- loss of interest in pleasurable activities
- being awake throughout the night
- alcohol and drug use
- staying home from work, college or school
- increased physical health complaints like fatigue or pain
- being reckless or taking unnecessary risks (e.g. driving too fast)
- slowing down of thoughts and actions.

- Treatments for Depression

Since there is no single cause there is no single best treatment. Nor is there general agreement among the experts.

❖ Antidepressant drugs can be prescribed by GP's and Psychiatrists to correct the imbalance of brain chemicals that occurs when people become severely depressed. This is a very complex business because there are many different types of anti depressant and it may not be easy to find the more appropriate one to use for a particular patient. There may be an element of trial an error involved.

❖ Cognitive Behaviour Therapy (CBT) is used by Psychologists to teach people to think about their life situation differently and to act differently. It tries to replace negative with more positive thoughts, helps them to think rationally and to use self talk to prevent depression reoccurring. It encourages the person to change the way in which he or she lives everyday life and reacts to everyday relationships and situations. This can be linked to the ideas on self esteem and emotional intelligence which we looked at earlier.

❖ Interpersonal Therapy (IPT) helps people to improve their personal relationships.

❖ Family Therapy uses family members to support the depressed person by giving them insights and techniques to use.

❖ Psychodynamic psychotherapy looks at earlier life experiences to explain current psychological problems. It is assumed that if a person gains some insight into the roots of their anxiety that will be better able to tackle it. This can be a very long term process with modest success rates which has its roots in Freudian psychoanalysis.

❖ Electro Convulsive Therapy (ECT) may be used in extreme cases who do not respond to other forms of treatment.

❖ Natural remedy clinical trials suggest that St John's Wort (Hypericum perforatum), for example, can have a positive effect on stress and mild anxiety. This is a natural and legal treatment available from pharmacies without prescription.

Stress and Anxiety

Some degree of stress can be a positive motivator but excessive stress produces anxiety which can be very damaging. People seem to operate best when they are in a state of relaxed concentration. To achieve this we must create the right environment, reduce threats, offer a supportive relationship and build self confidence. A mentor can help enormously here.

Unfortunately, sometimes the stress may have been present for a long time and the person concerned may have developed a way of reacting that takes a long time to change.

Stress and anxiety can lead to frustration and aggression (see next chapter). However, it can also lead to withdrawal into social isolation which might involve excessive daydreaming, fantasizing, and an obsession with computer games or internet chat. This can also be associated with substance abuse. If you suspect the latter you should encourage your mentee to access medical help or professional counselling.

ACTIVITY: Self Help Strategies For Depression, Stress and Anxiety

Here are self help strategies that you can suggest to your mentee. Think about your own life. How many of these match your life at the moment? How hard would it be to follow all of them?

- If retired or unemployed, don't be tempted to linger late in bed each day. Get up and get active.
- Exercise regularly—make it a habit. It does not have to be the gym or competitive sport. Brisk walking stimulates natural chemicals in the brain that can make you feel more positive. Try gardening.
- Take a pride in you appearance. You will feel better if you look better.
- Learn and use relaxation techniques and therapies. Practice controlled breathing.
- Experience sunlight each day, even if it is cloudy or wet—an early morning walk is great.

- Keep your caffeine intake modest. Don't take coffee in the evenings—it can disrupt sleep.
- Have a regular bedtime and don't stay up to the early hours *(except to watch English football on TV—as a reward for writing a book on mentoring)*.
- Cut out alcohol for a few weeks and only return to it in moderation.
- Read some self help books but don't go overboard on wacky ideas.
- Eat healthily. Cook for yourself. Minimize your intake of fast/junk food.
- Make an effort to be sociable. Try to get out of the house and meet people every day. Be a volunteer and help others.
- If you wish, tell your story to a supportive friend but don't be persuaded to recount traumatic events if you do not feel comfortable doing so. Consider joining a support group.
- Use self talk to challenge your own negative thoughts.
- Divert your attention from your worries by keeping active. Take part in pleasant, sociable, and low stress activities.
- St John's Wort is a mild, safe, natural substance that can help to improve your mood.

NOTE: Don't make this a guilt trip. These are a few suggestions. Feeling guilty for not doing all of these can reduce self esteem and make you feel even worse! So:

be kind to yourself. Give yourself some personal time to do things that you enjoy each day. Don't feel guilty for a few indulgencies but beware the booze. Enjoy music.

Chapter Ten

Managing Relationship Problems

A mentoring scheme could have the specific aim of supporting people with relationship problems. However, mentors will usually encounter personal problems as additional complications whilst working within schemes designed to address other issues. We can contrast people who have problems making and sustaining relationships with those who are facing damaging relationship conflicts. Typical situations that can emerge are: social isolation (perhaps a recently bereaved and retired person), poor communication skills (could be a teenager struggling to adjust to adulthood), conflicts with colleagues (raised by a mentee in a work place), conflicts with officials (homeless mentee seeks help of mentor when seeking accommodation), conflicts with parents (raised by a student in an educational mentoring scheme). Therefore all mentors should be prepared to discuss relationship issues, regardless of the initial aims agreed for their mentoring relationship.

Strong, close, and meaningful relationships with other people are crucial for human happiness and mental health. Are there any ways in which we can help people to create friendships or to repair damaged relationships? As mentors we are always one step removed from the relationship. We cannot observe it or intervene directly. What we can do is to offer emotional support, listen, and help the mentee to reflect on and think through relationships. We may be able to help them to improve their communication skills so that in conflict situations they are better equipped to talk to the other people involved and find a way forward. This can only happen if both parties are willing to work together to improve matters. Mentoring cannot force the unwilling. Unfortunately this means that occasionally we may have to support someone through the breakup of a relationship or refer them on for professional help.

General or Specific Relationship Problems?

It is important to distinguish between the mentee who struggles with relationships in general and the mentee with a specific problem relationship. In the former case, there are a number of possible contributory factors including the following:

- there may be deep seated psychological problems needing professional support,
- the mentee may be experiencing high levels of stress,
- the mentee may have become socially withdrawn after a major life event such as the loss of a partner, redundancy, or retirement,
- the mentee may be struggling to cope with adolescence,
- an illness or disability may have struck the mentee,
- the mentee may have developed low self esteem and lack the confidence to form new friendships,
- the mentee may lack self awareness, be domineering, trying to boss everyone else around,
- the mentee may have developed a negative mind set, become very self centred—offering little to others,
- the mentee may have a style of communication such as aggression or passivity, which repels others.

These factors are not mutually exclusive, rather they tend to group together and be mutually reinforcing. For example, a lack of self awareness, an aggressive communication style, attempting to dominate others, and a persecution mind set may characterise a manager who is under great stress at work and who is drinking alcohol excessively. Another example would be a quiet, anxious person who has recently separated from a partner. This person might well have a passive communication style, low self esteem and a negative mind set.

All the above factors are linked to issues covered in previous chapters where some advice has already been given. In summary, mentees benefit from emotional support, the building of self esteem, encouragement to develop greater self awareness (emotional intelligence) and awareness of the needs of others (social intelligence), help with communication skills, advice on combating depression and the setting of personal goals. Above all the mentee needs someone who will listen non-judgementally and who offers a trusting, supportive relationship within which worries and problems can be discussed in confidence.

Some mentors will have the confidence to work with mentees on these issues. Alternatively, a mentor who feels that giving this type of support is not for him or her, could ask the coordinator to bring in a more experienced mentor or to refer the mentee on to another agency.

Small Talk

Shaun was a 17 year old young man struggling with relationships. He dressed very unconventionally and his body language gave the impression of disinterest and indifference. In initial mentoring meetings, his mentor Andrea found it hard to get through to him. He seemed withdrawn from her and gave monosyllabic responses to her attempts at conversation. She felt inclined to tell the coordinator that it was not working out between them and that Shaun should be offered another mentor. Perhaps a man could get through to him.

The coordinator pointed out that a male mentor had been tried with Shaun but had experienced the same problem and pulled out. Andrea was asked to give it another try. She decided on some direct questioning to try to get Shaun to open up. After some hesitancy

---

Shaun revealed that he found most day to day conversation to be pretty pointless because it was usually about trivia and avoided anything important or controversial. She asked about his friends and discovered that they were largely confined to contacts via the internet with a small group who shared his interest in a minority science fiction genre.

It gradually became clear that Shaun's behaviour was a way of masking his shyness and difficulty in talking to people from other backgrounds and age groups. He found it impossible to talk to girls for any length of time. He was an only child of serious minded parents. Being physically quite clumsy, he had little interest or ability in sport and never seemed to fit in with other youngsters in his neighbourhood.

Andrea realised that she could play a very useful role in building Shaun's self esteem and could give him an opportunity to practice relating to an adult. She was also aware that, being an attractive young woman, there was a danger that Shaun could become infatuated with and over dependent upon her.

By showing a genuine interest in Shaun she began to build trust and to persuade him to talk more. They discussed communication barriers and she raised with him directly the role of small talk in conversation. She explained that much conversation is superficially about trivial topics that cannot be changed, such as TV programmes, the weather, shopping, and sport. However this kind of small talk serves important functions. It is non-threatening, fills awkward silences, gives people something in common, gives the opportunity to take turns in communicating and to show liking, cements friendships, demonstrates normality, and can simply be a vehicle for pleasant companionship. Andrea modelled the behaviour that she was encouraging in Shaun.

Shaun listened to what she had to say and gave it some thought. He recognised that being able to sustain conversation in this way actually did have some point and was a very valuable lubricant for relationships. Over the next few weeks, at each session, they spent some time practicing conventional small talk conversation. It was of course very self conscious which amused them both. Having shared a few smiles and giggles Shaun slowly revealed himself as a sensitive, thoughtful and occasionally witty companion. He came to see that he could not expect others to be interested in him if he showed no interest in them. Moving from self absorption to a genuine interest in the lives of others was the route to friendships.

By the end of the mentoring period, six months later, Andrea was very pleased at the change in Shaun's behaviour. He had actually become quite chatty and seemed to have grown in confidence. She felt that as he gained more experience, he could grow into a very capable adult.

Relationships Across Cultures and Subcultures

Relationships between people from different cultural backgrounds can be particularly fraught and can be complicated by misunderstandings, false assumptions and irrational prejudices. To make sense of all this, it is helpful to start with a much wider question: "What holds our society together and prevents it falling into permanent unmanageable conflict between groups and in personal relationships, as we each pursue our own goals? What restrains us?"

Essentially, we live within sets of shared rules. These are not just formal written laws or regulations. We are surrounded by a dense network of taken for granted unwritten rules, called social norms, of which we are barely conscious until someone breaks them. These cover every aspect of life. For example when we are in a queue we intuitively know how far away to stand from the next person. Too close and we are invading their personal space, too far away and other people will wonder if we really are queuing at all.

Many social norms are not universal. What is normal in one culture is frowned upon in another, often resulting in mutual suspicion and distrust. To follow up our previous example, what counts as personal space varies by culture. Physical closeness and actual contact are expected in some social groups but may cause embarrassment in others. Our society encompasses a range of variations to our culture which we call subcultures; each of which has its own life style, beliefs, values, customs and social norms. Subcultures can be based on factors such as social class, religion, ethnicity, and geographical region.

If someone uses obscene language in public place, it may be perfectly acceptable to many people but profoundly shock others. A more challenging example is the variations in norms concerning sexuality. Clearly pre marital sex has become normal in some sub cultures whilst still being frowned on in others. Attitudes to homosexuality also vary powerfully from subculture to subculture, all the more so because fundamental religious beliefs are involved.

Most countries experience migration in and out—Australia more than most. Migrants carry their cultures with them and these cultures can enrich the host society but they can also be a source of conflict. A multicultural society is an ideal to be strived for but in practice we often find cultural segregation. We may find our mentee to be caught between these cultures.

Cultures are not monolithic. Great variations can exist within them and they can overlap. Many individuals are born into one subculture before moving into another and may retain aspects of both or change their behaviour as they move from one group to another. For example, a young woman moves from a suburban, conservative, Presbyterian background to the inner city and goes on to live with a migrant from Europe with no particular religious affiliation and a very permissive lifestyle. She becomes part of his social world. Will she find it easy to switch between subcultures when she returns to see her parents or will she come into conflict with them by rejecting their values? Either scenario could happen.

Recent migrants may find their children adopting much of the way of life of their new society and experience great problems in accepting their children's changing values. Children may be torn between their parents and their new friends. Young people may be trying to fit in to their new society but its members may be suspicious of their colour, accent, dress and religion. A young Muslim migrant may have parents who stay within their own cultural group and are intolerant of any take up of western values whilst potential western friends are distrustful, critical and lack understanding. Here there is a very real danger that the young person could become profoundly alienated from our society and be seduced by extremist ideology. Who could this young person talk to? A friendly welcoming, non-judgmental, mentor could be the ideal person. Someone older, from the same cultural background who has adjusted successfully, would be the ideal. But a skilled and empathetic mentor from the mainstream culture, who has some insight into these issues, could also be a great help.

How do we respond when asked for support from a mentee who is involved in a culturally conflictual relationship?

Mentors can find it very helpful to do some prior research on the cultural backgrounds of prospective mentees. What are their basic beliefs and values? Are there any social norms, customs or cultural features which are distinctive and could cause misunderstandings? For example it is traditional in Sikh culture for men to carry a dagger as a symbol of their manhood and their faith. Carrying a dagger around with you at work or at school could be interpreted as a threatening gesture with the potential for violence. Yet for the Sikh it is an important symbol of cultural identity. In practice the daggers are often welded into their sheaths and are unusable as weapons. Some Sikhs only carry miniatures. In fact miniatures are usually the only form of dagger acceptable at school. Explaining this to outsiders can assuage their fears.

The assumption being made here is that prospective mentors reading this book will share the author's distaste for racist ideas and discriminating against people on the basis of their ethnicity or subculture.

We may be faced from time to time with mentees who turn out to be racist or intolerant of other cultures. The key is to promote understanding. Haranguing an intolerant person will not be effective. Active listening, questioning and challenging myths and misinformation are our tools. What is needed is to encourage our mentees to put themselves into the other person's situation and try to understand why they behave as they do. We might not be able to remove prejudice but we can at least combat some of the wilder negative stories about other cultures that continue to persist. As we saw in chapter three there is an ethical dimension here. We need to be non judgmental in the sense that we do not attack or denigrate the mentee as a person. However, being non judgmental does not mean sitting back and making no comment when the mentor displays blatant racism or uninformed prejudice. Make your views known and challenge your mentee but do it calmly and with respect, not in anger or irritation. We have a responsibility to challenge the prejudiced mentee to look at the world from different viewpoints.

Conflict Resolution

Conflicting relationships are not automatically a problem. Conflict is inherent in human societies and can be very productive when it challenges us to look at life from fresh viewpoints and draws our attention to people or issues that we might have neglected. It can stimulate us into action and heighten our experience of life. Conflict can be the parent of innovation. The real question for us is how to help our mentees manage conflict so that it becomes constructive rather than destructive of their most cherished relationships. Some techniques, notably negotiation, are outlined in this chapter but central to them are, as usual, our mentoring skills of: listening, questioning, empathising, challenging and encouraging assertiveness.

Supporting a Mentee with a Problem Relationship

Where a specific relationship is the problem, rather than relationships in general, that relationship may be the key to understanding the other issues that initially brought the mentee into the mentoring scheme. An example is the employee who has sought mentoring support to prepare her for promotion. Yet, as mentee and mentor get to know one another it becomes clear that she is convinced that her manager is blocking her promotion because she is a woman. Another example would be the school student seeking career advice who wants to study art but whose father is adamant that he must do mathematics and business studies. A third example would be a patient who has lost confidence in her medical practitioner.

What is our role here? If we have developed a trusting and empathetic relationship, the temptation is to be immediately indignant on behalf of the mentee and to begin to suggest strategies to defeat the other party. A close friend may take that line but a mentor should resist that temptation for three reasons.

- Our mentee may be misinterpreting, exaggerating or oversimplifying the situation. We need to spend time listening and asking questions for clarification. Talking the situation through calmly and rationally may help the mentee to see things from the other person's point of view and recognise that it is more complex and less one sided than it at first appeared. Use questioning to encourage the mentee to imagine how the other person sees the situation and understand why they have taken up their position.
- We have only heard one side of the conflict. Our mentee may have suppressed or discounted some of his or her own poor behaviour which would have led us to see the situation in a very different light.
- The mentee may have to continue in the problem relationship long after the mentor has departed.

In a dispute, there are four main options:

1. change your behaviour to accommodate the other party as a means of avoiding further conflict,
2. discuss the situation with the other party in an attempt to understand each other's position and to reach an agreement on mutual change,
3. end the relationship,
4. put up with continuing conflict.

Usually, the second option is the one most worth trying. However, there will be occasions when the mentee, after discussion with the mentor, decides he has been unreasonable and the first option is chosen.

Mentors should also recognise that there are occasions where ending the relationship is the only sensible option because the other party is behaving intolerably, will not cooperate or because the parties have completely irreconcilable positions.

Often the best help that the mentor can give is to support the mentee in repairing the relationship for the long term rather than in winning an immediate argument. Defeating someone in a dispute may simply create resentment, and a desire for revenge, which will make long term collaboration very fraught. Winning in the short term can mean losing in the long term. Whereas reaching a sensible compromise that leaves everyone's self respect intact and goes someway to meeting their goals, can be the start of building a better relationship. This is not the same as our mentee simply giving in to the other person. Explain the different communication styles to your mentee and explain that assertive rather than aggressive or passive communicators are likely to be more effective. By encouraging them to practice assertive communication, we can assist them to stand up for themselves without unnecessarily antagonising others.

Clearly some relationships involve bullying and violence and are exploitive and damaging. Whilst these may be very much the minority, attempting to repair and continue with such a relationship may only increase our mentee's distress with no prospect of improvement. If after a careful discussion with the mentee, we strongly suspect that they are in a relationship of the latter kind we should consider accessing outside help. For a child or young person we have a responsibility to report to the relevant authorities, any suspicions of abuse or harm. As we have seen we should do this through the mentoring scheme coordinator. We should also report any evidence of serious criminal activity. In respect of adults, you should discuss with the scheme coordinator any concerns that you have for the welfare of your mentee.

Remember that confidentiality should have been covered in your first meeting with your mentee where you informed her or him that you would have a duty to report serious concerns for their well being (see Chapter three). In discussion with your coordinator you might agree to report any criminal matter to the police or offer to refer your mentee to professional help such as counselling. Dealing with workplace reports of bullying was discussed in chapter eight.

Some mentoring schemes focus specifically on supporting people who have been abused. One example is Women's Aid, an English charity that coordinates a mentoring service for women who have experienced domestic violence. Women's Aid uses as mentors, women who have personal experience of domestic violence or who are experienced in working with those who have survived domestic violence. Hence the mentors know what their mentees are going through and can reassure them that they are not alone. A similar UK scheme is the Jan Foundation Lantern Mentoring Project. This project recognises the potential damage to children of family violence and believes that by giving mentoring support to the mother they are also helping to reduce the damage done to children. The Lighthouse Foundation in Melbourne is another organisation that uses community volunteers. In this case they mentor young people who have experienced homelessness. It is not uncommon for mentoring to complement other programmes run by the same organisation as is the case with the Lighthouse.

When we are in relationship conflicts we tend to find justifications for our own behavior and seek to blame others. Whilst the other person may indeed be behaving unreasonably, the source of the problem is often an inability to appreciate fully the other person's point of view and to communicate with each other in a considerate and effective way. As mentors we can use our skills to try to get out mentee to see the other person's point of view and we can suggest some strategies that they might employ to improve the ways in which they communicate.

Family Conflict

Sometimes conflict within families is long standing and passes from generation to generation. Here conflict is habitual. It is a learned way of relating to each other and as such it is very hard to break down. These situations are best dealt with by trained and experienced family therapists.

If as a mentor you find that your mentee is caught up in such a family, it would be sensible to work through your coordinator to refer your mentee on to a family therapy service which can work with all the family members.

If the issue is a more limited one, perhaps a recent breakdown in communication, you may be able to help. Often the conflict will occur when the behavior of one family member comes to be seen as a problem by the rest of the family. That member is then placed under a lot of pressure to correct their errant behaviour. For example the teenage son may be seen as staying out too late, 'getting in with the wrong crowd' and frequently rolling home drunk or staying out all night. In such situations rational discussion between the parties may have broken down and no real communication may be taking place. Here, if you are mentoring one of the parties try the basic strategy outlined below.

Resolving Conflicts

As we have seen previously, simply talking an issue through with a mentor can help a person to see it more clearly. Having someone who shows understanding, concern and empathy can itself calm a stressed person and generate more positive emotions. Example is a great teacher. As you talk with your mentees you can model the communication skills that they could use in their other personal relationships.

Having listened and discussed the situation, move on. If each meeting is simply a repetition of the same relationship history and catalogue of complaints, you are simply reinforcing negativity and cannot make progress. Challenge your mentee to think in new ways. Concentrate on a strategy for the future e.g. what could the mentee do to establish better relationships and avoid further relationship damage?

When your mentee asks for your advice on how to deal with a dispute, discuss active listing and explain the value of being assertive rather than aggressive or passive. Stress the importance of using temperate language, soft tone of voice and not giving off aggressive or rejecting body language.

They should not say one thing and imply the opposite by their facial expression or tone of voice.

Problem solving techniques (see chapter eight) and negotiation (see below) could be discussed, focusing upon the problem not the person. Frequently, in personal conflicts, the real, painful underlying issues, are repressed or avoided. Unless they are recognised and addressed, progress may not be possible. Whilst it is essential to clarify the current issues and focus upon resolving them, old grudges and resentments may need to be recognised since they may be the underlying source of mistrust. Having recognised them the parties must then be prepared to resolve them and show forgiveness or they will become major barriers to progress. Is your mentee able to recognise personal negative emotions? Does your mentee have the maturity to rise above them?

Often we see apparently rational people developing such a strong sense of grievance that they are determined to pin blame onto others and demand an acknowledgement of guilt and an apology. This will simply raise the emotional temperature and will probably provoke the accused into an emotional defense and counter accusation. We must point out this likelihood to our mentees and encourage them to move on rather than continuing to rake up old resentments. Therefore emphasise the importance of showing respect and consideration for others. Dislike of them is no excuse for behaving badly towards them—we must all learn to mix with people we dislike. Hence they should do their best to remain calm and not get drawn into exaggeration, threats or abuse. Avoiding sarcasm and niggling asides is important but humour can be used to lighten tension provided nothing is said that could be interpreted as a put down.

Another danger is the making of demands that the other party could not possibly accede to and which would humiliate them and threaten their basic interests. Try to see things as others see them and seek avenues that they can accept.

Mentees should be warned not to jump to conclusions about other people's motives and to avoid accusations about their intentions and feelings. They cannot be sure of these. Remember that they can state their unhappiness with what a person has said or done but not with what they are. ("what you said really upset me" NOT "you are a nasty slimy creature"). Successes is more likely if your mentee deals straightforwardly and honesty with others. Attempts to trick or mislead usually rebound negatively in the long term because they undermine mutual trust. Whereas focusing on solutions which meet everyone's needs and preserve everyone's self respect provide a good basis for a long term relationship.

Where the parties discuss a dispute together, it will only deteriorate into personal abuse if both parties lose their cool. If your mentees can remain calm, show respect to others and exercise self control they will be using the most important strategy of all to resolve a conflict.

Needs and Wants

Before delving into the use of negotiation to resolve or manage disputes, it is important to contrast 'wants' and 'needs'. Needs are our fundamental requirements as human beings to enable us to lead a healthy life. They include our basic physical requirements for food clothing and shelter but also encompass psychological needs including safety, social relationships, emotional ties and self esteem. Maslow famously placed needs into a hierarchy with 'self actualisation' at the top. Self actualisation is about fulfilling your potential as a person, gaining wisdom and being creative. Maslow claimed that few of us actually reach this peak.

Other researchers have proposed further needs. Whilst it is doubtful that these needs do, in fact, form a hierarchy it is useful to see them as being fundamental to our well being and prospects for happiness.

Wants on the other hand are things that we may desire but don't necessarily need. A person may want a luxury beachside home but a decent suburban house may quite adequately meet their housing needs. Moreover, recent research suggests that once our reasonable needs have been met, simply acquiring more money and property does not in itself make us any happier.

Indeed striving for more possessions can be a route to unhappiness because the craving for more can never be fulfilled. Much of this desire to continually possess more could stem from what sociologists call 'relative deprivation'. Someone who is continually striving to join a 'higher' status social group may base their self esteem on matching the income, wealth, and property of that group. But they will always find someone who has something that they do not possess. Hence they feel deprived by not having it. Seeking happiness through matching the possessions of others is self defeating.

How is this relevant to mentoring? Needs are fundamental and our mentee cannot simply bargain them away in any negotiation. A successful outcome to the negotiation should always meet the needs of the parties. Whilst we all have similar needs there may be many different ways of meeting them. When working with a mentee to prepare for a negotiation, it is important to stress the importance of identifying everyone's needs and not making demands which prevent them being met.

Mentor and mentee can also discuss wants. These are the less fundamental desires that may not always be able to be met if a reasonable compromise is to be reached.

Resolving Conflict Through Negotiation

(note the similarity with the approach to problem solving in chapter eight).

The basics of negotiating are well established and are set out in many texts on communication skills. Here is a summary of the key points.

- Do not think of it as a win/lose situation. A win for you in the short term can cause lack of co-operation and mistrust in the long term.
- Allow everyone to leave with their needs met and self respect intact.

- Aim at a solution where everyone gains i.e. WIN/WIN. Think of it as a problem you are tackling together rather than as a battle that you must win.
- Be systematic. If you are unsure where to start, try the following step by step process. Don't rush

ALL must agree that there is a problem/conflict and be willing to make a genuine effort to resolve it. This is usually because it is in their interests to do so.

Step 1

Arrange a meeting to discuss the situation at a mutually acceptable time and place for a discussion. Give everyone time to calm down and reflect before having the discussion. Put aside enough time for a full discussion and be prepared to set up further meetings to complete the process. Avoid alcohol.

- What is the real problem?

  You may find that parties differ on this because they see things from different perspectives and have contrasting feelings and interests. Listen to each person explaining their views. Don't attack them personally or interrupt. Ask questions for clarification. Ask yourself if there is a hidden issue that has led to the conflict. Focus on the problem not the person. Agree on the facts. Make sure that there is agreement on the nature of the disagreement before you move on.

- Be clear about everyone's essential circumstances, needs, wants, and goals.

  Recap your understanding to check it with them. Everyone should be clear about the requirements of others before you move on. What is their bottom line? Give reassurance that you would like to find a solution that everyone can live with and feel comfortable with.

Step 2

Examine all the alternative solutions together and bargain until all can agree. Do not denigrate the suggestions of others. Encourage everyone to put all their ideas forward and be willing to consider all proposals. You can do it like this.

- Brainstorm together all the possible solutions that anyone can think of, however unusual. Draw up a list of them before you discuss the advantages and disadvantages of each one.
- Take each option in turn. Discuss it and check it against everyone's situation, needs, wants and goals. List the advantages and disadvantages of each one. If necessary use a SWOT analysis to help you. Look at both the short term and long term consequences of every option.
- Agree a way forward—Identify the option or combination of options that comes closest to a workable solution which meets the requirements of everyone. Once you have found an option agreeable to both parties, restate it clearly to avoid any later misunderstanding. You may need to write it down to refer back to if further conflict arises.

Step 3

Arrange a follow up discussion at a later date—to check that there are no ongoing problems. Be prepared for further negotiation to resolve issues that may emerge as you implement your solution.

A Warning for your mentee.

Some people will agree to a discussion when put under pressure but have no serious intention of finding a solution because the present situation suits them. They can consciously or unconsciously use a variety of strategies to disrupt the discussion and try to bring it to an immature end. Watch out for these.

- Making lots of irrelevant points.
- Making personal attacks in order to provoke anger in others leading to a row, and then using this as confirmation that "this will never work".
- Dragging things out in the hope that you will get frustrated and give up.
- Asking for guarantees that could never be given.
- Bringing up old conflicts and trying to reignite long standing grievances.
- Trying to discredit some of those present.
- Appearing to agree and then raising new objections at the last minute.
- Escalating demands or making new ones when agreement seems near.

If you spot these, calmly explain that you feel they are unnecessary and suggest that they are blocking progress.

Can your mentee keep calm and focused throughout this and avoid personal attacks? If so, the negativity of others can sometimes be overcome. However on occasion you simply have to recognise that no agreement is possible.

It is also important when negotiating not to neglect the cultural imperatives and differences that we discussed above. For example an employer who demands that each worker wears a revealing uniform may be discriminating against employees whose culture demands modest dress. To wear such clothing may bring shame and cause conflict at home and among friends.

Let us look at a family negotiation to show how it might work.

Retiring from the Farm?

A church women's group in a rural community is operating a support group for its members. They have recently started to offer one to one mentoring to women on local farm properties.

Marjorie has been feeling low for some time. She confides in a friend who puts her in touch with the group. Noreen offers to mentor Marjorie.

As they get to know each other Noreen discovers that, at 67 years of age, Marjorie has had enough of working with her husband Brian and son Tony on their farm. She also does the shopping, housework, washing and cooking. She wants Brian to retire and hand the farm over to Tony so they can move to town.

Seventy year old Brian will not hear of it. Whenever she raises the idea he rejects it. She accuses him of selfishness and not caring about her. He sees her as selfish, knowing that he would die of boredom in town. He feels his life would be finished if he left the farm. Half his life has been spent building up his prize Herefords and he is not going to throw that away now.

Tony has worked the farm with his father since leaving school but is fed up of his dad bossing him around. In his view, his father's methods are old fashioned and Tony longs to be free to make changes. He is thinking of leaving the district with his wife and kids and is applying for farm manager's positions since he can't afford his own place.

Marjorie says that she still loves her husband but she can't take much more and is considering leaving him to go to live in town with her recently widowed cousin. She would be very sad to see her son, daughter in law, and grandchildren move away. It has left her feeling angry at Brian and sick with worry.

Noreen suggests that organising a family conference after a meal, where everyone is relatively fresh and relaxed, could be a starting point. To prepare for it they talk through everyone's needs and wishes. Noreen encourages Marjorie to be assertive in raising her feelings but cautions against ganging up with Tony and his wife against Brian. She proposes that Brian be given every opportunity to give his views and that the others listen carefully to him and tell him that they want to find a solution that he can accept.

Noreen advises taking the same approach with Tony before Marjorie gives her own views.

Once it is clear what everyone wants, they can put all the options on the table before talking them through to try to find one that they all can live with.

Noreen and Marjorie rehearse together what she is going to say. She also decides to talk to Tony in advance to explain her strategy and ask for his cooperation.

Noreen and Marjorie meet the following week to discuss how things went. Majorie feels much more positive. It seems that they have found a way forward that they can all accept. Majorie and Brian will move into town and Tony will move his family into the farmhouse and take over the farm. However, Brian will retain ownership of his Herefords and will run them on one third of the farm. Tony will also do some part time contract work for a friend to help make ends meet. Brian will be able to drive the 20 kilometres to the farm whenever he wishes. There is a spare bedroom in the farmhouse that he can use if he occasionally wants to stay over.

It is not a perfect solution but it goes a long way to meeting everyone's needs.

Dealing with Aggression

In some relationships, conflicts degenerate into outright aggression or even violence from one or both parties. As mentors it is unlikely that we will face any aggression from mentees. They are all volunteers too and our seeking our support. However, they may have to deal with others who are aggressive to them or they may be unable to control their aggression in some circumstances. Talking through the ideas below may help them.

High levels of frustration or threat can trigger automatic, aggressive responses in the older areas of our brain. We stop thinking rationally. Our body prepares for to fight. Our heart beats faster, our breathing becomes more rapid, and blood is diverted to our muscles. In this state we can lose self control and are inclined to argue with and abuse others. We may even physically attack them.

Some individuals seem to have a very low tolerance threshold of frustration and are quick to become aggressive. Anger and aggression are usually the result of frustration in people when:

- they feel that no one is listening to them,
- they feel threatened, humiliated and insecure; often this is a result of sarcasm or ridicule—a threat to their self esteem and self image (e.g. their partner has left and now lives with someone else),
- they have needs that are not being met (e.g. others have a partner but they do not),
- they feel that they can't cope with their situation or the demands being made upon them (e.g. overwhelmed at work).

Note: most threats are not physical—they are threats to a person's self esteem for example: by being ridiculed, criticised, failing at tasks, or not being accepted by a group.

Some people may become abusive and rude because they have poor communication skills and have to get themselves very angry before they are able to tackle a person who has upset them (such as a client who approaches benefit office with a complaint about underpayment of welfare payments).

If you need to have a conversation with someone whom you suspect will be aggressive towards you, choose your time and place carefully. Don't tackle them when they are tired and feeling under pressure. Talk where there are other people are nearby. Leave yourself an avenue of escape. Never have your discussion when either of you have had or are having alcohol.

If the other person's behaviour continues to be threatening and uncontrolled, don't be a hero, don't confront them—leave.

The best thing that you can do is to give an aggressive person the chance to express their feelings in words. Calming people down, by listening to them, showing concern and taking them seriously, usually makes them feel guilty about their rudeness. Once they calm down they may feel humiliated that they let their anger get out of control. Sometimes aggression turns to tears. So, explain to your mentee the difference between being assertive and aggressive. Suggest to your mentee:

- do not shout or lose your temper, keep calm and do not mirror their aggression—with any luck they will start to copy you,
- use body language and tone of voice to give calming messages,
- keep physically relaxed because it is impossible to be physically relaxed and truly aggressive at the same time,
- avoid confrontation—you know by now not to criticise the person even if you have to show disappointment with their actions,
- take their concerns seriously however stupid they appear to you,
- in a group be non-threatening and give the other person a chance to escape from the situation without loss of face.

"Why don't we have a private chat about this in . . . ." or "Why don't we go and speak to . . .".

If they calm down and you feel safe, give them some uninterrupted time. As always, use active listening. If possible, sit them down at right angles to you, in a location where you can be seen but where you can also talk privately. Ask non-threatening questions about their feelings and the circumstances that led to their outburst. Don't make promises that you can't keep but show a willingness to help. This may mean seeking someone else who is in a better position to help them or arranging a further discussion at a later date.

Some people cannot express themselves well and may not understand why they feel like they do. Sympathetic questioning may help but avoid making them feel even more stupid and immature than they do already by being patronising.

Georgina

Georgina found her home situation particularly difficult to talk about. She loved her partner and wanted their relationship to work. Unfortunately she felt that all the positive things that she contributed were taken for granted by him whilst he was quick to point out her defects and any errors that she made. When she challenged him about the unfairness of his behaviour he became very defensive and the conversation invariably descended into a shouting match and an exchange of insults.

In these circumstances the relationship was suffering and Georgina's self esteem was damaged. Georgina felt that her partner cared for her but was quite unconscious of the effect that his behaviour was having on her.

After talking through the issue with her mentor, Georgina resolved to try to be assertive without attacking her partner directly. She understood the need to choose the right time and place for a discussion and to avoid aggression. With her mentor she practised how she would explain her feelings and make positive non threatening suggestions to her partner that might improve the situation.

At her next mentoring meeting Georgina reported that she had tried the suggested strategy. She and her partner had been able to have a relaxed and friendly discussion. He blamed stresses at work for his "occasional thoughtlessness". Georgina felt that she had made a useful start but recognised that there was still a long way to go to improve her relationship with her partner. She was hopeful that she could use the skills that she had discussed with her mentor to make some real progress.

The Row

At this point it might be thought that we are seeking to sanitise relationships—to take all the passion out of them and turn every dispute into a calm rational conversation. Even if we wished to do this, it is highly unlikely that we could succeed. Could an occasional stand up row with anger, raised voices and extreme language, actually have benefits?

Sometimes the release of pent up feelings in such a way can have a cathartic effect releasing stresses and allowing suppressed feelings to be expressed. If this happens on isolated occasions, it could actually strengthen the relationship by stimulating the exploration of deeply felt emotions. Of course, if it is a couple, making up could be fun.

What we need to avoid here is a total loss of control where we say extremely hurtful things to the other person which may never be forgotten and permanently destroy trust.

Even when having a row, the rule applies of being able to express your own feelings and disagree with a person's actions without verbally or physically abusing them. Obviously it is essential to avoid getting into the habit of rowing whenever a problem arises.

Supporting the Mentor

In all types of mentoring, traumatic events will intrude from time to time. Mentors themselves will experience emotional stress stemming from these encounters. Hence it is very important that the coordinator is available to support the mentor, to give advice, reassurance and to simply listen and understand. Being part of a network with other mentors can also be a valuable support system.

There will be days when the mentor returns home, anxious and worried, needing to offload intense feelings. As we saw in the ethical dilemma in chapter three, it is important to recognise that confidentiality does not mean total silence. Feelings can be shared. An issue can be explained in general terms as long as the mentor does not reveal the identity of the mentee or give details that might breach confidentiality and make it possible for the identity of the mentee to be inferred.

Usually other people will have been discussed in mentoring conversations and their identities must also be protected. As long as these safeguards are maintained mentors should be able to share their feelings with a trusted partner, close friend or fellow mentor.

ACTIVITY—Thinking about your personal relationships

Think about your closest friend. What is it about the way that you relate to each other that makes you feel at ease in each other's company?

Think about someone that you struggle to communicate well with. What is it about the way that you relate to each other which forms a barrier between you?

In mentoring training these questions could be discussed in small groups to make people more aware of communication barriers (see chapter two).

CHAPTER ELEVEN

Organising a Mentoring Scheme

Any new mentoring scheme will usually be a response to a perceived need. It makes sense to check carefully that this need is a real one and that it is not merely a symptom of something more deep seated which should be tackled first. A careful assessment of needs should be undertaken before any decision to go ahead.

Clearly, the details of scheme organisation will vary according to the setting, the aims of the programme, its size, the target group, and the mentors to be used.

A great deal of community (as distinct from workplace or educational) mentoring takes place through public services, health services, and voluntary organisations. Often this is not labelled mentoring. Hopefully readers of this book will recognise it when they see it, whatever the label attached to it. Some of this is formally organised e.g. through voluntary support groups in the health or welfare fields. Other mentoring is very informal and occurs as a natural spin off from some shared activity

When initiating a new community mentoring scheme, rather than creating a brand new body, an existing organisation can often be used such as a local government department/agency, community centre, a not for profit voluntary organisation, church, school or college. This has great advantages including funding, premises, administrative support and insurance. Where the initiative for a mentoring scheme comes from outside an existing organisation, rather than set up an entirely new one it is well worth trying to find an existing community organisation that will sponsor or take on the scheme.

However, operating for or within an existing organisation can also lead to tensions. It will have its culture, policies, procedures and goals which might not always dovetail neatly with the principles of mentoring. Mentoring may be seen as the answer to a problem faced by the organisation. Hence mentors might be expected to persuade or direct mentees rather than supporting them to make their own decisions. These decisions may not always suit the organisation. Such a situation can stem from a misunderstanding of mentoring on the part of management. What they describe as mentoring might be better described as supervising, coaching or tutoring. Therefore, it is helpful at an early stage to have a discussion about the principles of mentoring, role of a mentor, the ethics of mentoring and what could be realistically achieved.

As explained in chapter six, senior people without direct experience of mentoring programmes may assume that it can be done with minimal resources, perhaps using volunteers in their own time. They may assume that once a mentor and mentee have been identified and paired up they can simply be left to get on with it. Such an attitude will almost inevitably lead to disillusionment on the part of mentors who will soon begin to drop out. Creating a support structure for mentors and mentees is vital.

Core Principles of Mentoring within an Organised Scheme

1. Mentoring is a relationship in which a more experienced person supports a less experienced one through a challenge, transition or difficulty.
2. Prospective mentors should be screened for their suitability including criminal background checks.
3. Some initial training should be given to new mentors.
4. A mentoring scheme should have a general set of aims. These should be fully explained to and be accepted by, both mentor and mentee at the beginning of the process.
5. Mentors and mentees should agree in advance how they will use their time together (sometimes called a mentoring plan) to avoid repetitious discussion which does not make progress.
6. Mentors should support mentees to develop specific personal aims and a plan to implement them (mentee's personal action plan).
7. Mentors should promote the independence of mentees.
8. Mentors should seek to win the trust of mentees, to empathise with them and develop rapport.
9. Mentors should always treat their mentees with respect and should endeavour to be a positive role model for them.
10. The mentoring relationship should not be prolonged unnecessarily.
11. Boundaries should be established around the mentoring relationship to protect both the mentor and mentee; such as restrictions on the time and place of meetings.
12. Both mentor and mentee are entitled to their personal privacy. The mentor has no right to demand personal information from the mentee that the mentee does not wish to give and vice versa.
13. Mentors should adopt a non judgmental attitude towards mentees. This does not require mentors to suspend their own beliefs and values.

14. Mentors should not attempt to convert their mentees to a political or religious belief system. Nor should they pressure them to join any organisation or movement.

15. Mentor and mentee should not form a sexual relationship whilst mentoring is in progress. If as adults they wish to have such a relationship they should withdraw from the scheme or the mentee should be allocated another mentor.

16. Once the mentoring has been completed, a mentor and adult mentee are free to develop a personal friendship if they both wish to do so. Great caution should be observed in any continuing relationship between the former mentor and a former mentee who is child or young person. Parental approval will normally be required.

17. Mentors should be non directive. They should ensure that any decisions made are genuinely the mentees own.

18. Both mentors and mentees should be volunteers.

19. Mentoring conversations should be confidential, unless otherwise agreed by both mentor and mentee, or unless the mentee reveals something which must be reported; such as criminal activity or circumstances which put the mentee or others at risk. This should be explained to the mentee at the first meeting.

20. Coordinators should be appointed to supervise and support mentors.

21. The progress of mentoring relationships should be monitored, and evaluated.

22. Unsatisfactory mentoring relationships should not be allowed to continue.

Management Committee

The starting point for a scheme will usually be the creation of a steering group of key people who will establish it on a sound footing. Such a group should include key stakeholders and enthusiastic supporters of the venture.

Once the scheme is in operation the steering group should become or be replaced by a more formal management group/committee which could include mentor representatives to bring their experiences to the discussions. Initially the steering group should clarify the aims of the scheme, gain the support of stakeholders and obtain resourcing for it.

Once the aims are agreed, the steering group should create a development plan which includes the following key tasks.

- To find the finance and other resources to run the scheme. These are usually underestimated.
- To appoint an experienced and trained person to manage the scheme, coordinate mentoring activities and support the mentors. The actual title of the post will vary from scheme to scheme. It could be called a coordinator, supervisor or organiser. Here we will stick to coordinator since it is a 'friendlier' less threatening word.
- To create (usually with the advice of the coordinator) a set of written policies, procedures, and a code of conduct. These should meet legal equal opportunity requirements for staff and mentee recruitment. Volunteers should be treated as staff even if they are unpaid.

Equal opportunity does not mean that schemes are prevented from targeting mentors of a particular age, gender and ethnicity. However, where this is done it must be because the aims of the scheme require it. For example the mentoring of women abused by violent partners could be exclusively by women mentors.

An outline of the proposed scheme ought to be produced before the coordinator is appointed so that the candidates for the post can see what is expected of them. They should be given a written job description/role statement specifying their duties and the qualifications, experience and qualities required.

For small local schemes the initial plan does not need to be very sophisticated but the main tasks do need specifying, time scales agreed, money and other resources found and the people who will carry them out need to be identified.

Clearly the role of coordinator is crucial. In smaller schemes this person may be the only one employed to run it and might only be part-time. In larger schemes a scheme manager may lead a team of coordinators, each of whom recruits and gives day to day support to the mentors. In the workplace the coordination job may simply be added to the duties of someone in Human Resources with the danger that they will not have the time to do it properly.

Aims

Aims should include:

- the target groups of mentees,
- the outcomes that it is hoped the scheme will achieve.

It is recommended that these are spelled out clearly so that everyone involved is in no doubt what they are trying to achieve. For example: "to assist recently appointed colleagues to adjust to their new roles and responsibilities" or "to reduce the level of drop out from training by offering individual support to trainees for the first six months of their programme". These aims should also be used after the scheme has been operating for a while, to evaluate its success. Therefore it is helpful if they are written in such a way that that they become measurable.

A big danger here is that initial enthusiasm will lead the steering group to specify aims that are overambitious, so that when the evaluation takes place the scheme will appear to have failed even where it has made a solid contribution to the lives of mentees. Stick to a few straightforward aims and make them realistic and achievable. You can always become more ambitious later, as your mentors gain more experience and skill.

Where an aim involves tackling a particular problem such as: school truanting, unemployment, or drug use, it can involve mentors trying to persuade their mentees to go in a particular direction. Yet, you will recall that a major principle of mentoring is to support mentees to make their own decisions. What if a drug user decides he wishes to carry on using? Is that a free choice on the part of the mentee which the mentor should not try to change?

The way to view this apparent contradiction is to remember that the mentee is a volunteer. A mentoring programme to keep people off drugs would state that aim at the outset. If the mentee volunteers for the programme it should be because they have made a decision to try to give up and steer clear of drugs. Hence the aims of: the programme, the mentee and mentor should all coincide. This will only happen if the aims are made very clear to prospective mentees at the outset and they agree to pursue them with the mentor's support.

Scheme Management and Coordination

The appointment of a scheme coordinator is absolutely crucial. Acting as a coordinator can be a very fulfilling role, bring much job satisfaction, leading to some wonderful friendships and generating an extensive network of contacts in the community. However, it can be a demanding role because the mentors will rely heavily upon the coordinator for advice and support. Ideally the coordinator will be enthusiastic, friendly, well organised and able to stay calm and make carefully thought through decisions when required. It is essential that the person appointed is trained and properly resourced.

In the author's experience, poor coordination and inadequate support for mentors are the most significant causes of failing schemes. The typical tasks of a scheme coordinator are set out below. Obviously there will be some variation from scheme.

At the setting up stage

- Create scheme policies and procedures including written guidelines for mentors and mentees. Submit to management committee for their consideration amendment and approval.
- Create a system for mentoring records and ensure that they are maintained and kept in a secure location.
- Promote and advertise the scheme. This may involve working with the media and giving presentations to organisations which might support the scheme financially and which might be a source of mentors.
- Set up a reputable accounting system to process and account for all income and expenditure.
- Ensure any necessary insurance, risk management and occupational health and safety policies and procedures, are in place.

At the recruitment stage

- Design and utilise application forms for prospective mentors and mentees including background information to facilitate matching.
- Contact potential mentors and mentees, selling the idea to them and gaining their trust so that they volunteer to participate.
- Brief and interview potential mentors and mentees.
- Organise mentor training and ensure that all prospective mentors undertake it. Give mentors the opportunity to obtain a qualification unit.
- Arrange background checks for mentors.
- Select and match participants.

Before mentoring starts

- Identify days, times, and locations for mentoring.

- Ensure that mentors and mentees have access to a telephone, computer, printer and photocopier.
- Ensure mentors and mentees are looked after at the venue when mentoring e.g. toilets and refreshments available.
- Create and distribute mentoring booklets to mentors.

During mentoring

- Attend the first mentoring meeting to perform introductions and check arrangements are all in place.
- Be available to support mentors and mentees during and immediately after mentoring. This could be by telephone or by being physically present nearby.

Ongoing

- Monitor by obtaining feedback after mentoring sessions, including attendance and record sheets.
- Establish a network of mentors that meets regularly and has email/ telephone contacts.
- Make additional training and development opportunities available to mentors.
- Use feedback from mentors and mentees to prepare evaluations of the scheme.
- Prepare and hold regular committee meetings giving feedback from mentoring.
- Include a formal evaluation and review meeting at least annually.
- Prepare submissions for additional funding.
- Prepare and hold celebration events from time to time.
- Arrange for ongoing marketing and publicity. Organise events (such as celebrations) that capture the attention of the media and the public. Produce regular press releases.

Let us look at some of these in more detail.

The Creation of Written Guidance, Policies and Procedures

A document should be produced which sets out the aims of the scheme and the principles of mentoring. It should specify the roles, responsibilities and duties of the, mentors, coordinators, manager and management committee. Rules should be included which set clear boundaries to the mentoring relationship to protect both mentors and mentees from inappropriate relationships and excessive dependence.

A code of conduct for mentors should be included (see chapter 3) or produced as a separate document. This must incorporate an explanation of how mentors should report any concerns about risk of harm to the mentee or others and any indications of criminal activity.

The document could give guidance concerning: the recruitment of mentees and mentors (see later), when and where mentoring should take place, and the duration of the mentoring relationship. Minimum training requirements could be specified.

The guidance might also explain how coordinators should support mentors and when and how mentors should seek the advice of coordinators. Record keeping, monitoring and evaluation arrangements could be included. A grievance procedure could be added which explains how mentees could raise any complaints against mentors but which also gives mentors a fair hearing. It might also be useful to set out criteria for the selection of both mentors and mentees based on the aims of the scheme and equal opportunity principles.

If young people are involved the policy should specify how parents are to be informed and parental consent obtained. It should include procedures concerning the giving of lifts to mentees and taking them out on visits (see later).

Documentation of this kind might be thought to be unnecessary bureaucracy. But it can help to avoid lots of unnecessary conflict and disputes down the track and can serve as an important protection for mentors and mentees if complaints are made. Mentoring can arouse strong emotions and opinions. It can also raise important ethical issues. Having some rules and guidelines to point to can take the pressure off individuals "The policy says we must do it this way" or "I had to report that—it specifically says so in the code", or even "I am sorry but I am not allowed to give you a lift home".

Insurance

Insurance can usually be arranged through the parent organisation. Mentoring may already be covered but this must be checked. Insurance will be needed for the premises being used. It may also be needed if mentors and mentees will be travelling together in a vehicle owned by the mentor or by the scheme e.g. to visit colleges, clinics or employers.

Recruitment of Mentors

Personal contact with a welcoming and friendly coordinator is the best recruiter. The successful coordinator shows an empathy with potential mentees and explains with examples how valuable and rewarding mentoring can be. A highly formal presentation with lots of powerpoint slides is likely to be less effective than a informal style. A presentation could be followed by an opportunity to discuss concerns and opportunities in a small group. Often potential mentors like the idea but are anxious about how to go about it and are unsure that they have the skills to tackle it. Hence initial training and ongoing coordinator support should be stressed. The social aspect of meeting other mentors and making new friends might also be explained.

Use written eligibility criteria. Not all volunteers are suitable and not all will be accepted. This needs to be made clear at the beginning and the basic principles of mentoring (particularly, being non-directive) should be explained.

Within an organisation it is important to stress that mentors are volunteers. Calling a meeting for interested staff, without obligation, is a good way to go. Application forms could be available at the meeting and those interested could be given the chance to fill them in on the spot or return them later. Managers who feel that particular members of staff would make good mentors could have a quiet word with them individually to encourage them to attend the meeting.

Where a scheme uses unpaid community volunteers, recruitment and retention are likely to be a central issue for scheme managers and coordinators. Local media are often happy to include news items requesting volunteer mentors and giving updates on the progress of the scheme. These may bring in some enquiries. First contact with the mentoring coordinator will be vital in turning enquires in to commitments. A prompt telephone response, friendly welcome and showing a genuine interest in the prospective mentor will all be helpful. Enthusiasm from the coordinator can be infectious. Just sending out a standard letter may not be enough.

Using existing organisations is often the most productive recruitment strategy. Coordinators can contact voluntary organisations, retired people's clubs, church groups, or local service clubs such as rotary, and offer to come and talk to members. College and university students are usually a good source. On some courses they can earn credits for voluntary work. Accredited mentor training and some practical experience of mentoring can help their employability later, particularly if they are training for the caring professions. It is also well worth while getting the backing of local councils. They may have community workers and volunteer coordinators who can recommend volunteers to you.

Retired teachers, managers, social workers, financial advisors and nurses often make great mentors because they may well have developed the social skills to deal with people under pressure or suffering distress.

Some companies such as banks and local credit unions may allow selected staff a few hours off each month to do community service. Mentoring is an ideal way for them to do so. It also helps to promote the image of the company. Coordinators should acknowledge the support of any businesses and public bodies in scheme publicity.

Screening of Potential Mentors

Potential mentors must be screened to assess their suitability. Police criminal background checks are essential for mentors working with children and young people However, there may be certain mentoring situations where having a criminal record should not disbar people from becoming mentors. Using ex drug users to support existing users who are trying to escape their addiction, could be a useful strategy.

Other screening techniques include the use of referees and application forms. Application forms are also useful for matching mentors and mentees. It is helpful if prospective mentees have a one to one discussion with a scheme coordinator. This could be a formal interview but an informal chat is often more revealing. The training programme is particularly useful for screening since opportunities for discussion of case studies or ethical dilemmas can reveal people with stereotyped and prejudiced attitudes who are clearly not suitable as mentors. Practicing mentoring conversations during training can also reveal people who lack the personal skills to mentor effectively.

Where a volunteer is keen to get involved but perhaps lacks the personal skills to mentor, it is worth looking for another role that they could play, such as assisting with scheme administration, rather than rejecting them altogether.

Unfortunately, in some situations (particularly workplaces) people may be instructed or persuaded to become mentors and mentees despite having skeptical or negative attitudes towards it. Others may approach it in fear. In chapter three the notion of mindsets was introduced. Mentors and mentees will come to mentoring carrying their characteristic sets of attitudes with them which may include aspects of one or more of those set out below. These are not meant to be comprehensive. They are merely a means of stimulating thought and discussion about feelings, attitudes and motives. They can be used in training and by mentors and mentees to help them think about demanding situations that they may be tackling.

Mind sets are often revealed if, in relaxed conversation during a coffee break, we simply ask a potential mentor "what do think it would be like to mentor someone?"

NOTE that these are not always a good predictor. Experiences can change mind sets.

ACTIVITY: MENTOR MENTEE MIND SETS

In respect of mentors, which of these mind sets are conducive to effective mentoring? Jot down your response in the right hand column. If this activity is used in mentor training ask each trainee to rate their own reactions.

- A positive, altruistic response (give 2 ticks).
- A response offering some hope of success (give 1 tick).
- A neutral response (give a question mark).
- A response which will act as a barrier to success (give a cross).

MIND SET	Perception of challenge	Response	Likelihood of success.
Anxiety	Fear of the unknown. *Will I be able to cope? This could lead me into trouble/conflict. What if I fail—what will they think of me?*	Fear Self doubt Caution Excuses	
Avoidance	Why the need for change? *I doubt if this is workable or worthwhile. It could be too much extra work. I might be exploited. What is the point?*	Scepticism Cynicism Rejection Negativity	
Opportunity	A chance to learn more about . . . . *I could develop new skills. I could lead. This looks interesting. We could try doing it this way.*	Confidence Optimism Curiosity Experimentation	

Self interest	What is in it for me? *Will it improve my promotion chances? Will I meet people who can help my career? Will I earn more money—get more perks?*	Questioning Calculation Negotiation	
Seeking attention or approval	Being at the centre of things. *I am delighted that they want me. People will think well of me. I can show off what I know. I will be accepted by the manager/team.*	Willingness Collaboration Sociability Popularity?	
Caring	Belief in its value *This is important. This is really going to help people. I/we ought to do it. I can make a contribution. I must find the time.*	Concern Commitment Compassion Empathy	
Persecuted	Cynical about the motives of others. *I am an outsider. They have never liked me. Why land me with this? I always get the rough jobs that no one else wants.*	Suspicion Conflict Aggression Mistrust	

Mentor Training and Qualifications

As we have seen in earlier chapters mentoring requires a range of skills and some background knowledge. Many mentors will already possess these skills but can benefit from becoming more consciously aware of how and when to use them to best effect. Some knowledge is applicable to any mentoring scheme whereas other knowledge may be only relevant to a particular setting; such as career development or working with adolescents. Therefore some initial training to develop knowledge and skills is essential for an effective mentoring scheme. Ongoing training/staff development after the mentor has gained some experience, is also very beneficial.

Training should be offered as a way of finding out about mentoring without obligation. Hence there should be no prior commitment on the participant to sign up as a mentor nor would the scheme be obliged to accept them if the training indicated that they were unsuitable.

Initial training should:

- introduce prospective mentors to the scheme managers/coordinator,
- introduce mentors to each other and to existing mentors,
- provide a means of mentor screening,
- explain the aims of the scheme,
- explain the principles of mentoring,
- explore self image and self esteem,
- explain the ethics of mentoring and introduce the code of conduct,
- explain the skills that mentoring requires and give an opportunity to practice them,
- outline the characteristics and needs of the group to be mentored,
- describe the support arrangements for mentors,
- explain how the scheme actually works including arrangement for mentoring meetings, record keeping, monitoring and evaluation,
- give plenty of opportunity for discussion and questions.

In the author's experience at least two days of training are required to cover the above but three or four days would be preferable. These need not be continuous days. A weekend course (perhaps residential) can be a good option. Alternatively, eight or nine two hour evening sessions should be adequate for most schemes. Where mentors are to be employed full time e.g. in education, a much longer training and induction would be required.

More specialised training would also be required if the mentors were to work alongside professionals, for example in the mental health field.

Ongoing training/development for existing mentors could involve presentations by visiting experts, updates from the coordinator or simply mentors sharing experiences, successes and concerns. It is important to make these pleasant social occasions where people have a chance to mix and chat. They can also act as a reward for mentors by incorporating a meal and a recognition certificate or small gift.

Although some mentoring qualifications do exist, to the best of the author's knowledge we do not have any formal accreditation systems for mentors or schemes that would authorise them to practice or license them in some way.

In the UK, National Vocational Qualifications are available in mentoring and some universities, such as Oxford Brookes, have post graduate mentoring qualifications. Prospective mentors in New South Wales, can take a level 2 unit called ' Prepare to Mentor' or a level 3 unit called 'Mentor Individuals and Groups' which can be upgraded into a Statement Of Attainment by the addition of a further 2 units. There is also a specific qualification in Aboriginal mentoring. The author has taught and assessed on all these Australian programmes. Not only do they provide valuable training they also enable the participants to decide whether they are really suited to be mentors and the trainer to assess their suitability.

In some other countries there are national organisations which have tried to set national standards e.g. Germany. No doubt a national accreditation system for mentoring would be useful when employing paid professional mentors. However, there is the danger that it could act as a disincentive to volunteer mentors. Accrediting schemes and coordinators would be preferable to accrediting individual mentors. We don't want to professionalise mentoring to the point where it is only open to people willing to spend a lot of time being trained and willing to make a major long term commitment.

Having one or more mentoring units, as part of a qualification, is a sensible option. One unit could be free standing for initial training. Further units could be added later for interested mentors and coordinators to build into a full qualification. Having some qualification units can be very valuable as an aid to screening and as a quality assurance mechanism for training programmes. It also gives reward and recognition to people who have given up their time to train. A mentoring unit can also be a useful addition to a CV for mentors who wish to go on to train or seek promotion in: human resources, health, education, or welfare occupations.

An Outline of an Initial Mentor Training Programme.

You can see that it is broadly similar to the structure of this book. Each session could take about two hours and should include individual and group activities with time set aside for questions and discussion.

- Session One What is mentoring? What are the aims of our scheme? The mentoring process.
- Session Two Introduction to skills and attitudes. (Skills and attitudes should be reinforced in all the following sessions, through examples, and practice using realistic scenarios).
- Session Three Ethics and our Code of Conduct.
- Session Four Developing mentees self confidence and self esteem. Understand human potential.
- Session Five The characteristics and circumstances of the mentees in our particular scheme. How can they benefit from mentoring?
- Session Six How to support mentees with personal/emotional problems.
- Session Seven How our scheme operates. Outline of duties and support arrangements. The mentoring network. Development opportunities for mentors. Contact details of individuals and organisations that we can turn to for assistance for our mentees.

> • Session Eight Review of the basic principles of mentoring. An existing coordinator and mentor answer questions. Final scenarios for skill practice and assessment. Self assessment of own attitudes and skills. Invitations to apply to become a mentor.

Matching Mentors and Mentees

Asking both prospective mentors and mentees to complete a brief application form can be very helpful in the matching process. The questions that we ask will depend upon the aims of the scheme, its setting and the age and circumstances of those involved. Obviously basic information including: gender, age, availability, and contact details, will be needed. Questions could also be asked about the applicant's relevant previous experiences. These will include: work roles, any training attended, qualifications gained (remembering to explain that these are not used to exclude mentors but merely to help with matching), together with any community work or volunteering experience. Questions about personal interests and hobbies can also be valuable but we should be careful not to probe into private matters that do not concern us. Attitudes are best explored during discussions at interview or during training.

Matching by mutual interests, or experiences, as revealed on application forms, is a sensible way to proceed. In the workplace, current work roles may be the key factor.

Some 'experts' suggest that gender, age, and ethnicity should be used to match mentees but the experiences of the author do not support this approach. Occasionally mentor and mentee can be of the same gender, age group and ethnicity and yet the relationship does not gel. In fact there are plenty of examples of retired people successfully mentoring teenagers, of women successfully mentoring men and vice versa. Sometimes a mentor from another ethnic group can open doors for a mentee or give them a new perspective on life.

This does need qualifying in certain circumstances. For example in a scheme to support women with breast cancer, only women mentors would be used. A sensible approach would be to invite the mentees to nominate a preference but also to give them the option of not stating a preference.

Matching by personality, using the judgement of the coordinator, is usually a sensible option. It is hard to beat the judgement of an emotionally intelligent and experienced coordinator. In industry personality tests have been used but this might come across to the mentee as a very mechanical and impersonal process. In any case it is not always clear whether a similar or contrasting personality paring would work best. Personality matching may only be needed in a minority of cases where the mentee seems particularly vulnerable or anxious. Sometimes a mentor who is calm, sensitive and gentle is needed. For others a mentor with lively, bright, cheerful and outgoing personality can be great. These personality traits usually emerge during training. If the coordinator does some of the training, or attends some of it to observe trainees, the attitudes and personalities of the prospective mentors can usually be assessed without difficulty.

Where a group of mentees are starting the process at the same time, an alternative approach (never tried by the author) is to invite all the mentors and mentees to meet together at an introductory session to explain the scheme. Then give them a chance to circulate and invite them to select each other or to nominate several preferences.

Mentoring Booklets

It is helpful to mentors to have a booklet setting out the basic principles of mentoring, scheme aims, code of conduct and the procedures to be followed. It should give guidance on the first meeting (see chapter two) and should have a list of useful contacts. Such a booklet can also include suggested activities that the mentor and mentee can do together to break the ice and pursue the aims of the scheme. Record sheets and feedback sheets should be included for submission to the coordinator

Mentees can also benefit from having their own files for recording their personal action plan, useful information, their thoughts on their progress and the outcomes of activities. See chapter seven for other suggested additions in respect of a 'My Career' version of this file.

Structured Activities

In some schemes it is helpful if the coordinator can offer a range of structured activities for mentor and mentee to tackle together. If these activities follow a logical sequence they can provide a scaffold for the mentoring meetings and help mentor and mentee to address the scheme aims. They are particularly useful at the beginning as an icebreaker.

An illustration of what a set of structured activities might look like was provided in chapter seven in the form of *the six question approach to career development*. You will recall that the questions formed a set of stages each of which incorporated suggested activities to help with career choice. Activities of this kind could be included in the booklets for mentors or mentees. Alternatively they might be included in the mentor training sessions with spare copies of activities being available from the coordinator.

A structured programme would not normally be mandatory for mentoring. It would simply be an option that mentor and mentee might decide to use; in full or selectively.

Supporting Mentors

In any scheme situations will arise where mentors feel out of their depth. There will be times when they struggle to establish a rapport with their mentee. Occasionally a mentee will reveal personal information or circumstances which are out of the mentor's range of experience and leave the mentor shocked or floundering. Occasionally moral dilemmas will arise, as we saw in chapter three. At such times it is essential that the mentor has an understanding and sympathetic coordinator to turn to.

The coordinator is not quite a mentor to mentors because the coordinator has a supervisory role and may need to direct the mentor (e.g. to keep the relationship within the specified boundaries). The coordinator may need to insist that the scheme guidelines and code of conduct are adhered to.

On rare occasions a mentoring relationship might need to be closed prematurely. None the less, the coordinator should use the usual mentoring skills such as active listening and questioning to support and encourage the mentor who needs some advice. Often all that the mentor needs is reassurance. Sometimes it may be information such as the contact details of another organisation that could be of help to a mentee.

Clearly, it can be an emotional business for both parties. When a mentor emerges from a session full of concern for a mentee and feeling stressed about what has just been revealed, there may be a need to share the burden. Given the confidentiality rules of the scheme, the coordinator may be the obvious person for the mentor to turn to. The more distant the coordinator, the more insecure the mentor may feel. Ideally the coordinator should be contactable during a mentoring session for immediate advice.

Whilst immediate availability is not always practicable, mentors should not have to wait for several days to get a reply to a telephone call or email. Face to face contact is preferable but a prompt telephone call is surely the minimum support that mentors should expect. If mentors feel unappreciated or unsupported they will soon drop out. What can be done to keep them onboard?

- Mentors need to be able to talk through issues that might have arisen during mentoring sessions.
- Provide good training and supportive written guidance, including a mentor booklet.
- The coordinator should contact the mentor regularly to check progress and deal with any outstanding issues.
- Ideally the coordinator should be contactable for advice immediately before, during and immediately after a

mentoring session. This facility may not always be used but knowing that it is there provides reassurance.

- In some schemes e.g. in schools, several volunteer mentors may come in to mentor at the same time. The coordinator should be there to greet them, to offer refreshments and to have a feedback session before they leave.

- The creation of a network of mentors which can meet periodically for social events and to share experiences and ideas.

- More experienced mentors could be used to mentor new colleagues as these colleagues embark on their first stint as a mentor.

- Praise, feedback and reassurance should be given. Coordinators should not assume that experienced mentors do not need this. We all need it.

Coordinators are themselves subject to stress. They need to be able to share their concerns with colleagues and members of the management committee. A small scheme may only have one coordinator. Here, it can be very helpful if the Chair of the management committee makes a point of meeting the coordinator regularly to create an opportunity to discuss any issues and concerns.

Visits

Before the scheme gets underway it is worth considering whether a policy is needed on travel and visits by mentor and mentee. In many schemes there are great benefits to be gained by the mentor accompanying the mentee on a visit. This could be a visit to a potential employer or to a careers fair for example. A socially isolated mentee may ask a mentor to come to an appointment with a doctor, lawyer or government official. If you wish to encourage visits do you pay your mentors expenses?

Where children and young people are involved written parental permission should always be obtained and it is strongly recommended that the mentor does not travel alone with the mentee. A second mentor (perhaps with her mentee) could accompany them or the mentee may be invited to bring a friend along. In the latter case they should both sit in the back of the car if the mentor is driving them. Alternatively a parent might bring the child to the venue. A risk assessment may be required and you should also ensure that you have insurance cover.

Monitoring

Monitoring involves regular checks on progress to make sure that everything is on track. It could lead the coordinator to intervene if a mentoring relationship is not working or if the guidelines (including code of conduct) are being breached. A coordinator can monitor through observation, looking at mentoring records (see below) and discussion with mentors. If any concern is aroused the coordinator may simply call the person being mentored to ask *"how is it going?"*

If the relationship is not working, is there a straightforward obstacle that could be fixed? If not, the coordinator should consider intervening to end the arrangement and perhaps offer an alternative mentor. Don't just leave it; stop it.

Records of mentoring, such as the one below, should be checked regularly. If mentoring takes place in a particular building such as a school meeting room or a community centre, the record sheets could be kept centrally by the coordinator and issued to the mentor upon arrival for a mentoring session. In which case, the record must be kept securely in a locked cabinet. In some schemes the mentee might have a personal file which is used to keep information collected during mentoring. This file could also be used to keep the recording sheets and could also be kept centrally. The file would become the property of the mentee once mentoring was concluded. Such an arrangement could be put in place where a mentee might otherwise lose or forget the file (e.g. a scheme in a school or one for homeless people).

We would not wish mentoring to become an irritating bureaucratic procedure, as sometimes happens with employee development schemes. However, it is not unreasonable to ask mentors and mentees to fill in a sheet where they record the dates and times of their meetings, state the objectives that they have set and briefly note the topics they discussed or practical tasks that they undertook. Here is an example of a simple recording sheet.

Record of Mentoring

Mentee   Mentor

Start Date   Planned Completion Date

Mentoring Aim (s)

Date	Activity	Action Agreed / Outcome

In some schemes a mentor might become unavailable for a few weeks. In these circumstances another mentor might step in as a temporary replacement where the mentee is in immediate need of support. The record sheet will help the substitute to see what has already been covered.

Evaluation and Review

An evaluation is a planned activity which might take place annually. It takes an overview of the scheme to assess how far it is meeting its aims, how well it is operating and to check that the resources allocated to the scheme are being used properly. Is it giving value for all the time and money being spent on it? An evaluation should always look at ways in which the scheme could be improved.

It is sensible to ask the coordinator, often with the help of an outside evaluator, to produce an annual evaluation report for submission to the management committee. The committee should consider the report and review the scheme to decide upon any improvements to be introduced.

The evaluation should look at the extent to which aims are being met. The scheme will have its overall aims but within it the mentee will develop more specific personal aims. Indeed the mentee may develop other personal aims which go beyond or are outside scheme aims. See this as a positive development and take them into account when evaluating; don't just base success on measuring overall scheme aims.

If there are quantifiable outcomes this evaluation is considerably easier. Obviously aims and outcomes will vary from scheme to scheme but there are some common questions which an evaluation might seek to answer.

- How many current mentors do we have?
- What is their age and gender distribution?
- How many mentors have we recruited and trained in the past year?
- How many mentors have dropped out?
- Why did they drop out?

- How many people have been mentored?
- What was the average length of a mentoring relationship?
- What were the outcomes of feedback from the mentees?
- What were the outcomes of feedback from the mentors?
- What proportion of mentees met the scheme aims?
- How many mentees were able to set their own aims and create a personal action plan with the support of their mentor?
- How did mentees rate their success in meeting personal aims?

A financial statement should also be required.

When seeking feedback from mentors and mentees, an evaluation form could be used. This might be a questionnaire that they are asked to complete themselves or an interviewer could be used. It is particularly useful to use an outside interviewer who has no vested interest in the outcome and who could ask follow up questions to tease out any difficult issues.

A simple questionnaire with tick boxes gives quantifiable answers but tends to lack in depth responses. The following questions might be included.

- What issues did you tackle in your mentoring meetings? (These can be stated in general terms without compromising confidentiality)
- On a scale of 1-10 how well did you get on together? (Where a score of 10 is extremely well and 1 is extremely badly).
- What personal goals and specific objectives did you agreed on for your mentoring relationship?
- What activities have you agreed upon in order to address your objectives?
- What resources, including staff time, did you use?
- How would you rate the effectiveness of the mentoring, on a scale of 1 to 10.
- What were the outcomes?
- How successful was the process?
- How could it be improved?

Knowing that they could be asked questions such as these should help to keep the mentoring on track.

Finally lets us look at a an example of a scheme from the author's own experience.

Scheme organisation—an example

Plan—it Youth New England, New South Wales, Australia

Plan-it Youth started on the Central Coast of New South Wales in the late 1990's. Retired people volunteered to mentor school students to help them prepare for the transition to employment, training and further education. The scheme was very successful and with the support of the New South Wales government, spread to other regions within the state. The New England Region adopted it in 2005, beginning with one school, Peel High School in Tamworth. The author was the coordinator for the first six months to get the scheme off the ground. Over subsequent years it has expanded to include the other two state high schools in Tamworth and schools in other communities across the region.

The following aims were adopted.

- To improve school attendance and to encourage students to engage with learning.
- To give extra support to pupils in years 9 and 10 particularly those who are thinking about leaving school.
- To reduce the number of young people who drop out of education and/or training early and fail to acquire the skills and qualifications needed for continuing employment.
- To assist students to think about the future and to prepare themselves for the transition to continuing education, training and employment.

A management committee has oversight of the scheme. It includes representatives of the main stakeholders including: the Regional Equity

Coordinator of the NSW Government's Department of Education and Training (DET), the coordinators of the scheme, the schools participating in the scheme, the mentors, and the Further Education College (TAFE).

Two excellent part-time coordinators are employed by DET to manage and support the scheme across the schools in the region. Each school provides an in-school coordinator to run it within the school. This is usually a teacher who is released from teaching for one period each week but potentially a member of the support staff could fulfil this role.

Mentees are school students, mainly in years 9 and 10. The idea is explained to them and they are invited to apply. Parental permission is required. Underachieving, uncommitted students, who are contemplating leaving school early, get priority, However all students are invited to apply and higher achieving students are often mentored.

Mentors are unpaid volunteers from the local community. They are subject to criminal background checks and they have initial training. Many are retired people, some are students, some work part-time and others are in employment but work shifts or are able to negotiate some time off with their employers to mentor. There is quite a high turnover of mentors. Some are university and TAFE students who move on after finishing their studies. Others use mentoring as a stepping stone to employment. This includes people who use mentoring to develop experience and skills working with young people before moving on to work in the education or welfare fields. A few use their mentoring experience to move on to more demanding voluntary work with people in need. However, there are also those who find mentoring very demanding and decide not to continue. A number of mentors are still with the scheme in 2011 having joined in its first year. Among the most consistent mentors are retired people in rural communities who know each other, have a strong commitment to their local school and form a strong network. Regional coordinators spend much of their time recruiting new mentors.

Mentoring takes place at each school during school hours. It usually happens once per week for one school period and all mentors attend at the same time. This makes coordination easier, facilitates networking between mentors and enables the school to release the students concerned with minimal disruption to their education. Usually between 5 and 10 mentors can be found in a school each week. The school provides refreshments and an opportunity to liaise with the in-school coordinator and colleagues at the end of each session.

Mentoring is usually one to one, in a public space such as the library or the staff common room. Each pair sits far enough from others for their conversations to be private but they are in public view.

The in-school coordinator is available throughout to field any queries or concerns. Mentors and mentee also have access to the careers library and to computers and the internet. Where the in-school coordinator is also the careers teacher, these arrangements work particularly well.

Celebration events are held several times each year. Both mentors and mentees are presented with certificates at the end of the process and they both have the opportunity to thank publicly one another and comment on the positive aspects of their relationship. Also included is a thank you from the scheme coordinators and perhaps also from a visiting supporter of the scheme who is well known in the community (such as the MP or a school or college Principal). Refreshments and the presence of family and friends can make this a very enjoyable occasion. If the press and local TV station are invited it can also enable the scheme to gain welcome publicity which can help to recruit new volunteer mentors and financial sponsors.

Evaluations over the years have demonstrated very high success rates in tackling drop out. Overwhelmingly those mentored stay in education and training or gain employment with training opportunities. Hardly any leave school without a training place or a job to go to.

The NSW government initially provided funding to pay the salaries and administration costs of a part-time regional coordinator. It also provided funding to the TAFE college which covered the costs of training new mentors. The author has been the TAFE trainer and has trained over

250 mentors for Plan it Youth. Unfortunately government spending cuts scrapped direct funding for the scheme in 2009 which placed it in jeopardy. However, it was so highly valued by schools that they provided extra money from their own budgets and it has continued to expand.

Some funding was also found from other DET budgets and from outside donations to enable the scheme to continue.

In removing funding the DET argued that many mentees were not in the category of being vulnerable to dropping out; which was the original purpose. The schools argue that confining it to that group would stigmatise the scheme and reduce its credibility. They also point to its value to other students.

If you would like to examine a range of other case studies, *Mentoring in Action: a practical guide* by Megginson, et al. is a good source.

Ten Key Issues that any mentoring scheme must address if it is to succeed.

- Creating a management group, with sufficient funding, to initiate and sustain a high quality scheme.
- Creating a set of clear and practical aims, guidelines, policies and procedures, including a code of conduct.
- Appointing a coordinator to manage the scheme, who possesses the skills, experience, time, funding and support to do so properly.
- Recruiting and selecting suitable mentors, including screening and the use of criminal background checks for all potential mentors.
- Gaining the interest and trust of potential mentees so that they volunteer to participate.
- Initial and ongoing mentor training and personal development opportunities for both mentors and coordinator(s), supplemented by written guidance.
- Matching mentees with suitable mentors.

- Ensuring that mentors have the resources that they need in order to operate effectively and they are linked to a network of key individuals and agencies.
- Retaining mentors by giving them immediate access to coordinator advice, personal meetings with their coordinator together with regular contact and social activities with fellow mentors.
- Ongoing monitoring of mentoring relationships and intervening when they are faltering. Regularly evaluating the operation of the scheme and introducing improvements.

Conclusion

Mentoring seems to be fashionable. Just surf the internet and you will find organisations across the world employing it in many contrasting contexts. Once you start looking it seems to be popping up continually. Yet it is a concept that is often misunderstood and misused. As we have seen, mentoring is a relationship where a more experienced person supports a less experienced one. However it is easily confused with coaching, counseling and teaching; with which it has some features in common. In industry it is sometimes also used to describe a form of personal sponsorship by a senior member of staff. The vision of mentoring that has been presented in the preceding chapters is a rather different one.

What is at the heart of this vision? In essence it is that mentoring should promote the independence and empowerment of the mentee. It is a side by side relationship where issues are worked through together using listening, questioning, challenge and discussion. It is important that the mentor does not dictate to the mentee or make decisions on the mentee's behalf. The whole point of the process is to support people whilst they develop the confidence and skills to become autonomous, independent, human beings who know how to plot their own course through life. This requires mutual trust and respect. Inevitably it entails the creation of boundaries to the relationship and a time limit on the process.

Effective mentoring is not easy. It is often stimulating and enjoyable but, at times, it can also make considerable demands on the mentor. Yet overwhelmingly, mentoring is not done for personal financial gain, glory or advancement. It is a generous personal gift of time, concern, experience, knowledge and support to another person. It is humanity at its best.

Further Reading

General Mentoring

Crawford, CJ. 2010. *Manager's Guide to Mentoring*, McGraw Hill, USA.

Du Bois, D. 2005. *Handbook of Youth Mentoring*, Sage Publications, USA.

Department of Education and Training. 2005. *Guidelines for Mentoring and Supporting Students.* New South Wales, Australia

Kay, D. & Hinds, R. 2007. *A Practical Guide to Mentoring 3rd edition*, How to Books: Oxford, UK.

McCarthy, W. 2008. *The Guide for Mentors: How to be a Valuable Mentor*, Focus Publishing: Woolloomooloo, Australia.

Megginson, D. et al. 2006. *Mentoring in Action: a practical guide.* 2nd edn. Kogan Page: London, UK.

Robbins, S, Judge, T, Millet, B & Jones, M. 2010, *OB: The Essentials*, Pearson, French's Forest, NSW.

Rolf-Flett, A. 2002. *Mentoring in Australia*, Pearson Education, Australia.

Zachary, L J. with Fischler, L A. 2009.*The Mentee's Guide. Making Mentoring Work for You*, Jossey-Bass: San Francisco, USA.

Skills Development

Brounstein, M. 2001. *Communicating Effectively for Dummies*, Hungry Minds: New York.

Daniel, B. & Wassell, S. 2002. *Assessing and Promoting Resilience in Vulnerable Children (3 volumes covering: Early Years, School Years, Adolescence)*, Jessica Kingsley Publishers, London.

Egan, G. 2010. *The Skilled Helper.* 9th edn., Brooks/Cole: Belmont, USA.

Nathan, R. and Hill, L. 2006. *Career Counselling* 2nd edn., Sage Publications: London. UK.

Slattery, P. 2001. *Youth Works.* Peter Slattery: Australia

Psychological Background and Brain Science

Dweck, C. 2006. *Mind Sets.* Random House: USA

Gardner, H. 1993. *Frames of Mind.* Fontana Press: London, UK

Goleman, D. 1995. *Emotional Intelligence.* Bloomsbury Publishing: London, UK

Goleman, D. 2006. *Social Intelligence.* Hutchinson: London, UK

Kitchiner, B A, & Jorm, A. 2006. *Mental Health First Aid.* University of Melbourne. Australia.

Nisbett, R. 2009. *Intelligence and How to Get It.* W.W. Norton & Co: New York, USA.

Ramsden, S. et. al. 2011. *Verbal and Non-verbal Intelligence Changes in the Teenage Brain.* In the Journal Nature, 19 October 2011.

Rose, S. 2006. *The 21st Century Brain,.* Random House: Sydney, Australia

Strauch, B. 2010. *Secrets of the Grown Up Brain.* Penguin Black inc.: Melbourne, Australia

Smith, A. 2004. *The Brain's Behind It.* Hawker Brownlow Education: Moorabbin, Australia.

Some Interesting Websites
(see also career sites listed in chapter seven)

www.bbbsi.org. (USA Big Brother Big Sister site)

www.beyondblue.org.au (for help with depression)

www.youthmentoring.org.au (a good support if you are mentoring young people)

www.mentoringaustralia.org (a national network for mentors)

www.internationalbusinessmentors.com

www.mentoring-association.org

www.dsf.org (the dusseldorp skills forum—an excellent source of ideas)

www.cancercouncil.com.au

www. connexions-direct.com.uk (site of a British service giving advice to young people, sadly being phased out at the time of writing)

www.womensaid.org.uk

www.mhfa.com.au (mental health first aid)

www.lanternproject.co.uk

www.lighthousefoundation.org.au

www.edmentoring.org (USA site)

www.ReachOut.com

About the Author

Gordon Holding has trained mentors and organised mentoring schemes in both England and Australia. He has taught in colleges in both countries. As a specialist in vocational education and training, he also worked as an education advisor, researcher, and curriculum developer for local and national governmental agencies in the United Kingdom.